So Many Sunlit Hours

... Whatever comes
One hour was sunlit and the most high gods
May not make boast of any better thing
Than to have watched that hour as it passed

Ezra Pound

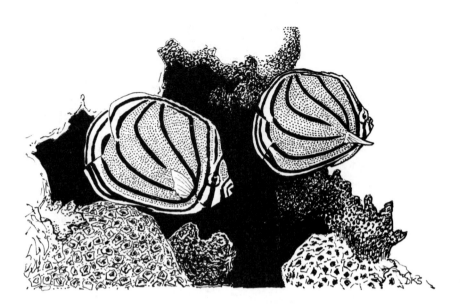

So Many Sunlit Hours

PHILIPPA SCOTT

Foreword by Keith Shackleton

 WWT The Wildfowl & Wetlands Trust

First published in Great Britain in 2002
by The Wildfowl & Wetlands Trust (Trading) Limited

A catalogue record of this book is available from the British Library

ISBN 0–900806–34–6

Editor: Judith Draper
Designer: Alan Hamp
Production: N. G. Hemsley

Colour reproduction by Reed Digital, Ipswich
Typeset in 10.5/13pt Photina
Printed and bound in England by Biddles of Guildford

All proceeds from this book will go to
The Wildfowl & Wetlands Trust

Contents

List of Illustrations

The *Lindblad Explorer* ice-bound in the Lemaire Channel. Peter and Lars
    Eric stand by.
The *Lindblad Explorer* fo'c'sle with an ice fringe on the bell after a stormy
    night in the Ross Sea.
Dafila at Cape Hallett, 1971.
Hot and cold: Falcon standing on the rocks by Knut Rasmussen's Glacier in
    Greenland. A heatwave on the way to Spitzbergen off the coast of Norway.
    Peter, Keith and a passenger sunbathing.
Philippa and her guardian Shau Liu at the top of the '51 steps' climb at
    Wolong Sichuan, China.
The Victoria Falls at sunset from the Zambian side.
Welcoming party for Peter: Harassis tribesmen at Yalooni in the
    Omani desert.
Peter, Richard Leakey and Aubrey Buxton looking at fossils near
    Richard's camp on the shores of Lake Turkana, Kenya.
One of so many sunlit hours: Philippa and Peter on Heron Island off
    the Great Barrier Reef.
Peter with a Shovel-nosed Shark in the channel at Heron Island.
Philippa swimming with a large Potato Cod in 'the cod hole' near
    Lizard Island, Great Barrier Reef.

Plates section 3, between pages 192–193
In New Guinea, on the boat ride up the river: Jacq Shackleton with the
    head man from the village of Pirien in the Asmat Region.
The reception at the Sultan's palace at Bau Bau on the island of Butong,
    Indonesia. No reception was ever quite like this again.
Asmat, New Guinea. The wood spirit, elaborately dressed in palm leaf
    costume, arrives at the village of Owus for a formal celebration.
Warrior canoes seeing us off from Owus for the long journey downriver.
Yasur Volcano in action on the island of Tanna in the New Hebrides.
    Rocks as big as Land Rovers were being thrown into the air.
Part of the vast crowd of tribesmen with their spirit Toka Poles at the
    Toka Festival on Tanna Island. The poles arrived after a long night
    of dancing in the woodland clearing.
Kakadu National Park, Northern Territory, Australia: a flock of Magpie
    Geese, just some of the many thousands. A Glossy Ibis in a lily pool.
Peter painting a fish on board the *Kimberley Explorer* on the the way back

All the photographs are by Philippa Scott ARPS, with the exception of the following taken by Valerie Taylor:

One of so many sunlit hours: Philippa and Peter on Heron Island off the Great Barrier Reef.

Peter with a Shovel-nosed Shark in the channel at Heron Island.

Philippa swimming with a large Potato Cod in 'the cod hole' near Lizard Island, Great Barrier Reef.

Frontispiece and chapter heading drawing by Dafila Scott, other drawings by Peter Scott.

Foreword

Sir Peter Scott died in Bristol on 29 August 1989; in sixteen more days he would have been eighty.

Few will disagree that in his lifetime he had done more, perhaps more than anyone on earth, to further the cause of wildlife conservation and respect for the natural environment. 'The Patron Saint of Conservation' was how Sir David Attenborough once described him – and he should know.

But to Peter this was a cause of worldwide importance, so he tackled it on a thoroughly international, worldwide basis. In Peter, and Philippa too, the word 'peripatetic' began to acquire a new dimension. Though they loved every moment of the shared adventures, the effort was always directed towards the furtherance of a goal. Wildlife, and the wilderness without which it cannot survive, were the beneficiaries.

Philippa had joined the Severn Wildfowl Trust, as the Wildfowl and Wetlands Trust was known in its humble beginnings at Slimbridge, in 1947. I first met her in the dining room/office of the SWT at 8 Edwardes Square in Kensington. She had applied for a post of 'secretary' as Miss P. T-P (Philippa Talbot-Ponsonby). I also recall her confiding, with a certain trepidation in her voice, that she did not know one kind of a wildfowl from another.

History will relate that she soon found out; she got the job and to all practical purposes, she still has it – fifty-five years on...

In the following Prologue she mentions *Lucky Me*, her first autobiography. *So Many Sunlit Hours* is the aptly named sequel, beginning where *Lucky Me* left off – when she became Mrs Peter Scott. The wedding was in Reykjavik, Iceland, in 1951 and she had the distinction of being 'given away' by Europe's, possibly the world's largest ornithologist (in terms of physical displacement) – the great Finnur Gudmundsson.

The concept of sunlit hours ran into sunlit years and there is hardly anywhere on the earth's surface – at least in the less travelled parts – that has not been touched upon and thereby helped to enrich a kaleidoscope of memories. With scuba diving added to Philippa's attainments, often all one saw of the Scotts in those years was two lines of rising bubbles.

Throughout this time Peter kept up his Travel Diaries, accumulating chronicles filled with lovely drawings – fish (lots of fish), birds, insects, flowers, mammals – all annotated by handwriting legible as a typewritten page. But it must be said that Peter's prowess with a camera was less than legendary, and P. T-P's skill in that direction was called upon to complete the record. Moreover her own diaries, backed by an enviable memory, shaped all these family encounters with wild animals, wild places – and wild people, too, into a cohesive whole.

I wince at the use of such a truism but it applies to so many throughout history – 'Behind every great man, look for the great woman'. Those of us lucky enough to have known the Peter and Phil magic will be the first to appreciate just how much this symbiotic match brought to the world.

Assuredly Peter found the second forty years of his life – the Philippa years – the most rewarding. So also did the cherished causes that were his love as well as his life's work.

KEITH SHACKLETON
Woodleigh, Devon

Prologue

In April 1990 the first part of my autobiography was published. I called it *Lucky Me*. It seemed to me that if Peter Scott was the happiest person he knew, then I was the luckiest. The book started and ended with my marriage to Peter, and covered the whole of my life until our wedding in Iceland in 1951.

I was lucky to have shared Peter's life for over forty years. Now, living on my own and paddling madly to keep my head above water, I am aware of the legacy he left me. Everything I have now he gave me: my children, my interest in wildfowl, my circle of friends, my scuba diving and interest in coral fish. He gave me so much and although I shall never stop missing him, I do know how lucky I am. This book is about some of the many things that happened to me after our marriage.

CHAPTER ONE

Family Life

It was autumn 1951 and a lovely breezy day. Peter and I were on our way north to join the rocket-netting team in Scotland. By this time we had a regular team of about ten people who helped us to locate, catch and ring the Pink-footed Geese for the population study of the species. The Pinkfeet were already in large flocks. On the way we stopped off to walk on Rockliffe Marsh, which lies at the eastern end of the Solway Firth. It is a huge area of salt marsh with innumerable creeks and pools – a wonderful place. In the winter there are both Barnacle and Pink-footed Geese. Peter knew it from his shooting days. I had seen it from the air once when we were counting geese from a small aircraft. Also I had seen the clouds of flying geese settling there as we watched from the car, dangerously parked on the metal bridge on the main road north. But to walk on it was something else. And that day was special because with a surge of unbelievable happiness I had discovered that I was pregnant. We were a couple of hundred yards apart when the keeper caught up with Peter and spoke to him. Then he came over to me. 'I've been talking to your father,' he said. Peter and I went on our way north, laughing about the keeper's mistake and rejoicing in our other news.

The euphoria of pregnancy lasted through all the nine months and my condition did not prevent me from enjoying a hectic visit to the United States in November, followed almost immediately by a trip to the Wexford Slobs in Ireland to see Greenland White-fronted Geese. The Greenland Whitefronts were special to Peter. He had named them, 'described' them as they say in ornithological circles, only two years earlier. They were his geese. They were different from the European Whitefronts with their yellow legs and darker plumage. Knowing the large flocks of European geese at Slimbridge, it was interesting for me to see the Greenland ones. Peter's enthusiasm for everything we did together, whether it was watching wild geese, showing me the Empire State Building, or just the exciting experiences of travelling, carried us along on waves of happiness.

That first year Christmas was the only bad break. On Christmas Day Peter was to broadcast live from Herm in the Channel Islands, on what in those days was a Commonwealth-wide programme. Unfortunately the week before, my mother was taken ill with a thrombosis and I had a lonely five days nursing her at home. Peter returned to take me back to Slimbridge since it did not seem practical for me to stay indefinitely. That was a difficult period. A nurse was with her when she died suddenly a week later.

Our daughter Dafila was born in London in June 1952. Somewhere in the back of my mind I had felt sure that she would be a boy. She was beautiful, good natured and utterly irresistible from the start. With a baby, a nanny, my step-daughter Nicola for part of the school holidays and Hugh Boyd, our resident biologist, our cottage was becoming rather crowded. During the day there were two secretaries in the cottage as well, and John Yealland, Curator of the Wildfowl Trust, also had his meals with us, though he slept in the farm cottage opposite. And then Nicky said she wanted a dog. If we were to have a dog, Peter said, then it must be a decoy dog. And that is how we came to have a delightful Shetland Collie called Piper, who was brought up with Dafila, trained for the duck decoy by me, and lived until he was fifteen.

In 1953 I was again pregnant, with Falcon. The cottage was bursting at the seams: there would not be room for the new baby. Housing was still under licence from the local authorities due to post-war shortages of building materials. When the inspection committee came to look us over we crammed the cottage with all our staff and family. However, it was not the numbers that impressed them, it was our tiny bedroom above the studio with the steep stairs leading up into it. That, they thought, was insupportable. So we were issued with one of only fifteen licences out of over 100 applications.

When she died my mother had left enough money for us to build a house and to loan money to the Trust to convert the adjacent cow byre into living accommodation for our staff. Peter Bicknell, the architect, was an old friend of Peter's from Cambridge days, so they worked happily together designing what was to be a unique house overlooking a new big pond in the enlarged Rushy Pen, the first occupied enclosure at Slimbridge. Nicola, aged eleven, put down the first brick and Dafila, aged seven months, laid the foundation stone on 27 January 1953; it did not occur to us that it might be embarrassing for her later in life to be thus dated. This was to be Peter's dream house, with a studio and picture-window facing as nearly north as possible. To achieve the correct outlook we had to make the studio wing of the house curved, with a flat roof.

At that time the Rushy Pen outside the house was still open to the public. People walking along the other side of the big pond would often stop and look through binoculars at us while we were in the studio or having our meals in the dining-room. Sometimes we had fun watching their reactions if we cupped our hands to our eyes to stare back. Some would look embarrassed and shift their view slightly; some continued to look but would also wave; others would turn quickly away.

Our move into the house overlooking the newly dug pond in the Rushy Pen, where on a cold day Peter Bicknell had been able to go skating, was quite dramatic. On Sunday, 7 February I was smitten with a threatened miscarriage, brought about by fetching and carrying my belongings into the new house. I had to be carried down the steep, dangerous stairs from the cottage bedroom and taken to our lovely bedroom in the new house. Peter slept on a mattress on the floor. Later the bed was raised to window height and I spent three months bird-watching from it. As spring came so the activity of the mallards increased and I was forever watching multiple rapes. The month before Falcon was born was spent at Peter's mother's old home, 100 Bayswater Road ('Leinster Corner' as it was always known). Peter's stepfather, Lord Kennet, had kindly loaned us the house, together with domestic help. Kensington Gardens were opposite, so there were walks with Dafila and Nanny. There was the occasional theatre but it was not quite like the pre-Dafila's birth sojourn in London, when we had gone to the theatre almost every night armed with a cardboard box wrapped in brown paper for me to put my feet on. Peter had already become involved with many more activities and was often away. Just before Falcon's birth he had to be in Switzerland for an International Union for the Conservation of Nature and Natural Resources (IUCN) meeting but he got back just in time.

When we were first married I had been determined that, whatever else, I would have a nanny for my children. Luckily my mother's bequest made this possible. I knew that temperamentally I was unsuited to a wholly domestic life and in any event I intended to share as much of Peter's life as I could. There were, of course, problems. Young nannies tended to come and go, either hopelessly lovesick for a staff member, or to marry a Wildfowl Trust warden. We wondered if it had to do with all the courting and copulation on the ponds. Nannies were expendable, wardens were not. There were periods when I looked after the two children and enjoyed it, and there were also times during the school holidays when Peter had to be away and I insisted on being with the children. Leaving them to go abroad was always terrible, but I know that I suffered more than they did. From childminders and dogminders I have since learned that dogs suffer from absence far more than children!

CHAPTER TWO

To South America

In 1953 we accepted an invitation from Colonel Biff Goss, whom we had first met in Iceland and who had visited us at Slimbridge. We were not only to be guests for a week at his plantation home in Georgia, but also to join his expedition to South America for the Cleveland Museum of Natural History. I am not sure why he invited us to join his party, which consisted of himself, his wife and a taxidermist from the Cleveland Museum. Biff was to collect specimens for the museum, and Rendell Rhoades, the Curator, was to do the skinning. The shooting and collecting part was obviously not going to be much fun for us, but on the other hand it was a wonderful opportunity to see out-of-the-way places where Peter could add new water-fowl to his life list. Neither Peter nor I had been to South America before. I hated leaving our nine-month-old Dafila, but luckily we had a very good nanny at the time.

When we stopped in Santiago for three days Peter and I were looked after by Mr A.W. Johnson and Mr Goodall, author and illustrator of *The Birds of Chile*. We also met a third distinguished author, Dr R.A.Philippi. It was Mr Johnson who drove us out to look for Black-headed Ducks. Sometimes known as cuckoo ducks because they lay their eggs in other ducks' nests, they rejoice in the delightful name of *Heteronetta atricapilla*. That day, 14 March, Peter wrote in his diary:

'Drove out from Santiago through countryside with beautiful wayside flowers, many introduced trees, poplar, acacia and eucalyptus. There were nice horses in the fields, being ridden by decorative Chileans wearing broad-brimmed hats, broad belts and sometimes bright ponchos. We went through a river valley leading from the central valley to the coast range, where afforestation had been extensive – mostly with blue gums, some pines and rows of weeping willows growing along water courses. Suddenly we topped a rise and there in front of us was the Pacific Ocean – as blue as could be. A little holiday village nestled in a bay – Cartagena (pronounced Cartahena of course) – and a little to the north of it was a pool – a large pond just behind the sand dunes. This was a known haunt of the Black-headed Duck. The lake was called El Peral. From the dunes we could see great numbers of birds scattered among the floating weed all over the surface. There were many birds on the lake and each one was carefully scanned. But no *Heteronetta*.'

After a picnic lunch and much searching we were taken to another eucalyptus-fringed lake where:

'For the next hour we had a thrilling view of as many new and exciting birds as I can remember for many years. There were at least 2000 ducks below us, scattered, feeding and resting among the floating weeds. It was such a view as we have so often had along the shore opposite St Cerf's island in Loch Leven. But instead of being familiar birds, they were wild birds, which we had not previously seen in the wild state. The sun was full upon them, the nearest 70 yards, the furthest a quarter of a mile. I began to go over the ducks bird by bird.... I worked on across the flock and suddenly there it was, plain as a pike staff, preening itself – an unmistakable Black-headed Duck – the enigmatic and euphoniously named *Heteronetta atricapilla*.'

It seemed that Mr Johnson and Mr Goodall had never recorded the birds on this lake before. Yet we saw three. The co-author of their book, Dr Philippi, had never seen one alive in thirty years of bird-watching in Chile. Peter comments:

'It is of course remarkable what good 12-power binoculars will reveal where rather bad 7's and 8's have previously been used. And then the specialist in any bird group had the advantage over the general ornithologist. These things make us think that perhaps we may yet make some useful discoveries during our trip.'

Mr Johnson told us that he had found Black-headed Ducks eggs only in the nests of Coots and Night Herons. We returned for tea to the beautiful farm – the building all in a Spanish architectural style with bougainvillea growing in profusion. 'In the brilliant evening light,' wrote Peter, 'it looked even more beautiful then earlier in the day; horses, sheep and Spur-winged Plover were mixed in the paddock.' There were two tame Black-necked Swans in with the chickens. The garden was a riot of colour with oleanders and a magnificent flowering begonia with its trumpet-shaped organ blooms growing over a large tree. It was an enchanting place. But we still had to see the Skimmers, who apparently skim particularly by night. There was a long drive down to the sand dunes and Mr Johnson was worried that we might be too late. The sun had gone down half an hour before we reached the shore. We set off to walk along the beach to the river's mouth. There was a strange eerie mist over the waves in the green light of the afterglow. It was our first time on the shore of the Pacific. We felt elated and excited and ran hand in hand. We found the Skimmers, about 180 of them flying down the river with some gulls. Their aerobatics were impressive even in the half light. I was proud to be able to show Peter the Southern Cross as we walked back. He had not seen it before, but I was born under it in South Africa and enjoyed every opportunity of seeing it.

From Santiago we flew in a DC3 down the west side of the Andes, passing a series of volcanoes. After a stop at Puerto Montt we flew (without oxygen) over the mountains to land briefly at Balmaceda. Here we saw our first geese – Ashyheads or Uplands – on the airfield and on to what was then the southern-most city in the world, Punta Arenas (nowadays McMurdo in the Antarctic must have that distinction). Compared to the golden glow of Santiago, Punta Arenas looked dreary. 'Why have you brought me to this awful place?' I asked Peter.

Biff Goss had friends and contacts in high places and so it was that we found ourselves being driven out into the country by a general who had been Chilean Military Attaché in Washington. If we had hoped for an ornithological excursion, we were disappointed, as was Biff Goss. After about an hour in the car he said to the general, whose English was not very good, 'How far is it to the nearest ostrich?' This subsequently became an oft-quoted phrase, living with us for years. The objects of this special outing were a fox farm and a rock garden, which we never saw. We did, however, see dolphins and our first Steamer Duck, which gave us great pleasure.

In the next few days there followed a few excursions with conflicting interests. Biff Goss was collecting specimens, so from time to time, as his guests, we had to watch him shoot certain species and then be photographed holding the bird up by one wing. As Peter was making a film of this trip with his Kodak 16mm camera, the disturbance to the birds before we had reached them was, to say the least irksome. On some of the outings we found ourselves playing a tiresome game of leap frog, with the film-crew sometimes racing ahead of us. On one occasion while we were trying to get close to a flock of *Banduria* (Straw-necked Ibises) we were in terrible disgrace because we had gone ahead in the station wagon containing not only Biff's camera but all the guns as well.

For me one of the highlights of the Punta Arenas visit was a ride round the racecourse. On the previous day we had been to the races and had all put money on a horse called Peter Pan, in honour of Peter's godfather, J.M.Barrie. He did not win but I was promised a ride on him the following day, though as it happened I rode another horse instead, accompanied by a local jockey on Peter Pan. We had a splendid twosome race. It was my first and only venture onto a racecourse and I found it very exhilarating.

In spite of the guns and the collecting for the museum we saw an incredible number of birds, all new to us, and Peter produced some film which we were to use later for lectures in aid of the WWT. Biff's boss's connection with the museum opened doors for us with local VIPs and we were treated to much hospitality all round. One of the most exciting days was a trip in a small wooden schooner to Islas Santa Marta and Santa Magdalena to look at penguins. Here in the Straits of Magellan we were to see our first Southern Ocean sea birds – albatross, Antarctic Skua and petrels. As we approached Magdalena there were many Blue-eyed Cormorants flying around. Terns were sitting on the long floating strands of kelp and dolphins jumped around in front of the ship. We had some difficulty restraining some people from shooting at the gulls and skuas, without any hope of retrieving them, and a Chilean naval officer was trying to shoot at the dolphins. On shore we found that the Jackass Penguins had retreated to their burrows from where they eyed us first with one eye and then the other, turning their heads with comic curiosity.

On 12 March we arrived in Tierra del Fuego. Having read Lucas Bridges' *The Uttermost Part of the Earth*, we were full of excitement in anticipation of the wildlife that we would see on this remote island, the 'Land of Fire'. The 600,000-acre estancia Caleta Josephina which we visited on the west side of the island consisted of a settlement with a huge and impressive shearing shed and some thirty white buildings with neat red corrugated roofs, set inside shelter belts of trees. Situated on the open pampa with no other trees or hills within miles, and first viewed on a very windy and rather bleak day, it nevertheless had a curious charm. Looking out of the window as we went into the house we saw Ruddy-headed Geese browsing at the foot of the garden – our first view of them in the wild. The following day brought another ornithological first: Silver Teal (*Anas versicolour fretensis*). We learned with some dismay that they are locally called blue teal or pepper teal, which only goes to show how important the scientific names are.

The best way to get around in Tierra del Fuego is on horseback. It was not Peter's favourite means of transport, but nevertheless we set out happily on some well behaved horses belonging to the Huntleys at the estancia. Peter actually recorded it as 'a lovely ride'. The birds were delightfully tame. The worst hazards were the Caruro holes which peppered the ground. Caruros (*Ctenomys magellanicus*) are said to look superficially like ground squirrels and are about the size of a mole, but we never saw them. What we did see were hundreds of rabbits: white (or at any rate partly white) and of various sizes. Only a few were short-eared and good runners like the English wild variety. These Fuegan rabbits had been introduced by accident and clearly show their descent from the Belgian hare and other domestic breeds.

Returning from the lagoon we came to an open hollow, free from Caruro holes, and decided to have a gallop. 'In the middle,' Peter wrote, 'my horse suddenly opened the throttle and went like the wind.' The numerous blankets and rugs under the saddle had slipped over the horse's rump and finally over its tail. This was not the first time I had seen Peter carted home at speed on a horse. I reined mine back in order to avoid a race, but I am afraid that I could not resist peels of mirth. When Peter eventually managed to stop we decided that in the strong wind it was too difficult to replace the rugs so we rolled them up and attached them to the saddle. The horse, however, did not wish to be remounted. As Peter put his foot in the stirrup it reared, gave a neat little wriggle, and there was Peter flat on his back. His second attempt was successful and we rode back to the estancia with no further problems.

Leaving Caleta Josephina we headed east to join the rest of Biff Goss's party on the Argentinian side of the island at Estancia Maria Behety. The journey across country was accomplished in a farm truck and took most of the day. Recent heavy rain had turned the track into a quagmire. The fact that Peter kept stopping the driver in order to film such things as Seed Snipe, Guanacos and rabbits delayed us further. On the way we passed the Chilean Police post and then a little further on the Argentinian border post of San Martin. Here a policeman copied the particulars of our passports onto a piece of paper, without marking the passports in any way at all. The piece of paper was then given to what appeared to be an old fisherman who shambled off with it to a tiny hovel next door. The policeman searched our luggage, expressed surprise at the number of cigarettes we were carrying and counted the magazines of cine film. Repercussions from this little interlude were to catch up with us later.

After passing through Rio Grande with its rather charming statue of Eva Peron we drove on along the dirt road, flanked on either side by hordes of rabbits, across rolling pampa until we came to Estancia Maria Behety nestling in a hollow. The settlement was the largest we had seen and had, at that time, the world's largest shearing shed. Our delightful host, the farm manager, was Duncan McKay, a Scotsman, and here we met up with the Goss party. The reunion was friendly enough but it was not long before our conflicting interests upset Peter.

From Maria Behety we all went to stay at Viamonte, the home of the Bridges-Reynolds family. The owner, 'Auntie Ber', was a splendid old lady in her mid-seventies. She was a sister of Lucas Bridges. Her son Robbie Reynolds was a dedicated ornithologist and had met Peter at one of his art exhibitions in London before the war and had corresponded with him for about twenty years. The Viamonte connection had been ours not the Cleveland Museum's, so we were a little sad that this place was to be invaded by the trigger-happy section of the expedition.

Our first excursion took us to a bay at the mouth of a river where Clarita Goodall (Auntie Ber's daughter) told us that the Kelp Geese were wont to congregate on a shingle bank. The geese were indeed there: beautiful little white ganders with their well camouflaged, almost-black females. No sooner had Peter started taking some distant shots with his cine camera when once again we were overtaken by the shooting party. They walked down to the shore and shot at the geese as they rose up ahead. Biff Goss had not been close enough to kill a Kelp Goose, but eventually he walked up to a trio. One flew off, leaving a pair sitting; Biff shot the female. The male did not move. Biff walked a few paces nearer and killed the male standing faithfully by his mate. Peter wrote: 'If this has to be done for science it is one thing, but if it is to be regarded a sport, it is quite a different thing. What particularly disgusted me was when Biff sent his wife and later tried to persuade little Puchachoto to go down to the beach "just to be able to say you shot one". This cannot be connected with science and can only be supposed to mislead someone into thinking it is a difficult sport. By this time I was very much disgusted at this ignorant carnage perpetrated on the flimsy excuse that Kelp Geese were needed by the Cleveland Museum. (We heard later from Rendall Rhodes that the museum had several skins.) In the car proceeding from here to the picnic site I was rash enough to ask Biff whether he had enjoyed walking up to geese and knocking them over on the ground. The result was a certain coolness during the rest of the day.' I shared Peter's feelings and it was a relief when the Cleveland Museum party left us with our birdy friends at Viamonte. If Punta Arenas had seemed awful, Tierra del Fuego had made up for it in a big way with the birds, the interesting countryside with its huge areas of grassy pampa, the leaning Antarctic beech trees and our charming hosts.

Since that first year when I had been so shattered by the sight of Punta Arenas and had complained about it to Peter, I have been there again three times on my way to the Antarctic peninsula. It no longer fills me with gloom. It has, of course, grown enormously and is not at all unattractive as southern cities go. For me now it is one of the stepping stones to that magic continent, Antarctica.

From Tierra del Fuego we flew north to Buenos Aires. On reaching our hotel we were informed that we had not arrived in Argentina: there was no entry stamp on our passports. It was late evening – too late to get in touch with the British Consul – and we were tired and hungry. The police were called. We could not have a room. Finally we were allowed to go to a near-by restaurant before being taken to the police station. On condition that we were back in the police station by nine o'clock the next morning, we were eventually given a room in the hotel. It took the whole of the next day to get our papers sorted out. Such a waste of a day, and so hot that Peter hated it. If I did not like Punta Arenas, then Peter did not like Buenos Aires. I wanted to see the city, he did not. 'This is how our marriage will end,' he said, 'because you like the heat and I like the cold.'

A contact at the Zoo took us on two excursions to see some ducks and was helpful, but the question was, 'Where from here?' Peter wanted to go to Corrientes, a huge marshy area just south of Paraguay. He described it as having tall reeds, so I envisaged a flat water-logged country with nothing to see but a huge reed bed. I could not imagine how one could see any ducks or other water birds. After some discussion we decided to go to the altiplano in Bolivia instead. For years afterwards that word 'Corrientes' was used to indicate something marvellous which I had prevented Peter from doing. In later years there were places I could quote as being my 'Corrientes' – places which Peter had persuaded me that we should not visit. In any case, we had such a marvellous time in Bolivia that for the time being Corrientes was forgotten.

Having decided to go to Lake Titicaca in Bolivia we discovered that it was not all that easy to arrange at short notice, but we managed to wangle some diplomatic visas through the good offices of the British Consul in Buenos Aires and set off for La Paz on 3 April in an unpressurised plane not much bigger than a DC3. It was quite a long flight, with a break on the way at the foot of the Andes, where the vegetation was incredibly lush and alive with tropical insects entirely new to us both. In those days no one minded if you wandered around a small airport building during refuelling. Peter was so excited that he wanted to stay there.

The next leg of the flight took us high over the Andes. Oxygen masks were lowered and they were certainly welcome. It became very bumpy and most of the passengers, as well as the steward, were sick. Peter and I, on the other hand, were hungry and were pleased to be given some lunch since we were not due to arrive until 1pm, though it was difficult to eat wearing an oxygen mask. Strangest of all was to get out of the aircraft at La Paz airport, at 14,000ft, and to see those passengers who were going further sitting in the plane still with oxygen masks on.

A car, sent for us by the ambassador, Mr Lomax, took us to the city of La Paz, situated slightly lower than the airport. On arrival at the British Residence we were informed that Mrs Lomax was awaiting us for lunch-eon. We discussed the problems of acclimatising to the altitude and she told us that one of the worst things was to eat too much. Out of politeness we did not dare to tell her that we had already eaten lunch.

The Ambassador arrived mid-afternoon. The Foreign Office had just given him a new car and he was very anxious to have it photographed at high altitude to show how good it was. Would we like to come? First we were shown the amazing talcum hills near La Paz. Then we went up another thousand feet or so, where the car was parked in a suitably imposing place, with mountains behind and snow in the foreground. It was about then that His Excellency told us he had brought his previous visitor, an American, to this view point but he had been so affected by the altitude that he had had to spend the night in an oxygen tent. We fared better but we did find sleeping difficult since one's normal night-time breathing rhythm simply does not cope with the thin air and the extra need for oxygen.

Peter was particularly anxious to see Torrent Ducks – beautiful, slimline, elegant birds which live in the white water of fast-flowing rivers. H.E. kindly arranged for us to be taken to a guest house belonging to the hydro-electric power company on the Zongo River. It was a long drive, first over a 16,000ft pass where we saw Andean Geese and then plunging down terrifying hairpin bends into the deep cleft of the valley of the Zongo River, which is one of the sources of the Madiera, a main tributary of the Amazon. At about 9,000ft the tree line begins, and for the first time in our lives we were in a real tropical rain forest with tree ferns and humming birds. The valley echoed with the roar of the river with its continuous series of cascades and waterfalls.

The only people we saw were a few silent, impassive looking Indians with their betel-nut-stained teeth, who worked for the hydro-electric company and spoke no English. The isolation and these strange silent people were slightly frightening, but the guest house was comfortable and we were well served for our one-night stay. The following morning we walked up the valley in the steaming heat and suddenly through a gap in the trees we could see Torrent Ducks. At that time not many ornithologists had seen them and very little was known about their behaviour. Photographically it was not much use to me but we watched the ducks for some time and Peter made notes and sketches of their behaviour.

The next day we returned to La Paz by lorry and reported to the Embassy office. H.E. was anxious to get rid of us in order to avoid the celebrations of the anniversary of the last revolution which were about to take place there.

It could turn nasty, he said. So the next day we were put on a train to Guaqui, the rail and boat terminal on Lake Titicaca. Our host at Guaqui was a delightful Englishman called Tom Pryce, manager of the railhead. His house was comfortable enough but his Indian cook seemed to be doing her best to poison us all: the food was very unpleasant and on the second day I suffered badly from its effects. This meant that I could not go on the lorry drive with Peter to another part of the lake, and having started out and then felt ill, I had to walk back alone through the village. I must admit that I found it pretty frightening. The natives were not openly hostile but there was no doubt that they resented Tom's presence there, and probably any other white face. Some years later Tom came to a sudden and mysterious death on board the ferry boat at Guaqui.

We had three days there and spent a certain amount of time in balsa wood boats looking for ducks. Around its edges the lake was shallow and there were reeds growing quite far out. We succeeded in catching four Puna Teal and four Sharpwing Teal which we wanted for the Slimbridge collection. Boxes were made for them in the railway workshop and we took them back to the Embassy Residence where they were put in H.E.'s bath and I was put to bed and given custard apples and orange juice to settle my upset stomach. During the night one of the Puna Teal escaped but was found in the garden. The ducks travelled to England separately from us – not, I think, in the diplomatic bag but certainly with the help of our friend the Ambassador. Our own journey back by air took us to Antofagasta, where the plane broke down, then back to Buenos Aires and Rio de Janeiro, where another plane broke down. At all the places where we were delayed Peter was out and about with binoculars and movie camera, something that was not easily explained to local security men who were usually carrying guns.

Film material from this trip provided us with a number of opportunities for lecturing around the country in aid of the Wildfowl Trust, including a lecture in the Royal Festival Hall. As Peter was the first person to use the Festival Hall for this purpose we were excited to find it filled to capacity.

CHAPTER THREE

Fun and Games Down Under

In 1956 we embarked on a world tour which took us away from home for
three months – too long as far as I was concerned because it was so heart-
breaking leaving my children. Our expedition was made possible by two
different organisations. We were to provide material for a series of wildlife
programmes for the BBC, with Charles Lagus as our cameraman. Charles
had already travelled with David Attenborough on a filming trip to
Australia so he probably knew more about it than we did. Almost as important as the filming was the fact that this was the year of the Olympic Games
in Melbourne. Peter was Chairman of the International Yacht Racing
Union and Chairman of the Jury for the yacht races, so he was in
Melbourne in an official capacity, the first of several Olympic Games that
we attended. We stayed in Scott's Hotel which should have been a good
omen but was not. The bedroom, small and cold, looked out on to a well in
the middle of the block. One could only see a small bit of sky by putting
one's head outside and craning upwards.

The middle of the week was occupied by the Olympics and the weekends were for filming wildlife for the BBC. We had spent ten days in northern and western Australia on the way and had learned a lot about
Australian bureaucracy, developed a taste for steak and eggs for almost
every meal, including breakfast, and added several species of ducks and
geese to Peter's life list. Most special among the birds were the huge flocks
of Magpie Geese near Darwin and our first sight of Pink-eared Ducks not

far from Perth. We also experienced heat at Darwin such as neither of us had
known before. It was just working up to the rainy season. The endless eucalyptus forests on either side of the road were far from interesting and were
aptly described by an early English pioneer as 'trees which make no shade and
where no birds sing'.

Of our two weekends away from Melbourne I found the excursion to
Flinders Island more interesting and exciting than an attempt to film Pink-
eared Ducks in the Griffiths area west of Canberra. To reach the island in
order to see Cape Barren (or Cereopsis) Geese, we flew first to Launceston
in Tasmania, where we had to change planes and found ourselves unexpectedly let in for a formal elevenses picnic with speeches. From
Launceston we flew to Flinders Island – an hour's flight in a DC3 with more
elevenses and tea served en route. It was so bumpy that I still have a vivid
picture of what looked like ropes of tea hanging from the ceiling of the
aeroplane as it suddenly soared on a thermal then dropped like a stone
several hundred feet. Luckily Peter and I refused the tea, but sitting near
the back we had a good view of our fellow passengers' misfortunes.

We only had a few hours on Flinders Island, but it was memorable
for its high mountains, lush vegetation, wind-swept trees and the local
hospitality. From there we set off by boat with our host, the distinguished
Australian ornithologist Dom Seventy, for Fisher Island which had been his
study area for Mutton Birds (Short-tailed Shearwaters) for nine years. In
my diary I wrote:

'The island, which was about two acres, had a small two-roomed
asbestos hut on top and is covered with tussocky grass, white everlast-
ing flowers, slabs of granite and large patches of pink mysembryanthe-
mum between the shore rocks and grass. It all looked very beautiful in
the low evening sunlight. Before going to bed that night we went out in
the dark to count the Mutton Birds coming in to their burrows. Each
year the birds are harvested by the Tasmanians, who take the young
birds by digging them out of their burrows. Some are eaten fresh and
the remainder are salted.'

After a breakfast of eggs and bacon cooked by a delightful Irishman who
was with the party, we set off to look for Cape Barren Geese and saw our
first on Little Dog Island. There were more on other islands but mostly in

pairs and never any great number. It was going to be difficult to film them. A strong, cold wind was blowing, but the sun shone and there was that lovely clear light that seems to happen only in the far north or south. The stark mountains of Cape Barren made a wonderful background to the little low grass-covered islands and rocky reefs.

We stopped off-shore from Little Woody Island. Peter, Charles and I went ashore with cameras to try to stalk some geese and to find ourselves somewhere to hide, while the others landed on Wood Island and drove the geese over to us. Our stalking was only moderately successful, as the geese were pretty wary. We hid ourselves as best we could among some large rocks. There were no trees, only low scrub and the long grass, so a hide was not possible. In among the grass were large patches of a plant with the delightful name of 'bidgee widgee'. It was in full seed and covered with little round balls the size of mothballs. They had little hooked spikes all over them which stuck on our socks and trousers. As we walked, the balls broke into hundreds of seeds, each with its spiky end, and soon the lower part of our legs were encased in seed.

As we sat waiting for the geese and trying to camouflage ourselves, I saw an enormous tarantula spider about four inches wide walking up Peter's leg. It was brown and a bit furry. We tried to keep it, but it finally hid under a stone where we marked it down in order to photograph it later.

A pair of Cape Barren Geese flew over, then later about thirty or forty, but none came and settled anywhere near us. Finally we saw that the party on the other island had finished their drive so we moved out, filmed the spider and packed up. I went back up the hill to look for Charles's exposure meter while Peter went to see if there were any geese over a ridge and down near the shore. As I stood on top of the hill I saw Peter appear suddenly, running, and then I saw a large flightless goose ahead of him. He caught it and I went back to look – getting there just as they were ready to hand it over to me while Peter caught another and Charles filmed the chase. There were three flightless birds but we only caught two. I held them both and they were beautiful and friendly. They struggled very little and soon became quite quiet unless I moved. Charles filmed them in close-up and then we decided to take them back to the boat in case Dom Seventy had any rings for them. I carried them back across the island and over the hill. Here I was sheltered from the wind and for the first time felt really hot. The geese became heavier and heavier and I got hotter and hotter. When in sight of the boat I finally sat down on a rock above the shore and shouted, but they were all below deck and no one took any notice. So I tucked one bird lightly under each knee where they sat quietly while I stripped off layer after layer of clothes. At last I heard a shout from the boat and the Irishman came over in the dinghy to fetch me. While he was on his way the geese started eating the bidgee widgee off my ankles.

We released the geese from the shore, collected a huge, lovely, red octopus from the seaweed and filmed it in the dinghy, where it slid around poking its tentacles up the sides and around the seats. Back on Fisher Island we had cold roast Mutton Bird for supper. They are extremely oily, with lots of subcutaneous fat. Luckily I was very hungry and managed to eat most of the meat off my bird.

On the Monday we sadly said goodbye to Fisher Island, the Cape Barren Geese and the Mutton Birds and headed back to Melbourne and the high life. En route we were waylaid once again in Launceston where we faced an unexpected civic reception in the Town Hall. It was kind of them but we were not prepared. On arrival back in Melbourne in the evening, we were told that the yacht racing jury were at daggers drawn and were refusing to meet again without Peter. So he went straight to a meeting while I returned to the hotel. Later I went out to dinner with Peter's Olympic driver while Peter worked until midnight. Fitting in our wildlife filming commitments and the Olympic jury entailed a lot of hard work for him. On the day when we went to film at the Healsville Sanctuary, about thirty-eight miles out of Melbourne, Peter still had to go to his jury meeting on our return. Then, after a difficult day when the Press attacked him because an Australian yachtsman had been disqualified from a race (thus losing them a gold medal), he had to give a lecture twelve miles outside the city. It was 10.15pm before he started his lecture, to twenty people, and afterwards his driver and I watched him over tea and buns going the colour of ashes. Luckily the next day was an easier one.

There were other excursions, including one to Philip Island, which is a sanctuary for Koala Bears and notable for its colonies of Fairy Penguins. At the fenced-off area of the beach near the penguin burrows we waited till dusk to see them coming in from the sea to feed their young or to change places with their mates in the burrows. The 'Penguin Parade' is one of the Southern Hemisphere's most popular wildlife spectacles.

*   *   *

Left Dafila and Falcon decorating the Christmas tree,1960.

Below Nicky outside the studio window at Slimbridge feeding Nenes in the Rushy Pen.

Above Peter in the studio on a filming day with the BBC. Dafila and Falcon looking on.
Below Peter with Mervyn Cowie (Director of Kenya National Parks) after opening the lodge at Paraa in Uganda, 1961.

Above Local dug-out boat coming in to land on Aride Island, Seychelles, 1971.
Below My childhood home at Beauchamp, in South Africa, revisited in 1962.
Thaba Pachua in the background.

Left Peter at the foot of the statue by his mother, Kathleen Scott, of his father, in Christchurch, New Zealand.
Above The colony of incubating King Penguins at Volunteer Point, Stanley, Falkland Islands. *Below* Tenzing and his wife Daku at Volunteer Point, Falkland Islands, 1978.

Above Swan Lake in winter with Bewick's Swans seen from the house tower.
Below Peter and Dafila looking for Bewick's Swans from a mound on the tundra on the Yamal Peninsular, USSR 1978.

Above Peter conversing with a sea lion on Hood Island in the Galapagos.
Below George Holton, distinguished American photographer, with large Galapagos Tortoise on Alcedo Island.

Above Philippa stroking a well-fed Komodo Dragon on the Island of Komodo, Indonesia, 1977.
Below Komodo Dragons feeding on a dead goat.

From Melbourne we went to Sydney where we were looked after by that great man Sir Edward Hallstrom, founder of the Taronga Park Zoo. On his farm outside Sydney he kept koalas and kangaroos, and he also owned a private zoo at Nondugl in the Wahgi Valley in New Guinea, in the name of the Hallstrom Trust. Sir Edward took us straight to Taronga Park and drove us round in his car. During the drive he told us a curious story about an ostrich crossing with a cat and a black kitten hatching out of the egg. It was difficult to know what to say.

The following day a car picked us up from the hotel and whisked us off to Sir Edward's office at his refrigerator factory. Just as we arrived he swept in accompanied by a nursing sister. He sat down in a large armchair which was a bear carved in wood and started giving instructions, opening his mail and talking on the telephone all at once. Most of his telephoning was connected with organising our trip to New Guinea and the possibility of taking Salvadori's Ducks to England for the Wildfowl Trust. These ducks are unique to New Guinea. Not many people had seen them, so this trip was very special.

Two days later we flew up to New Guinea with exciting views of the Great Barrier Reef beneath us. It was the flight from Lae on the coast of New Guinea up to Nondugl in a DC3 with bucket seats that was perhaps the most interesting. There was no road and this was the only way to get there; it entailed numerous stops on grass airstrips with mist-decked mountains rising all round. At one such stop the plane was refuelled by locals in their traditional dress. The men had mother-of-pearl crescents and many coloured beads hanging around their necks, more thin pieces of shell stuck through their noses and headdresses with bright plumes. They carried a variety of weapons. Some had long knives, some bows and arrows, some axes. They were wild and decorative and we filmed them. Rain storms blotted out the mountains from time to time, making it all an exciting adventure.

On our first night in Lae we discovered that it was a paradise for insects. Peter kept two praying mantis and a moth in our mosquito net overnight so that we could film them the next day and we took them on with us to Nondugl. The mantis pair had copulated that first night and the female ate the head off the male while they stayed together, providing more material for the film. The zoo at Nondugl was remarkable and wonderful. Here for the first time we saw some Salvadori's Ducks on a pond in a beautifully designed enclosure. Mr Shaw Meyer, the director of the zoo, was cutting up meat for them. They were strange-looking ducks with splay tails which stuck up, the back end high in the water. They were striped, black and white, as Peter had painted them for the *Waterfowl of the World* by Jean Delacours, and had broad yellow bills, dark brown heads and very pale breasts. The zoo was entirely for preserving native species and was not open to the public. The aviaries were planted with creepers, shrubs and trees. The birds of paradise were not easy to see but the whole place was well designed to accommodate the animals which were there. We were allowed to go in with the tree kangaroos, which are very engaging animals. They were even fairly friendly.

We spent some time searching, both by Land Rover and on foot, for wild Salvadori's Ducks in the forest, but only found Black-Headed Ducks and Grey Teal. At least we had seen them in a natural setting in the zoo and had had a wonderful time filming the many other small animals which were brought in to us by the natives. We had also enjoyed the people themselves, who were delightful and of course immensely colourful when dressed in their 'Sing Sing' finery with headresses made of birds of paradise feathers. Taking off from Nondugl in a small aircraft was not easy as there was thick fog hanging about in the mountains – in fact it was pretty frightening – but after one false start we made it and fortunately the Qantas flight from Lae for Sydney had been held for us.

It was the end of December when we flew from New Guinea to Cairns not really knowing what was in store for us, except that Charles had filled us with the desire to go snorkelling on the Great Barrier Reef. He had snorkelled when he was there with David Attenborough.

Peter had been told by Konrad Lorenz that looking at coral fishes was something he must do before he died. This was our chance. We were met at Cairns by someone who said he knew exactly what we wanted to film – which seemed strange because we didn't know. The press knew all about it too, he said. This was reminiscent of our experience in Tasmania and my heart sank into my boots. Gone were our four undisturbed days skin diving. Mercifully a compromise was reached, though it was years before we lived down the story among Australian naturalists of how Peter Scott the ornithologist had gone to Cairns and had insisted on fish watching instead of bird watching. Honour was satisfied when we made an excursion as guests of honour of the Harbour Board Trust to the bird island, Michaelmas Cay. But there at least we could indulge in both pleasures and Charles could do some filming, too, although it was not too easy as some of the sixteen people from our boat tended to stride ahead with their Box Brownie cameras.

All that happened on Christmas Eve and we carefully planned our Christmas Day which we decided to spend on Green Island, about an hour's run out from Cairns. At that time Green Island was wonderfully unsophisticated, but it did have an underwater observatory built into the coral reef. This has since been enlarged and improved and copied in other parts of the world. For Peter it was magic. I had problems with the lack of oxygen as there was no air conditioning but I was able to appreciate the beauty of the underwater world for the first time.

I had problems, too, learning to use a mask and flippers. It was not quite as easy as I had thought. The fact that I had to be filmed with Peter wading out to the reef when I was so hot and sticky that my bathing dress had split did not help. Plunging my head into the water and breathing through my mouth produced an unaccountable claustrophobia. Then I got cramp in my foot. It was not easy to explain to Peter and Charles why I found it so difficult, but I persuaded them to leave me so that I could persevere quietly on my own. Suddenly, as I tried again, I saw a marvellous fish with blue round its nose and on its back and with its eye about half way along. I was so excited that in that moment I won the battle with my mask and snorkel. Ever since then the Pig-Snout Trigger Fish (*Rhinecanthus aculeatus*) – sometimes called Picasso Fish and known in Hawaii as Humu Humu nuku nuku apu aa – has been one of my favourites. It lives in fairly shallow water and is often over the sand. I was in the water for an hour and a half. Peter and Charles were in for so long that I began to worry about sharks and whether we would catch the boat back. It was two and a quarter hours before they came ashore.

Those few days in Cairns were immensely significant. Peter was hooked on fish watching and from that time on we could not visit any tropical country without going to the coast and the nearest coral reef. A long day's flight on 26 December via Townsville and Brisbane to Sydney was wearing and it was a bitter disappointment that among the mail waiting for us there was no news of the children.

After a short night in the hotel in Sydney we left for New Zealand where we were to spend two days at Government House with Sir Willoughby and Lady Norrie. We had a few problems because of course we had to look respectable for dinner on the first night and some of our things had gone to the hotel where Charles was staying. Inevitably, and as always, we had a lot of luggage because of our multifarious activities such as snorkelling, filming, and bird watching, for which we needed reference books, etc. Peter had another problem which made him feel very uncomfortable, not only for social events but in particular since he had to give a public lecture the day after we arrived. Because he had spent so much time in the sea using a very ill-fitting snorkel he had a swollen, sore mouth. The good thing was that I had news from home and a letter from four-year-old Dafila.

New Zealand remained memorable for me for many years as I was always coming up against things that I was not allowed to do because I was a woman. Things have changed since then, but at that time it was quite astonishing and particularly annoying when Peter and I were separated for that reason. The first time it happened was in connection with a visit to Takahe Valley where a strange gallinule type of bird, previously thought to be extinct, had recently been rediscovered. At first the authorities were not going to allow Peter to go there but he said that as a well-known ornithologist in our country, he could not possibly go back to England and say he had been refused permission to visit the sanctuary up on the mountains on South Island. After a lot of persuasion the powers-that-be said they would take him but not Charles and certainly not me because no woman had so far been allowed to go there.

So Charles and I were taken to a hotel and sworn to secrecy about Peter's whereabouts, while Peter and his government official sponsor flew him up to the remote valley. Wherever we went in New Zealand the Press were always there and Charles and I found it a little difficult to explain why we were staying overnight in the hotel. We both felt annoyed at having to invent lies about Peter. The reason we were pursued by the Press was because of Peter's father's departures in the *Discovery* and then in the *Terra Nova* from Lyttleton and Port Charmers.

The Royal Albatross sanctuary on Otago Peninsula was another source of irritation. I was not allowed in – because I was a woman. Peter and Charles went in with the warden and filmed a bird on her nest close to the path, so tame that you could touch her. The sad thing about New Zealand was the amount of introduced animals – it reminded me of the attitude I had known in South Africa where people referred always to England as 'home' and longed for everything English.

We were looked after by members of the Acclimatisation Society, the nearest thing one could get to a group of naturalists. Because of our interest in waterfowl they kept taking us to see great herds of Black Swans, introduced from Australia. They were incredibly wild, as in New Zealand they are a game bird. They were also very numerous. Having seen huge flocks of them on Lake Ellesmere near Christchurch I was not very enthusiastic about long walks to look at others on North Island. I found myself walking with a delightful, friendly girl to whom I confided my irritation. The next day I went down to breakfast at the hotel to find Charles chuckling. There was a headline in the local paper which said: 'Mrs Peter Scott says she will scream if she sees another black swan.' I am not sure whether Peter was very pleased, but how was I to know that my nice friend of the previous day was a journalist? She had not said so.

One trip that was a treat and great fun was to the Trios Islands to see Tuataras – strange lizards with a pineal eye. That boat trip, the visit to the gannet colony at Cape Kidnappers and two exciting days on horseback at a station north-west of Gisborne looking for Blue Mountain Ducks were the highlights as far as I was concerned. Searching for Brown Ducks near Waipu eighty-four miles north of Auckland was also fun. We finally found a pair of these extraordinary little birds, which could be classed as 'not showy, but rare', under a bridge on a main road. In captivity they have an amazing capacity for climbing out of their pens.

Our time in the North Island had been very rewarding and we had made some good friends among the ornithologists there. But we needed a holiday and it was with a great feeling of release that we finally boarded a plane for Fiji on 15 February 1957.

CHAPTER FOUR

Fish Watching in Fiji

We arrived at Nandi airport on Fiji in a tropical downpour which continued all night and on into the next day. Our destination was Korolevu on the south coast of the main island of Viti Levu. We only had a week in hand, so it was important to get there as soon as possible. In the morning we were told that we would have to go quickly if we were to get there because the river beyond Nandi was in flood. There was no time to repack so we took two taxis, putting our luggage in one while we went in the other with two Indian drivers. We crossed one river which was high, and about three miles on the far side of Nandi we came to the other river. A line of cars each side showed us that the traffic was no longer moving and the bridge in between was invisible. Some people started to walk over, but the water was well above their knees and about three feet above the bridge. We turned back, stopped in Nandi to buy mackintoshes and then headed back for the hotel. In the meantime the other river had risen and we only just got across. The floorboards of the taxi were awash – and it was still raining. We repacked in order to reduce our baggage, left Charles' camera equipment behind in safe custody and set out after lunch when there was a slight respite in the weather and the tide was low. With just the one taxi we did a long detour to avoid the worst of the first river and arrived back at the bigger one as the rain started again with a vengeance. This time two boats with outboard motors were acting as ferries and miraculously there was a bus going to Suva on the other side which could drop us off at Korolevu.

So we were ferried across and boarded the bus. It broke down at one point, but luckily it was in a village and we had tea while it was mended and in half an hour we were on our bumpy way again.

We had never been to a tropical island before and it is difficult to describe the impact that it made on us. In those days there were not hundreds of travel brochures with palm trees and sandy beaches as there are now. Korolevu had a small hotel with twenty-five thatched rooms (or 'burres') set among the coconut palms, each one just yards from a beautiful sandy beach, with the blue-green sea beyond. Because of the floods we had it almost to ourselves. The fringing reef came right up to the shore so here at least we could go snorkelling as easily and as often as we liked. It was difficult to keep Peter out of the water: his interest and excitement with the coral fish was intense.

We were supposed to be on holiday, but Peter persuaded a rather reluctant Charles to retrieve his camera equipment from the hotel in Nandi so that some fishes could be included in the *Faraway Look* film series of our world tour. Without an underwater camera this was not easy, but ingenuity prevailed. With the help of the hotel manager, we constructed a glass tank. While Peter lay on the surface with his mask on, directing us, Charles held the glass down, hopefully in the right place, while I did the filming by holding the camera in the glass box. Of course neither Charles nor I could see exactly what we were filming so the exercise was fairly hilarious and not entirely successful. We also set the tank up on the shore, caught some fish, with difficulty, and filmed them in the tank.

We may have started our snorkelling on the Great Barrier Reef, but this was a fish watcher's paradise. Peter could spend hours in the water watching their behaviour and, since there were few books then, identifying them with difficulty. I have to admit that I was rather frightened of sharks, especially when one followed us along the outside edge of the reef. But Peter seemed already to have an understanding of shark behaviour, and swimming hand in hand with him I was reassured. Sometimes we were accompanied by a delightful Fijian called Walai, who had huge feet and could sink vertically through water to about twenty feet. On occasion he retrieved our dropped snorkels. He took us to see the chief in his village. All the houses were 'burres' similar to our own bedroom, made of bamboo and tied with lianas, although of course without the sophistication of such things as showers. Walai had been in court the day before we came because he had not cleaned out the communal lavatory. A man of great dignity, he obviously had no intention of doing so.

Peter's enthusiasm for fish watching was sometimes rather frightening. On our last night at Korolevu, after the lovely Fijian staff had sung their haunting farewell song 'Isa lei', Peter conceived the idea of going snorkelling in the dark in order to see the nocturnal fishes. Charles and I chickened out, but we sat on the beach with torches and Peter agreed to shine his torch back towards us at frequent intervals to show where he was and that he was all right. Of course he forgot after a while. At first we could see a little pool of light through the water, but as he went further the light disappeared. The little group on the beach, including a Samoan girl and her husband who were with us, fell silent and anxiety crept over us. But after what seemed an interminable age we saw the light again, a long way out, and gave him a beam from our torch. He came back thrilled with having seen Squirrel Fish, which come out at night.

Fiji was one of our most memorable holidays. A whole week on our own, with no pressure and an idyllic setting. Peter went back to Korolevu in 1966 on his way to and from the South Pole. It had changed somewhat by then, after a serious fire had burned down most of the burres, but he enjoyed seeing the fishes again and got a wonderful welcome from Walai who still remembered him.

From Fiji we went on to Hawaii where it was important to try to find and film the rarest goose in the world. We had ten days of fantastic American hospitality on Oahu and the big island of Hawaii. We spent some time staying with Mr Shipman, near Hilo. Peter had been in touch with him before the war, when he had offered to send Peter some Nenes. He still had tame Nenes, both at his house by the shore and also at his ranch inland at Ainahou, but we were not to see a wild Nene on this occasion. We visited the state Nene breeding project on the saddle between Mauna Loa and Mauna Kea (this, Peter said, was too high and too dry an area, for releasing Nenes). We walked in the mist over the lava hillside and saw an old used nest site, but never a real wild goose. Mr Shipman was a wonderful character who never slept after 4am and was surprised that we found it difficult to get up earlier than 8am after an evening spent socialising. His house, which was dark and damp, was full of priceless objects and his bedroom piled high with unopened Christmas presents.

Mr Shipman kindly took us to the far side of the island where we stayed

with Mrs Mona Holmes at the Hind Ranch. It was about fifteen miles inland
and situated on the side of a little cone called Puuwaawaa, which means
'the hill of the canoes'. We had two lovely days on the sea snorkelling and
fishing, going out from the harbour at Kailua. I had never before seen such
huge shoals of Yellow Tang and we also had the thrill of swimming with a
large Grouper, which was bigger than me, off the coast where the Captain
Cook monument is. We were sad to leave such a wonderful place, but
Hawaii had one more activity to offer of special importance to Peter: his
first underwater attempt with an aqualung. The place, just by the
Honolulu aquarium, was not ideal since the water was rather murky and
there were not many fish. It was a new experience and Peter was in for
about forty minutes. Charles and I snorkelled and saw a scorpion fish for
the first time.

There were two more stops on our way home. The first was in California,
where we met up with our old friend Jean Delacour, Director of the Los
Angeles Museum and then went up country into the Merced Valley to look
for geese. I do not know what I had expected of California, but from reading my diary it obviously did not come up to expectations. It rained, or was
dull and cloudy, most of the time. We did see a lot of geese and I remember
a lot of coots, who made a big impression on me. I became convinced that
they would take over the world. We also visited the San Diego Zoo with Jean
where I would have preferred to have spent time looking at the animals
rather than meeting so many people. Six days in California was enough for
me, but New York was still to come.

We had happy memories of New York from our visit in 1951 and our
hosts were kind and friendly. Peter was committed to lecturing to the
members of the Audubon Society and for the first time some of my slides
were shown to the public. These were photographs from New Guinea.
I had had the film processed in Honolulu and it was fun to see them on
the screen.

The day before we left New York we inaugurated The Wildfowl
Foundation at a meeting in the bedroom of a distinguished American
ornithologist called Pink Guthermuth in the Savoy Plaza Hotel. In
addition to a lawyer and two other American friends there was our old
friend Roger Tory Peterson. The object of the Foundation was to collect
tax-free funds for the Wildfowl Trust. It provided the Trust with quite

substantial funds over the years, before finally being wound up in December 1995.

We arrived back at Slimbridge on 13 February 1957. It was with enormous relief that I found my son was pleased to see me. I had been worried that he would no longer feel I was his mother – he was still only two years old, and three months is a long time at that age. Dafila, at four, was more securely bonded to me. But all was well. However, I did tell Peter that I would never leave my children for so long again – and I never did.

CHAPTER FIVE

The Enchanted Isles

Between our return from the world tour in February 1957 and our next foreign trip, life went on as usual at Slimbridge. For me there was the pleasure of my children. Thanks to my mother's legacy we continued to employ a nanny, and for the most part they were a great success, the last one staying on until the children went to boarding school. She then continued for a while as cook/ housekeeper. Sadly for us, she married and eventually left but it was thanks to her that I was able to accompany Peter on many of his business trips. He had by now become a well known figure. His radio programmes and the *Look* series on BBC television were very popular. He was frequently recognised in public places. I suppose we must have been a little self-conscious about it because we felt the need to acknowledge to each other that anonymity had left us, and we had to be on our best behaviour. The catch phrase was 'Annie has gone', Annie being Miss Annie O'Nimity.

Travel, however, was the essence of our lives. We loved sharing the adventure and the excitement of new places. By this time Peter was involved with the BBC Natural History Unit at Bristol. The *Faraway Look* series from our world tour had been a success and the BBC was keen to use Peter again.

There was talk at the IUCN of the possibility of setting up a Charles Darwin research station in the Galapagos Islands. IUCN was not in a position to fund an expedition to look into the project, but Peter managed to persuade the BBC to send us out there together with Tony Soper to make another film for the *Faraway Look* series. Once again I was faced with leaving my children for several weeks. Dafila was six and a half and Falcon four and a half, but I left them in good hands. How could I miss such an exciting adventure?

We left England on 5 January 1959 and flew via New York to the Virgin Islands. There we spent twelve glorious days filming pelicans, swimming and sailing round some of the outlying islands, which had deserted beaches. I collected and packed up masses of shells to send to the children. We rode to the top of Sage Mountain and filmed Peripetus, a primitive worm-like creature which excited Peter. He was less excited when his horse ran away with him on the way back to the stables (it had pretended to be lame on the way out). From the Virgin Islands we flew to Trinidad, where we stayed at Dr Beebe's Research Station at Simla in the Arima Valley. William Beebe, the great and famous naturalist, was then eighty-two but his mind was as sharp as ever. Peter had met him before and much of the first day was spent talking. David Snow was working on the birds locally and Dr Jocelyn Crane on butterflies. There was plenty for Tony to film. There were also two American photographers, Russ and Jane Kinne, who were to have a significant influence on me. I kept in touch with them for many years and they helped me greatly with my photography.

We visited the Spring Hill Estate, belonging to Mrs Asa Wright, a splendid Icelandic lady of seventy-two. She gave us lunch after we had visited the gorge where the Oil Birds live. Seeing these amazing birds, with a 3ft wing span, which live in a cave was exciting. Wearing a bathing dress, I climbed down a stream and then down a waterfall by ladder into a 3ft pool. The birds, which have heads like hawks, flew about uttering wild squawks and a clicking sound. Alas! I had never used flash before and my photographs were not very successful.

Our next port of call, after one night in Panama City, was Barra Colorado Island in the Panama Canal. We stayed at the research station belonging to the American Museum of Natural History, which is quite high up the hill and surrounded by dense tropical forest. It was a naturalist's paradise. During our four days based there we saw so many exciting animals. We had our first view of Masked Ducks, in the Chagres river, from a boat. There were Howler Monkeys, White-faced Monkeys, Coati Mundis, Peccaries and a Tapir close to the building. Also arrived that day was an orphan baby Kinkajou, the most adorable animal. There were Tree Frogs,

Leaf-cutting Ants, weird stick insects and many more wonderful exotic creatures. Alone in the forest with a tape recorder I saw a strange long, black animal with a red head, a Tayra – a marten-like creature rarely seen.

The next leg of our journey took us via Panama City to Quito, 10,000ft up in the Andes. During all this time poor Tony had to cope with endless frustrations over his camera and film equipment. Between the three of us we had thirty-nine pieces of baggage. Our object in Quito had been to see Torrent Ducks, and this we achieved on a day excursion with some ornithologists.

Our expedition began seriously when we arrived in Guayaquil, on the coast of Ecuador. Here we had help, in the form of a Jeep, to take us round the town, shopping for provisions for our six weeks in the Galapagos Islands. It was very hot and humid and there was an earthquake during the night which we felt at 5am in our hotel room. But everything was completed in twenty-four hours for our departure by air next day. This was the first commercial flight to the Galapagos by a company called LIA. We set out with our film equipment, personal luggage and food, for the airport. Sitting forlornly in the middle of the airfield, on the grass beside the runway, was a table with a typewriter and a weighing machine beside it. This was LIA. There were five other passengers who had already begun to fortify themselves with whisky. We took off in a Curtis, a vast freight plane with bucket seats. The Galapagos Islands are known as The Enchanted Islands because the early sailors could not always find them. They had the reputation for sinking into the sea. It is a case of next stop Japan if you do not find them and rumour reached us in our bucket seats that the radio beam was not working.

After three and a half hours in the air it was a relief to land on Seymour on a gravel airstrip among the tall cacti. There was a four-kilometer walk down to the little harbour, where the Patrol Boat *La Patrouillera* awaited us. It took all day to get our luggage down by hand cart. Peter and I slept out on the quay under the stars after dining with the Captain of the Patrouillera in his cabin.

At that time the islands were under the control of a naval governor. The patrol boat was for our use, courtesy of the Governor, for two trips round the islands. The boat had a crew of ten, most of whom were remarkably inefficient, with the exception of a tall black man called Pedro who seemed to understand more about boats and the sea than the others. The Captain was very young and spoke not very good English. We dined with him every night down below in his tiny cabin. The meals, always the same, consisted of one fried egg with rice, tea the colour of dish water and some fruit, if there was any. It was unbearably hot below deck. I sat on the Captain's right and tried to make conversation with him, while Peter, Tony and Chris Zuber, a photographer from *Paris Match*, sat on the other side and talked shop about filming. Luckily our picnic meals ashore on the outer islands were fairly satisfying, but meals on board and any we had with our hosts in Santa Cruz or San Cristobal were definitely thin.

Chris Zuber had cadged a lift off our party. It was not easy to get around the islands in those days. He and Tony must have slept below in cabins. Our luggage was stowed below but Peter and I slept on deck every night on air mattresses. If it rained, we moved to the wheel house and I slept on the chart table and woke sometimes to find both Peter and Tony on the floor.

We had established a base in Santa Cruz with the Castro family before we left on the first boat trip which took us to Tower Island, James and Las Plazas. Everywhere we went the wildlife was fantastic and it was hard to know where to begin photographing and filming. At that time I was using both colour and black and white film. The Frigate Birds were displaying on Tower and I do not think I have ever seen such a splendid performance by them since. Wherever we went we were the only people on these uninhabited islands. Peter's *Travel Diaries Volume I* describes the wonderful time we had with the birds, sea lions and seals and the fishes we saw while snorkelling.

Tower Island was six hours steaming to the north of the main group of islands. We had only been there one day when the crew announced that we were very short of water. In the tremendous heat, and with no water on any of the other islands, the situation seemed serious. On the third day we woke the Captain and the crew at 5.45am and set off back in order to call in on James Island on the way. At 8.30 I saw we were off Marchena and got Peter to look at the chart. We were ten miles off course in twenty miles. It was worrying that the navigation was so poor. It was also cloudy and hot and there were stinging flies. When we went ashore on James Island we found that four of us trying to film twenty-one rather wild flamingos was difficult. Chris of course said he had film of them at five metres, which was 'fantastique'. His film shots were always 'fantastique', which could be rather – no, *very* – irritating.

By this time the drinking water was the colour of tea, but none of us had been ill. We encountered a fishing boat which had run out of gasoline. We were able to help by towing it and we got a slop-pail of water from them, also the colour of tea, and some prune jam. 'Very good for the stomach,' the Captain said. Our beer and Coke were now finished and the tea, lemons and pineapples were all gone. We spent a morning looking at Fur Seals and Sea Lions on the shore. In the afternoon, miraculously, it rained. We persuaded the crew to fix up an awning to collect drinking water. We all put on bathing things and washed in the rain and had a good frolic. This made us so hungry that we opened a tin of corned beef, which made us feel better. The tow rope to the fishing boat broke six times on the way to Las Plazas, but we got there in the end.

Nowadays the land iguanas are very tame, as they are used to being fed by tourists (which is no longer permitted) but at that time they were extremely wild and we had great difficulty in getting near one. We had a great chase through the bushes, and finally caught one in its hole. Swimming with the Sea Lions was a new and wonderful experience until a big bull suddenly appeared, looking very aggressive. It was surprising how quickly the three of us managed to get out on to the lava rocks.

The Captain was in a hurry to get away. Chris wanted to stay. Feeling was running high on board. They refused us water, but promised to make tea at 3pm. We got back to Academy Bay on Santa Cruz at 5pm and were glad to have our first wash in fresh water at the Castro house. It was hot and we were very sunburnt. The only contact with the mainland was the arrival of the boat, the *Ancon Trader*, which was due once a month from Guayaquil. Its arrival was heralded by the cries of a slightly mentally deficient lad, who used to shout 'el barco, el barco' at about the time it was due, even if it was not in sight. All the inhabitants rushed to greet the boat. The water on Santa Cruz was brackish, which meant that liquid refreshment was especially welcome. The islanders had long since run out of Coke and beer so supplies from the mainland were an occasion for a really good binge in the 'pub'.

Three days after our return with the *Patrouillera* we set off, on foot, up the mountain on Santa Cruz on a tortoise expedition. All the islands are volcanic. As you get higher the vegetation thickens and the atmosphere becomes more humid. High up in the forested part we were to stay with Mr and Mrs Hornemann, who had a farm. It was drizzling as we set out and stiflingly hot among the trees. The rocky mountain path was slippery with water and deep mud in places. But the Hornemann lunch was amazing by Galapagos standards: roast pork, potatoes, tomatoes, avocados and rice pudding with fruit juice. Mr Hornemann was a German philosopher aged about seventy. He had built his house thirty years before and was the first settler in the interior. Everyone had told him it would be impossible to live there because there was no running water. His wife was also German and they had a delightful thirteen-year-old son, Sigvart, who spoke five languages and did most of the work on the farm. Half a mile further off in the woods was another farm belonging to the Kastdalens, who were Norwegian. Alf Kastdalen was an excellent naturalist and helped Peter with some of his ornithological queries. He had a useful library and was memorable for having the largest feet we had ever seen.

The following day we donned our wet-weather clothes and set off westward for tortoise country. The party now consisted of our guide, Caesar Moncayo, his ten-year-old stepson, two pack donkeys, Chris Zuber and Tony. There were two more donkeys, one for me to ride and 'Peter splendid on a horse'. There were also three large dogs, rather like reddish Alsatians. As an exercise in filming Galapagos tortoises it has to be said that the expedition was not a great success. It rained most of the time and there was too much competition between us and *Paris Match*. The biggest tortoise we found was fairly shy, although we managed to get some film of it during a brief period when it stopped raining. The trouble was that it put its head in if approached too closely.

We had bought a bottle of brandy in Guayaquil 'for medicinal purposes' and carefully divided it into three. When darkness fell and we had eaten our baked beans out of mugs we decided it was time to have some 'medicine'. But we had not reckoned with Chris, who began passing Tony's share round in an expansive way. Since Chris had poached most of the best opportunities for filming tortoises, we were not feeling particularly generous with such a scarce commodity – in difficult circumstances little things matter a lot. The only good thing was that we had taken jungle hammocks with us, and here at last they could be useful in keeping us fairly dry for the night (we had not reckoned with the islands' lack of trees so this was the first and last time we used them).

The trek back to Academy Bay the next day was tiring. We set off, a wet, weary and rather miserable party, to walk for six hours, barely stopping, with only a pineapple and a small piece of chocolate between us for food. The track going down the hill was even worse than when we had come up. We were soaked to the skin, covered in mud and scratched by the vegetation.

In the Castro house we had a tiny bedroom upstairs, with no door. There was a store room next to it for the camera equipment, etc. Water had to be carried upstairs. Tony was staying chez Moncayo at the other end of the village. In the pub we had to share one bottle of beer between the four of us since that was all there was. We were unable to leave the next day because the *Ancon Trader* had taken all the available local fresh food, so with a couple of extra days on Santa Cruz we joined the German Angemeyer family and the Belgian De Roys for various filming interludes. The Angemeyers had a fine house on the point, accessible only by sea. They had Marine Iguanas and Sea Lions on their verandah, which they fed.

Our second expedition in the *Patrouillera*, still with Chris along with us, took us first to Elizabeth Bay for the penguins, then to Tagus Cove, which had cliffs painted with the names of ships. Chris received good marks from us here for catching some mackerel which improved our evening meal (for some unknown reason the crew never bothered to fish). The highlight of this trip was perhaps Fernandina, the island with the most spectacular and highest volcano. Here there was a large colony of the fascinating Marine Iguanas. They are different on every island, but nowhere else did we see such large colonies of them as on Punta Espinosa and further round the rocky shore. Peter and Tony filmed them laying eggs in the sand and, using masks and snorkels only, feeding under water. There were also flightless cormorants; very few of these amusing birds remain on any of the islands – it is an endangered species and inevitably very vulnerable. There were Sea Lions and a remarkably tame Galapagos Hawk.

We picnicked each day under the same mangrove tree with a Mangrove Warbler singing above, Sea Lions and Red Crabs in the pool below and a colony of Marine Iguanas on the rock opposite. We had four blissful days at Punta Espinosa. By the fourth day a mosquito bite on my leg had gone septic and turned into a tropical abscess. It was huge and exceedingly painful. The weather was very hot and the crew had drunk all our small and precious supply of Coke so we decided to head for Academy Bay via Elizabeth Bay, where we hoped to get some penguin sound recorded. But the ship's generator spoiled that.

It seemed a long six-hour journey back to Academy Bay in stormy weather with rough seas and nothing to eat. By this time the abscess on my leg was about the size of an orange. On arrival we visited the 'sick berth attendant' at Academy Bay, who gave me an injection of penicillin which we had brought and told me that the abscess would have to be opened in San Cristobal. I had a bad night. In the morning we left for Wreck Bay at 6.30, arriving about 11am. I went straight to the naval doctor. He spoke no English, but I understood that he said he must operate. I lay in a bare room upstairs with the rain coming in through the open window onto the bed. Peter said that he could not bear to see me hurt, and retreated to the far side of the building. A nurse held my hand while the doctor stuck a needle with local anaesthetic into the large lump. He then operated. It all seemed rather Somerset Maugham. I was thus temporarily immobilised. The pressure was gone but my leg was still extremely painful. The doctor put me on a course of acromycin pills, which made me feel sick. Peter and I were given two camp beds in the basement of the naval barracks and had our meals brought to us there. At night I woke to hear something gnawing near my pillow. A rat was running round the room and next day I found it had been chewing at the piece of chocolate in my night bag. After two nights of misery in the barracks the doctor drained a large amount of poison out of the lump on my leg and we left in the *Patrouillera* for Hood Island.

With a large crater in my leg I could not swim, but I enjoyed being ashore on the island. The Waved Albatrosses were not there at that time of year, but there were lots of Blue-faced Boobies with young at all stages, Frigate Birds displaying, Tropic Birds along the cliff edge and the brightly coloured Hood Marine Iguanas. It rained and we all slept in the wheel house, where the Captain related stories late into the night. We had tried to persuade the crew to kill a goat for us to eat but they could not be bothered, even though Chris offered to clean and prepare the meat. The Captain dressed my wounded leg and announced on the first day that it would have to be cut open again. But the second day was not so bad. The crater was half an inch wide and deeper than that, with pus still forming, but of course eventually it healed.

After three days on Hood Island we returned to Academy Bay. There was a good deal of confusion about how to get us back to the airfield on Seymour. Karl Angemeyer offered to take us, but the plan changed every few hours through the night. There was a lot of packing which I did while Peter painted in his diary. Finally we set off in Karl's boat. It was a long haul in a rather slow sailing boat. We spent the night anchored off Las

Plazas with the boat lurching and rolling. After coffee at 5am we set off up the coast and through South Channel to Seymour. Peter kept us entertained reciting the whole of *The Hunting of the Snark*. I remember very vividly how utterly exhausted I was during the last few hours we spent between the landing on the island and our departure soon after midday. It was extremely hot and there was the two-mile walk up to the airstrip. The flight back was not much better than the flight out. There were more people, no toilet facilities and the aeroplane smelled like a lavatory. Tony, as always, was quiet, kind and efficient, coping with the huge pile of luggage at either end of the journey.

In retrospect, I think that that particular Galapagos expedition was probably the toughest trip of all the ones on which I went with Peter. There were so few boats around at that time and very few inhabitants of the islands. With the lack of fresh water one did not stand much of a chance if something went wrong at sea. But although it was tough it was wonderful. Little did I know that I would return to those Enchanted Isles later.

CHAPTER SIX

Up, Up and Away

The early sixties were busy years. So much was happening in Peter's life. In 1960 he was installed as Rector of Aberdeen University, which meant regular visits to Scotland. On one occasion the students threatened to kidnap him in aid of charity. That worried me but luckily it did not actually happen. Peter was supposed to be writing his autobiography but he was not enjoying writing. He had taken up gliding. The Scotts have this thing of becoming obsessed with some activity which has captured their interest. If Peter was going to be a glider pilot, then he had to be in the top league, which meant giving time and energy to it. He would be sitting at his drawing-table and, looking out of the window, he would see that there was the right kind of sky. Nympsfield Gliding Club, just at the top of the hill opposite us, is only twenty minutes away. Regardless of what was in his engagement calendar he would be into his car and off. On one occasion Esmond Knight, the distinguished, partially sighted actor, and some friends arrived, having made an appointment to see Peter. Not knowing that they were expected, I opened the front door and told them that Peter had gone gliding. Esmond was furious, though he later forgave Peter.

Mike Garside, his PA, had to cope with Peter's frequent unexpected absences and also with having to go and retrieve him when he landed his glider. Mike was to become the most important member of Peter's gliding crew and won the prize one year for best crew member at the National Championships.

Peter eventually finished his autobiography but deadlines had come and gone because he had spent the advance royalties on buying a new glider. *The Eye of the Wind* came out in 1961 and in 1963 he won the British National Gliding Championship. But that was by no means the end of his gliding activities.

I suppose the gliding era of Peter's life was the most difficult for me. We shared so many interests but this one defeated me. Peter took me up several times in his two-seater Eagle, but it was not for me. I am not really happy in the air. I prefer terra firma or the ocean. When the glider gets into a thermal the plane goes up with a jerk. It is like a bumpy ride in an aeroplane. I groaned each time it happened and it naturally annoyed Peter who had been waiting for just this 'lift'. So I gave up trying and Peter could then indulge in something more exciting and aerodynamic than a two-seater.

There were years when his movements were often unpredictable. I became a gliding widow and sometimes felt quite sorry for myself, though as a friend said, 'Better than it being another woman!' I tried to participate by going with Mike as part of his crewing team at all the major competitions. But the gliding fraternity was like most organisations – everyone knew each other and had a common interest. I found it difficult to fit in, although some of the retrieves, with Mike driving, were fun. I became quite good at navigating and Mike was very tolerant whenever we got lost. The competitions were enjoyable if the weather was good but many hours were spent on cold windy airfields waiting for a break in the clouds.

Throughout this period I had two young children and my teenage step-daughter Nicola who, although a good bit older, was very much part of the family. I needed the children and they (nanny or no nanny) needed at least one parent. We did have one family gliding holiday at Perranporth in Cornwall when the object for Peter was to obtain his 300km distance flight with a south-west wind from the gliding club nearby. I was sole crew member for this and as it was before we had radio communication we had to use the hotel as a reporting base. One day Peter set off in excellent conditions and I left in the car with the 40ft trailer and instructions to call the hotel every hour. I drove and I drove across England, calling every hour. No news. I remembered that Peter had said he would cross the Channel to France if he could. I began to wonder what I was going to do when I reached Dover and how I would manage in the narrow streets with my long trailer. As usual it had been a last-minute decision to set off and I did not have much money with me. Eventually, halfway across England,

I received a message from the hotel that he had landed about forty miles back from where I was. The trouble with that system was that the pilot could call just after the driver had called and the driver could be going for another hour. Later we had radio contact. Peter's call-sign was 'Drake' and I was 'Mallard'. 'Mallard to Drake. Do you quack?' I called.

My roots are in Africa. I can never get away from that. Peter had not been to Africa so our visits together to Uganda and Kenya in 1956 and again in 1961 were interesting for us both. East Africa is very different from where I was born in South Africa but there were smells and bird sounds sufficiently similar to make me feel that I was coming home. There were new things, such as eating mangos in the bath, fishing for Nile Perch below the Murchison Falls, and elephants wandering about outside the bedroom. By 1961 I had acquired a macro lens for my camera and Peter was enthusiastic about helping me photograph insects and other small animals. Catching chameleons became an important objective whenever we stayed in a house with a garden. They are not easy to find. I asked Cecil Webb, from London Zoo, whom we met out there. 'Just look in a bush,' he said. I spent hours looking in a bush but it was ages before I found some, captured and photographed them, then released them later.

At Paraa, the headquarters of the Murchison Falls Park which Peter officially opened in 1956, we slept in great luxury in a room built for the Queen Mother. Here one of our chameleons gave birth to eleven babies while we were out one day; and on another occasion we came back to find that a Praying Mantis's nest which we had brought in had produced a multitude of young which were climbing all over the curtains. It was all good material for photography. Much of these two trips to Africa is recorded photographically in a book we published in 1962 called *Animals in Africa*.

From Uganda we went to Kenya where we were the guests of Dr Mervyn Cowie, Director of the Kenya National Parks, and where Peter was to open the Nakuru National Park. The opening proved to be quite eventful. To start with we were late arriving at Nakuru because Peter and John Williams, the distinguished ornithologist, had stopped to look at every bird on the long drive from Nairobi. On arrival we learned that the water in the lake was unusually low, leaving a large area of soda-strewn mud and dust around its edge. Peter, the Governor and Mervyn were all to make speeches. A platform was set up on the dry part of the lake edge, but a strong wind got up and blew clouds of white soda dust all over everybody. Peter was wearing his tropical navy blue suit which was soon white.

The speeches over, the Governor invited Peter to join his party in the Rolls-Royce, and Mervyn was told to guide him in his Land Rover. It soon became apparent that we were sinking into soft mud. The Governor's driver noticed, swerved away and then sped off back to town. The Cowies and I were left stuck in the mud with a heavy vehicle and no help in sight. Mervyn and I did our best but there was no moving the Land Rover. Peter was due to give a lecture at which I was to operate the slide projector so I was a little worried, but it was nevertheless a laughter-provoking situation. We sat there in the mud for some time before a small figure was seen walking towards us through the soda mist. It was Peter. He had organised help but it would take a while for the rescue vehicle to come out so he had decided to come on foot to join us.

Mervyn had organised a wonderful itinerary for us which included a visit to the Serengeti and a tour of the Leakeys' dig in the Olduvai Gorge. Of course I longed to go fossil hunting, especially with Falcon's museum to think of, but did not dare even to pick up a stone in case I was thought to be trespassing. One of the highlights of the trip was camping on an island in the Galana River in the Tsavo National Park. I loved the red elephants – red from the Tsavo soil – and enjoyed watching them coming to drink opposite our camp. One evening they decided to investigate the camp, which caused some excitement. The warden pelted them with Doum Palm nuts and they eventually decided to leave us in peace. When I was a child in South Africa I used to catch scorpions in match boxes and send them to my brother at school in England. The Tsavo scorpions were bigger than anything I had ever seen. We put one in a soup plate so that I could photograph it showing scale. It was not a pleasant thought that I might find one in my shoe in the morning.

Like all our holidays from 1956 on we had to look at the coral fishes, so we asked to go to the coast. As in Australia our interests were misunderstood and we found ourselves staying in a hotel in Malindi, where the other guests were competitors in a big-game fishery competition. After only one night in the hotel we found ourselves happily ensconced as guests of two delightful people with a house right on the edge of the sea just south of Malindi. Archie Ritchie, then aged seventy-four, was a retired and very distinguished Director of Kenya National Parks. His wife Queenie liked to go snorkelling on a lilo, taking their Dachshund called Footsak ('footsak' is what you say angrily to a dog when you want it to go away.) Archie also had a tame Lilac-breasted Roller. They were devoted to each other and were always together. 'Good boy, Chirpie,' Archie would say as he fed it tit-bits. I was warned not to wear red nail varnish on my toe nails since Chirpie could be vicious. Another delightful animal on the premises was a toad who lived behind the books on a shelf.

Our visit to Malindi was pure holiday. Much of Peter's time on the 1961 trip was used for conservation propaganda. There were people he had to meet and speeches and talks to give. I remember being very tired when we arrived at Tree Tops. Mervyn Cowie wanted us to see all the famous wildlife places in Kenya and our time at some of the places was very short. It seemed awful to go to bed at Tree Tops when there might be a sighting of some special or rare animal at any moment. My chief memory of the visit is having tea outside on the roof, where we were joined by cheeky baboons and my scone was snatched from my hand on the way to my mouth. I have never been fond of baboons.

Peter managed to fit in a day at a gliding club and we had one day driving round the Aberdares National Park which had lovely scenery but not many animals. All these wonderful things took place in four crowded weeks in January-February 1961.

It was thanks to Peter's gliding obsession that in 1962 I was finally able to re-visit my old home in the Orange Free State in South Africa. I was born in Bloemfontein at the time when my father was farming at Westminster, close to the border with Lesotho. He died there in 1930 and my mother moved the family back to England when I was twelve. For me it had been a terrible break. I hated England and pined for the wide open spaces and sunshine of the land of my birth.

Peter's gliding ambition at that time was to achieve the Diamond Badge, which requires a distance flight of 500km. The weather, prevailing winds and geography of Britain make it difficult, even taking dog-legs into account. South Africa offers good opportunities with the splendid cumulus clouds. An invitation from Everard Read to stay in Johannesburg and open a wildlife painting exhibition fitted in admirably with Peter's plans. What he had not anticipated was that he would be confronted with the offer to borrow a glider pilot's sailplane the day after our arrival in order to attempt the 500km flight. The weather was right and he could not miss the opportunity, but what a challenge! A sailplane of a different make to his and totally unknown country. Needless to say, he did it. He flew from Baragwanath aerodrome, achieved the required dog-leg via Bloemhof and landed at Lindley. Lying all day in the Read's garden, I was very anxious about him. Finding one's way across the wide open spaces of Africa must be very different from navigating in Britain, with its crowded landmarks. It was a tremendous relief to hear that he had landed safely and I was delighted to learn that I could travel in the aeroplane that was to fetch him back.

The Reads' house in the suburbs of Johannesburg had a spacious garden. We were given their large bedroom where Peter could paint when there was time and Ev took us bird watching in the neighbourhood. A great wildlife enthusiast, his picture gallery – the Peter Wienning Wildlife Art Gallery – was full of exciting paintings by both South African and contemporary European artists.

For me the highlight of the visit to South Africa was going back to my old home at Westminster. Ev Read lent us his car and we drove there from Johannesburg, passing through Kimberley, where we were interested to see a flock of Greater Flamingos on a lagoon close to the diamond mining activity. We stayed with a friend, Mrs Thatcher, who had been a contemporary of my mother's. Her house was on the Duke of Westminster's estate, then owned by Lady Mary Westminster. Her son Michael was manager of the estate farms. I had known him as a rather poisonous little boy, so it was amusing to meet him again as an adult with considerable charm.

I was very impressed by the total lack of security in the Thatcher house. There were just the two old ladies (Mrs Thatcher had a companion) out in the country with only a few black people living anywhere near. No doors were locked at night. If Peter wanted to go to the loo in the night, he had to walk out of our bedroom, round the house and in at the front door. This was a very different situation from our friends in Kenya, where every door and window was locked and barred at night.

The day after we arrived we drove over to 'Beauchamp', my old and much loved home. The owner of the farm was an Afrikaner doctor with an English wife. They had no children and Mrs Dupreez had devoted her energies to the garden, which had been my father's delight. There had been stone terraces, rose beds, an avenue of fir trees, violets growing in their shade, a pergola with grape-bearing vines, a huge asparagus bed and, of course, well kept lawns and flower beds with every kind of annual and perennial flowers.

It was a risk to come back to this paradise. What if I were disappointed? I knew it had fallen into sad disrepair after my mother sold it in 1932.

We arrived at the front gate with its two stone pillars at the end of the quarter-of-a-mile drive. The house, which is on the side of a kopje, looked much the same. The pale yellow rough-hewn stone walls were as warm and inviting as ever. The red tile roof was still there. If the garden was not exactly the same, that did not matter. It was well kept and full of colourful shrubs and flowers. Thanks to Mrs Dupreez it was all as enchanting as ever: a magical place with the sun shining on it and the air clear and dry.

We were taken over the house, which was not much changed, and I was even able to show Peter the cupboard from which my brother Evelyn and I had clandestinely tried out our first gin and orange juice. Perhaps things were smaller than my memory of them but the most striking difference was in the distances. Thaba Patua (or Patchwa), the beautiful square-topped mountain opposite the house, now seemed very close. The farm to which Evelyn rode on his pony for lessons was only three miles away yet it had seemed many miles.

We climbed the kopje behind the house to enjoy the view of the hills of Lesotho not far to the east and Thaban'chu to the west. The sky was dotted with wonderful cauliflower cumulus clouds casting shadows over the veldt. Other farm-steads between us and the mountains could be seen with their red roofs peeping through their surrounding clumps of gum trees. Later we went to the railway station. As a child this journey was in a buggy drawn by two grey horses, Peter and Paul, crossing a donga (a dried-out river bed) as we went. Now there was a proper road. The store was still by the station yard, with all the wonderful things you would expect in an isolated farming community. What I had always loved were the brightly coloured rugs worn by the Basuto people. There were some on the shelves and the store still had a characteristic smell. We bought a tie for my brother and then walked onto the platform where a notice gives the height in feet (over 5000) under the name. The station had tremendous significance for me. On our return from summer visits to England it meant we had arrived home. After I left South Africa as a child I dreamed of Beauchamp for many years. The house, the farm and the station all featured in these dreams. After our visit in 1962 the dreams ceased, or became very rare. But two days later I shed tears as we left to return to Johannesburg. They were, I explained to Peter, because I could not cry when I left in 1932 – it hurt too much.

The Reads could not have been kinder to us. The social event which I remember best was the party they gave for us in their house. After all the guests had left and only the family and relations remained, they invited the two African servants to join us and we danced into the small hours. This impressed me because it was against the strict apartheid rules. I was also amazed to learn that children of English-origin parents were not allowed to go to the same school as Afrikaans-speaking children.

The painting exhibition duly opened and our nostalgic visit to Westminster over, it was time for wildlife. Once again the Reads generously lent us their car and we spent a few happy days in the Kruger Park, before going off to see the Parks in Natal where we were taken round by Colonel Jack Vincent. We visited Umfolozi, where we were introduced to quite a number of White Rhinos (*Ceratotherium simum*) for the first time. There is something very endearing about these great animals which at that time were quite numerous in this area. Peter noted that we had become 'ceratotherphiles'. We also saw some Black Rhino (*Diceros bicornis*) which were rare. From Umfolozi we went on to Hluhlue and on again to Mkuzi. The game viewing in all these parks was excellent. We were especially thrilled to see Nyala, although I was disappointed that we could not get close enough to photograph them. The bay at St Lucia produced a wonderful ornithological spectacle with hundreds of White-faced Whistling Ducks. They have an enchanting call which accounts for their local name 'Weesie weesie ducks'.

We could not leave South Africa without finding somewhere to look at fishes underwater. Santa Maria, off the island of Inhaca in Mozambique, was the most promising and provided us with some spectacular fish watching. But if the coral fish were plentiful, so were the mosquitos. Both were memorable. When I look at Peter's diary for that period I am amazed at the amount of things we did and places we visited during the six weeks we were away. From South Africa we went north and spent some time in Tanzania. Once again we were thrilled by the wonders of the Serengeti and Lake Manyara. Most memorable were the great herds of Wildebeest in the Serengeti and the mass of butterflies on damp places on the track down into the Ngoro Ngoro crater.

Our homeward route took us to the Sudan via Nairobi. Here we stayed with Mervyn Cowie again. We added a few chameleons from his garden to the one taken from the Ngoro Ngoro crater, and headed for Khartoum. After three hours' sleep in the Grand Hotel overlooking the Nile we were put on a small aircraft belonging to the Forestry Department and flown to Port Sudan where we planned to look at the coral fishes.

The chameleon that we had caught above the crater turned out to be extremely interesting. We named it the 'Oldeani Monster' after the area where it was found. It was not as easily tamed and handled as the other two species we had – *Ch jackson* and *Ch bitaeniatus* – hence the additional name 'Monster'. Some years later, thanks to the excellent painting of it in Peter's diary, it was recognised by Dr Schukker as the rare *Bradypodion uthmoelleri*.

On arrival at the coast we were welcomed into Port Sudan by the Commissioner for the Red Sea Hills, a large friendly man with a gusty laugh. He provided us with a programme for our visit which included a tour to the dead city of Suakin and its harbour. Suakin was the principal port of Sudan until the beginning of the 20th century. In 1905, when ships were growing bigger and the harbour of Suakin was incapable of expansion, work was begun on a new harbour forty miles to the north. It was completed and officially opened in 1909 as Port Sudan, and from then onwards the town of Suakin was dead. The number of inhabitants fell from 30,000 to 3000 and the great buildings began to fall into disrepair. Fifty years later it looked as if it had been bombed. After collecting the Mayor we drove across the causeway to the island where the city had been and which now had a Rest House maintained in an old bank building. From there we had a good view of the harbour where we saw a few scattered Greater Flamingos in the lagoon. After a tour of the harbour in a motor-boat we changed and put on masks and snorkels to have a look underwater. Although not marvellous it was interesting.

His Excellency the Commissioner arranged for a carpenter to construct some special boxes in which to keep our eight chameleons. Catching grasshoppers for our captives was rather time consuming but before long we had some eager assistants among the local small boys. Our large hotel was very empty and, although basic, was comfortable and conveniently close to the harbour. On the second day the Fisheries boat (which Peter described as 'a sturdy tub with an antediluvian engine') took us to the Wingate Reef. Here at last we saw fishes such as we had never seen before.

There was a wall, the water was clear and the fishes were superb. Santa Maria had been beautiful but here the outlook was on a grander scale. The coral cliff fell away to blue depths, the ravines were bottomless. The most beautiful sight against the deep blue of the deep water were the shimmering shoals of golden red Anthias, the apple green Chromis and the sheer quantity of small brilliant fish. We stayed in the water for ages and got very cold. It was after all early March and we were in the northern hemisphere. We went into the town and bought Shetland wool jerseys – the only available garment that would keep us warm in the water.

On our last day we were taken out to Sanganeb Lighthouse in the fortnightly tugboat. Here the water was warmer and I was able to stay in longer. We swam in the lagoon and again on the outer side of the reef in clear water of great depth with wonderful fishes.

We arrived home on 10 March, together with our suitably housed chameleons. They all survived and were kept in a small conservatory adjoining the house next to the studio. I called it the 'Animal Room'. Although they were a joint interest it was my job to look after them, which I enjoyed. They are delightful animals to keep as pets because they are slow moving and easy to handle. The most difficult part was keeping the live animals that they needed for food. The worst problem was breeding locusts, a good dietary change from flies, and meal worms which were easy to keep. The locusts had voracious appetites and had to have fresh grass every day.

I bred some of the chameleons to the third generation and kept records of their diet and behaviour. These were the small ones from Kenya (*Chamaeleo bitaeniatus*) which are viviparous (have live babies). The egg-laying ones were more difficult to breed. I did have some success with *Chamaeleo dilepis*, the rather more common one, but failed to keep the young alive for more than a few months. Sadly I finally had to give them up because I could not get anyone to look after them while we were on our travels (the locusts were the problem) but fortunately I found a good home for them in London.

Two Horned Frogs (*Ceratophrys ornata*), which Peter brought back one year from Argentina, survived with us for many years and grew from about four and a half centimetres to about ten centimetres across. They had little protruding horns and were a beautiful emerald green with chocolate markings. They never did anything. They just sat. Once a week they were fed on small pieces of raw steak which had to be offered with tweezers, because after sitting and gazing at it for a while they would suddenly leap for it. Their mouths were about three inches wide and their jaws shut with a snap. They were called Humpty and Dumpty and fascinated our visitors. They came to a sad end by drowning but not before they had given us a lot of pleasure without much work.

The chameleons from our South Africa trip were the first inmates of the Animal Room but later we kept all sorts of different things. The indoor plants were definitely my business because I was supposed to have green fingers. I was not quite so enthusiastic about the larvae of the various moths and butterflies which interested Peter – with good reason. In my childhood in South Africa I used to run barefoot most of the time. Outside the back door there was a huge weeping willow, which at certain times of the year was covered in caterpillars of the Emperor Moth. They grow to a very large size and are as thick as your finger. At that stage they would fall to the ground and more than once I ran out and stepped on some, leaving a nasty yellow mush which oozed between my toes. From then on I had an aversion to caterpillars of any kind. I was, however, a dutiful wife, fed Peter's 'treasures' in the Animal Room when he was away and collected the plants for them to feed on. Most often they were Hawk Moths, 'the racehorses of the moths world' as Peter used to say (the Hawk Moth figured large in the painting used for the cover of this book).

All these animals were good photographic subjects and Peter was extremely helpful in getting them to pose for me. Many of the larvae pupated successfully and hatched into beautiful, perfect insects. Once when Peter was in hospital I took him a cage with the larvae of the Hercules Moth, complete with its food-plant foliage, so that he could lie in bed and watch them. The nurses were fascinated.

The most beautiful animals which we kept were the little Madagascar Geckos. They are brilliant green with red spots on their backs. We bred them successfully but the young were so small and fast moving that it was almost impossible to contain them. For a short time we had two small snakes but they, too, escaped and I have to admit that I was not so keen on them. The prettiest one was found in the garden, months after it had escaped. It had survived an English winter but not the lawn mower.

The Animal Room at Slimbridge could not have lasted as long if it had not been for a noble and loyal staff. When the children were small there was always a nanny and there were secretaries. Noblest of all perhaps was

Mike Garside, who drove the children to school when we were away and kept an eye on everything during our all-too-frequent absences. Staff in the Wildfowl Trust assisted with food for the chameleons. There was always some animal in the house which needed looking after, even if it was only dogs in the later years. After the animals, I kept a variety of house plants as a hobby which mostly survived our absences from the house. They linger on today, in the care of a dog minder when I am away.

In the 1960s the single most important thing that happened to us was the founding of the World Wildlife Fund. From the moment that it was inaugurated our lives were never quite the same again.

We had the Director of the Delta Waterfowl Research Station, Al Hochbaum, from Canada staying. He was an old friend of Peter's and they had long talks about conservation in general and waterfowl in particular. Peter had been to a meeting of the IUCN (now Conservation International) and was much concerned about the lack of money to support the good work being done by that organisation. After Al Hochbaum had left I remember Peter in a pensive mood, standing in front of the fire in the studio at Slimbridge. He was worried, he said, because he wanted to be involved, to do something positive, to take some action to help the conservation of nature worldwide. He had discussed this with Al, and Al had told him that he should stick to waterfowl and the Wildfowl Trust. Peter asked me what I thought. I had no hesitation in encouraging him to go for the wider issue. That was what he wanted and that was when the World Wildlife Fund finally took root in his mind. Max Nicholson and Peter had conceived the idea on a flight back from Brussels, but someone had to do something. Talk was not enough.

Several people in the field of nature conservation were deeply committed and involved but it was Peter who was the driving force and the man of action behind it all. In 1961 it was Peter who approached Prince Philip and persuaded him to be President of the British National Appeal. And it was Prince Philip who suggested Peter approach Prince Bernhard to be President of the International Appeal. Prince Bernhard was about to hand over the International Equestrian Federation (FEI) to Prince Philip. Peter rushed off to Claridges to see Prince Bernhard. The Prince was dressing for an engagement so Peter was taken up to his bedroom and then invited to join him in a taxi to continue their conversation. The deal was clinched and Prince Bernhard agreed to take on the Presidency of the International Appeal of WWF.

I recount all this because there have been several accounts of the beginning of WWF and of course inevitably it had a considerable bearing on our joint lives. There were meetings in London which Peter had to attend and I became a committee member of the Wildlife Youth Service, run by Cyril Littlewood. I went to London regularly for their meetings and sent my two children to the WYS adventure camps twice in the summer holidays. Although not officially involved otherwise, I supported Peter wholeheartedly through all those early years. There came a stage when his workload was such that he acquired a wildlife assistant to help with the office work. He then kept three people busy in the office – a PA (Mike Garside), a secretary (Dougie Eccleston) and a wildlife assistant. I, too, was still involved with the secretarial work.

From being Chairman of the British National Appeal at the beginning, Peter ended up as Chairman of the World Wildlife Fund International. Forming National Appeals worldwide took time and effort. It also meant frequent visits to the first headquarters of WWF International at Morges, in Switzerland. In those early days we entertained a number of potentially influential people at Slimbridge, with the object of enlisting their support for wildlife and conservation. Notable among them were the banker, Ernest Kleinwort, and his charming wife. Later Ernest was very involved with both WWF and the Wildfowl Trust, and he and his wife became good friends.

Like any big organisation, it took time to get WWF off the ground. There were the inevitable personality problems which Peter, with his charm and innate diplomacy, managed to settle amicably. He enjoyed drawing the Panda for the WWF logo, aided by Gerald Watterson from IUCN. He was greatly saddened when it was altered so that it could easily be computerised. He felt that the Panda no longer had a friendly expression. The change to a longer name also worried him, but all these things happen in the name of progress. It is gratifying now to see so many Panda car stickers, even if the logo is not the original drawing. It shows how much interest in conservation has grown. Fundraising is still difficult, but the seed was sown and continues to grow.

Those were very full years. There was the Loch Ness Monster – or perhaps

not. Various people had come to Peter about possible sightings. One
summer Peter and I camped on a hillside above the Loch hoping to see
something, but without success. There were other visits to Loch Ness
which I always enjoyed, including the time when Peter put on a wet suit
and with a tank went exploring under water. It was Robert Rhines' photographs of a strange diamond-shaped object that looked like a fin which persuaded Peter that perhaps there really might be something there. If there
were an unusual creature in the loch, there was no law that could protect
it unless it was named; somebody, for example, could capture and remove
it. For this reason Peter decided to stick his neck out and name it. So it was
officially named, with an article in Nature, *Nessiteras rhombopteryx* which
means the 'Nessie monster with diamond-shaped fins'. Some smart alec
declared this to be an anagram of 'monster hoax by Sir Peter S'. The
naming did not happen until 1975, so the affair of the Loch Ness monster
lasted a long time as far as the Scotts were concerned.

I remember very vividly a family describing to us what happened to
them. They were sailing along in their yacht near the north-eastern end of
the loch. Everyone was down below except for an older boy at the helm. He
suddenly called down that there was a huge sand bank ahead: what should
he do? His father altered course. But the sand bank moved and started
coming towards them. One of the children took a photograph with a small
camera – but with a 35mm lens it was not close enough to look
spectacular. The sand bank was large, the father had a small child on board
and he did not like the look of things, so he bore away. When they reached
the lock a man standing on the bank said he too had seen what he thought
was a very large animal moving close to the boat. Not wanting to become
involved in publicity, the family kept quiet about their experience. They
were sure that they had seen the monster but did not wish to make a fuss
about it. I found the story very convincing. I do not think Peter ever really
thought there was such a large unknown animal in the loch but it did seem
worth investigating – and why not keep an open mind?

Gliding, WWF and the BBC notwithstanding, there was still time to have
fun with the family. In the summer of 1962 we teamed up with the
Winters and took a cottage at Gigaro on the south coast of France. Peter
and I drove down with Dafila and Falcon, and on the way we visited
some of the battlefields of World War II. These were places which Peter

remembered and tried to find. We stopped at Clères for a few nights to visit the distinguished ornithologist Jean Delacours, who was then in his eighties but still lived in his château and looked after his extensive zoological park. I suffered the usual worries of a mother with two young children visiting rather grand premises. They were very well behaved, of course, though they did become rather bored with nothing to do except wander round the zoo.

The park was encircled with a high wall and had a fairly main road running along one side. On the other side of the road was an additional area with a stream running through it, where some of the more precious and special waterfowl were kept. It was all too much like home for Dafila and Falcon, so we went off exploring outside the village, leaving all my expensive camera equipment with Peter. Falcon chose the most exciting looking deserted lane and we found a grassed-over tunnel. It was not extensive and not easily explored but it at least provided a suitably interesting diversion from the birds.

In bed in the château that night I suddenly remembered my cameras. It was after midnight and Peter was dozing off. Horrors! He had left them in the small outside waterfowl garden and had forgotten all about them. Supposing it rained? So he dressed and crept downstairs and out into the park. The big gates were locked, but edging his way silently along the bottom of the wall he found some more gates in among the trees. Here he managed to scramble over, drop down onto the road and cross over into the garden. The camera bag was still there. But coming back he had problems crossing the road. Some bicycles came by and a car. It would not be a good idea to be caught climbing in, so he had to wait a while. He then found it much more difficult to climb the gates from the road side. In the meantime I was lying in bed worrying, not about my cameras, but about Peter. Had he been caught? Had he fallen? It was an enormous relief when he crept quietly and triumphantly back into the bedroom. He had had to walk past some of the chimpanzee cages and they had threatened to give away his presence. I was immensely touched that he had done all this for me.

We met up with the Winter family at Gigaro, not far from St Tropez. With John and Rachel were their two sons, Mark and Giles, and their daughter Julia, who was about the same age as our Nicky, who joined us later. We had the little beach almost to ourselves and all the children enjoyed snorkelling, which was made so much more interesting with Peter telling them what everything was.

One night there was a memorable thunderstorm and we all stood outside to watch it. We went for drives and nature rambles; one day we drove to St Tropez to have a look and came back by a small road which took us to the top of a hill, where we were faced with a large notice saying 'Danger de mort' which excited the children. All in all it had been a very successful holiday. Two weeks were just right.

Our next foreign holiday with the children was in April 1964 with a repeat in 1965. We had been offered the sole use of a delightful little bungalow on the sea shore a few miles out of Nassau in the Bahamas. I had written to a lovely quiet, very rich man, Stanley Smith, whom we had met the year before and who had delivered the throw-away line, 'That is my guest house, if you ever want to use it just let me know', as we drove past on the way to lunch at his rather larger house. He was a world expert on orchids and one of the nicest and most generous people imaginable. When I wrote to him he replied with a two-page letter in long hand saying 'Yep, she's yours...' He explained at length that he would be away but we could use his boat, the *Emgent*, together with the skipper; that we would have a car at our disposal; and that we were to use his credit card at the supermarket – 'It riles us if you don't use it'.

There was a lawn sloping down to the shore and a coral reef just a little way out. The children had learned to snorkel in France but this was different because of the coral and the beautiful, interesting fishes. Peter and Dafila had an adventure when they unexpectedly found themselves face to face with a large shark when swimming in the dark with only one small torch between them. We had a glorious week sailing down the Exuma Cays, living on conch chowder cooked by the skipper, seeing more and more wonderful coral and fishes and exploring the little uninhabited islands. Falcon named one island 'Funnyland', mapped it carefully and listed all the strange 'Funny animals' that lived on it.

Visiting the supermarket was almost as exciting as exploring an island. None of us had ever been in one before. I had some difficulty in controlling Peter and Falcon, who found all the sweet things like ice creams irresistible. We were even able to arrange for Dafila to practise the piano in the house next door (she was working towards an exam so it was important to her).

On our second visit we arrived in the half dark in the evening and heard wild shouts and cries from the garden and by the shore next door. Peter shot off to investigate and found that our neighbour's husband was said to be attempting suicide by drowning and was in the sea some way out. He had taken the boat and there was panic and pandemonium. Peter flung off his travelling clothes on the beach, swam out to the boat and, as I understand it, rescued the poor man.

Later there were other holidays abroad but nothing was ever quite as carefree as those two Bahamas Easter holidays. There were no commitments for Peter; we could do what we liked; everything was new for the children and they seemed to enjoy the sea as much as we did. Sadly Stanley Smith died soon afterwards. We have since met his charming Chinese wife in Hong Kong at WWF events.

CHAPTER SEVEN

Of Swans, Shoes and Ships

Our lives were changed for ever in February 1964 when we enticed the first wild Bewick's Swan onto the pond outside the studio window. Wild swans had been visiting the New Grounds for some years in small numbers, but they always settled on the big pond on the other side of the premises. Peter was determined to get them to come over the lane to the pond outside the studio window. We brought the tame Bewicks over, as well as some North American Whistling Swans, to act as decoys. It worked and our first Bewick's Swan came in on 9 February, followed the next day by a few more.

Peter immediately recognised the difference in their face patterns, and Dafila, who was absent from school because she had 'flu, became as interested and excited as her father. They both drew the face patterns and we decided to give them names so that we would know them if they came the following year. The very first one was called Maud because she had taken up with one of the Whistling Swans (Maud was the artist Whistler's mistress), and we had persuaded her to come into what was virtually our garden. Soon after came the Major. He was top of the peck order and bossed the others around. There was Pink, who had very pink 'lips' and his mate Rebecca. Amber was very dark yellow. Lancelot, a particularly splendid looking bird, was named by Keith Shackleton after a character based on Peter in a yachting magazine for which Keith wrote. Lancelot's first wife was a very large and beautiful swan called Victoria. For a long time Lancelot was our most faithful swan, coming every season for twenty-six years. His arrival was always reported in *The Times*.

Peter enjoyed the naming and, of course – when he was not too busy – drawing and painting their faces. Some of his favourites were Caesar and Keeper, Harvey and Maria, Ruff and Reddy, The Colonel and His Lady, Asie and Flu, Mr Wrong and Lefty. Later came Hyle and Fling – I think that was the influence of our Scottish swan researcher, Mary Evans (now Mrs Geoffrey Matthews).

Before the wild swans came into the Rushy Pen it had been open to the public. From the time the Bewicks came in we started to close it for the winter months and opened it again when the swans left in the spring. For us, living in the house, it was very nice not to be under the public eye. Some years later we closed it to the public altogether.

The swans affected our lives in many ways. Inside the house we had to be careful how we moved when we were near any of the windows overlooking 'Swan Lake', as it came to be called. Peter was quite fierce with visitors. Keith Shackleton loves to relate how we were told to move 'like the hands of a clock' in front of the studio window. Peter and I frequently crawled across the space on the floor in order not to be seen by the swans. Outside noises and movements were carefully monitored by Peter. The cause of any flush or disturbance on the lake had to be immediately identified. On no account were the swans to be disturbed. They definitely recognise individuals, so as far as possible only two or three people were regular feeders on the daily rounds. Visits by the film crew to film Peter in the studio were nail-biting affairs and crew members were frequently in trouble for making sudden movements.

For me these visits were totally disruptive. I was banned from my own living-room, doors were left open to accommodate electric cables, the dogs escaped, it was cold and everyone had to be kept quiet. I was an outsider in my own house.

The swans were always a joy and still are. It is very exciting to see who will be the first to return in October. Sometimes they are new birds, sometimes old friends. At first Peter and I kept the records, but by the second year we had enlisted the support of a swan researcher, who came to the studio every day to do the daily register and make observations. Dafila soon became the expert, even though her visits from school were rather infrequent. A farmer told her he could identify 1000 sheep and that was a challenge to her to do the same for the swans. Her work on the swans and also her musical skills earned her a scholarship to Millfield School to take her A levels. When she was sixteen her headmaster, Jack Meyer, awarded her £200 to go to Holland to see if she could identify Slimbridge swans on their migration stop-off. This she did, to the amazement of a distinguished Dutch ornithologist, proving that it was the named bird she said it was by waiting half an hour until it upended on the canal and showed its ring number. Individual recognition of any wild animal, especially a bird, was not at all common at that time.

In winter the presence of the swans dominated our lives. The fact that the numbers increased every year was exciting and suggested we were doing the right thing for them. At first they used to come in for the day and go out at night. In later years they changed their habits, staying in at night and going out between morning and tea-time feeds. They did this in order to find a luscious wet field where they could feed on grass, since they needed their 'greens' as well as the corn provided in the pens. We started the idea of having flood-lights one year when Prince Philip was coming to stay so that he might enjoy the spectacle after dinner. Studying their habits and always mindful of their needs, Peter decided at some stage to install night-lights for them. After the flood-lights had gone out they should there-fore still feel relaxed and know who their neighbours were as they roosted on the islands close to the house. There was no doubt that they appreciated this, and I have noticed that before the swans arrive the ducks tend to roost in the dim light rather than in the darkness beyond.

The shape of the lake changed over the years, as extensions were made to provide better runways for the swans. Unlike Mute Swans, which can fly quite slowly with their broad wings, Bewicks need a long runway for take-off and landing and seem to prefer alighting on water.

The first time that we had a hundred wild swans at Slimbridge was in 1966 when Peter was in Antarctica having been to the South Pole to make a film for the BBC. He promised to call me from Antarctica and I was warned in the afternoon by the telephone operator that the call would come through at 2am. This gave me time to decide what was the most important news to give him: certainly that there were a hundred Bewick's Swans on the lake. It was a great moment. I set my alarm clock and woke up Falcon. The telephone rang. 'Is that Mrs Scott? I have a long-distance call for you. Will you pay for the call?' My Scottish blood answered 'How much will it cost?' 'Oh! come off it Mrs Scott, it's your husband calling you!' I never was at my best in the early hours! Later I learned that although it was from Antarctica, the call was not actually from the South Pole.

The swans have always been a special interest and a great joy to the Scott family: a legacy which Peter has passed on, not just to Dafila and me but to thousands of other people who have visited Wildfowl and Wetland Trust Centres at Slimbridge, Welney, Caerlaverock and Martin Mere. There is more to it than just the beauty and romance of their long migration from northern Russia: there is the study of their habits, their behaviour and their breeding successes, which will ultimately help to make sure that the species has protection from the many threats of modern life.

In recent years when we have caught them for ringing we have X-rayed a number of them and found that thirty-three per cent are carrying lead shot in their bodies. Yet they are protected in every country through which they fly on their migration route to the far north of Russia. The lead pellets are not all of the same calibre, which means that the shots come from more than one source.

For me, and for other people who have been able to identify a swan, there is a deep sense of privilege in looking at a bird which has come back for its second, third, tenth or twentieth winter from its far-away breeding grounds on the tundra, and in being able to say, 'I know you. Thank you for coming back'. As I write, the record is held by Lancelot (now dead) and Casino. We knew Casino in her first year as a cygnet. She has been coming for twenty-six successive years.

The America's Cup year, in 1963, was not much fun for me. It seemed a little ridiculous that so much money and energy should go towards a race between two yachts which were built specially for one race and did not form part of the normal yachting scene. However, for Peter it was an honour to be invited to be helmsman of Anthony Boyden's *Sovereign*. It was a great challenge and he spent much of the summer training in Dorset while I was at home with the children. When he left for America in August it was the school holidays. I took the children and the Shetland Collie for two weeks to Scotland before flying to the States to join Peter, who was living with the rest of the crew in a large house close to the sea, which they had christened 'Mildew Manor'. The rest of the wives had gone with their husbands earlier and I arrived as a new girl at Newport, Rhode Island, and found it difficult to fit in. Our America hosts were friendly and hospitable but among the British community on Rhode Island there was an undercurrent of jealousy which I found very unpleasant. The crew of the other would-be contender which had failed to be selected were inevitably critical of *Sovereign* and her crew. It was a period of much angst and finally some sadness. Peter had told me that I would know on the first day's race whether or not *Sovereign* would win. He said that it all depended on which boat could go fastest into the wind. There was no doubt that *Constellation*, the American boat, could and did. The only hope was to out-manoeuvre her. People have tended to make a great issue of the effect on Peter of not winning. I was with him all the time and know how he felt. I think what he minded most was that he felt he had let Tony Boyden down. But Peter was not the sort of person to allow this setback to ruin his life. Once at home he applied his mind to other things.

Sailing was one of Peter's spare time enthusiasms which I had never had the opportunity fully to share with him. There was a period when we used to go to Cowes every year for the regatta. As Chairman of the International Yacht Racing Union (IYRU) his opinion was much sought after on new types of sailing craft with the hope of their being accepted as an Olympic class. Centre board Catamarans were new on the scene and Peter was delighted to try them out. This was only possible when the weather was too rough for racing and it gave me the chance to learn something about sailing when Peter took me as crew. That day there was a lot of wind, the sea was wild and I enjoyed it all. The speed was tremendous. We were to go about when suddenly the sheet jammed in the cleat. The side we were sitting on rose in the air and it looked a long way down to the water. Peter said very coolly, 'I think we are going to capsize.' I wondered which way I should fall – backwards or forwards. It looked uninviting and a long way down to the water. I had not been instructed for this eventuality. But the cleat unjammed and we sank back. That was my first experience of sailing. Another year Peter was lent a Swallow and I was allowed to be number-three crew member with him and John Winter for the races. We did not win but I enjoyed it. On another occasion I took part in the races crewing for a young friend of Peter's whose wife had decided she did not like the rough weather that day. My skipper was helpful in telling me exactly what to do and I found it enormously exhilarating. Leading the dancing with Prince Philip at the Royal Squadron Ball that night crowned the day.

Less happy was my experience with a Norwegian couple when we were staying on board the Norwegian Royal Yacht in Norway for the National Regatta. Peter was crewing for the King. These were not centre board dinghies but boats with a cabin and mostly a crew of five. I thought it would be more fun to go racing than to stay on board all day and the Commodore of the Yacht Club invited me to join his crew. It turned out there were just four of us – the Commodore, his wife, their twelve-year-old son and me. I did not have a clue what to do and as all the orders were given in Norwegian, the sea was rough and I was superfluous, they finally decided to put me in the cabin to get me out of the way. I am not normally sea sick and I was not then but I did feel very ill and unhappy. They were all enjoying themselves because even with their much depleted crew they came in second in the race. But after that experience I decided yachting was not for me.

That must have been in 1957 because I remember we were all very interested to see the first Russian satellite in space – the Sputnik. *The Daily Telegraph* listed the times when it could be seen going overhead. One clear evening after dinner, at the appropriate time the guests all went out on the afterdeck and saw a bright object moving across the sky. But the King was dozing. His daughter, the Princess Astrid, woke him but panic and pandemonium ensued because it is not proper for the Captain in naval uniform to come on deck without his hat and this could not be found. We all ran in circles trying to find it and eventually his Flag Lieutenant produced it just in time before the Sputnik disappeared over the horizon.

On that same visit there was the affair of the sling-back shoe. Before joining the yacht we had been sightseeing and had then gone on to the Palace. As we walked up the steps at the main entrance the strap of my sling-back broke. As we joined other guests in an anteroom there was I hobbling about with one loose shoe. The King's equerry offered to make an impromptu repair. Our fellow guests were sympathetic and were all offering advice and help. Sellotape or a staple were on offer. The job was not complete when there was a rustle of anticipation, wide doors slid back and there was His Majesty the King. I tried to hide but found myself in a central position attempting to curtsey with one loose shoe. A titter went round the party. The King saw there was something amiss and the Equerry had to explain. Needless to say His Majesty was suitably amused and charming.

CHAPTER EIGHT

Antarctica the First Time

In 1966 Peter had been invited by the BBC to visit Antarctica and the South Pole to make a programme about the scientific work being done at the various stations there. Previously he had always avoided Antarctica for fear people would suggest he was trading on his father's name. He said, with some truth, that there was more abundant wildlife in the Arctic. By that time, however, having made his own name, carved his own niche, he felt he could safely go. He would have liked me to have been the first woman to visit the South Pole, but I was not allowed to.

My turn came two years later. Lars Eric Lindblad came to Slimbridge to visit us with his wife Sonja. This was the beginning of the tourist expeditions to far-away places organised by their American-based company Lindblad Travel Inc. Lars had already been down to the Ross Sea in 1967 in a ship called the *Magga Dan*. He was planning to do it again the following year, but wanted Peter to lead another expedition at the same time on the Antarctic Penninsula side in a Chilean ship called the *Navarino*. Peter was doubtful. But then he looked at me. 'Perhaps you would like to go?' he said, and then asked Lars Eric if he would take me too. And so it was on. This was to be the first of twenty-six tourist expeditions which we went on for Lindblad. On this occasion Peter was to be joint expedition leader with a delightful American, John Cadwalader.

We left London on 29 January 1968 with a party of about thirty people. Our journey to Buenos Aires was routed by way of New York, where Peter and I were met and taken aside by Mrs Sonja Lindblad, who told us that the *Navarino* had broken down in the Drake Passage on the previous trip and so had never reached Antarctica. It had been repaired, she told us, but it was obviously worrying news.

The onward flight was not without problems. A nine-hour delay at Caracas – where we were left stranded on the aeroplane at the far end of the runway with no crew on board – cemented friendships in the group. At the next stop, Asuncion, we were joined by an American called Dr Peterson from the previous aborted trip, who spread alarm and despondency among our passengers by telling them that the *Navarino* was going to be very crowded since the party of Americans from the first trip had opted to stay on board for the second. They were, he said, waiting at Punta Arenas and would of course get first choice of cabins. It began to look like all-out war between the Europeans and the Americans. By the time we arrived in Buenos Aires we had been travelling for thirty-six hours. On arrival we immediately had to go to a party at the English Speaking Club, where Peter was to present the *Animals Magazine* Photographer of the Year Award to a young Argentinian called Francisco Erize. The press were there in numbers and so was the British Ambassador. (*Animals Magazine* has since become the *BBC Wildlife Magazine*.)

After a further flight next day to Rio Gallegos followed by a six-hour bus drive we finally arrived at Punta Arenas. Here again there was trouble because there were not enough single rooms in the hotel for those who had requested them. I was learning the hard way what it is like to be a 'tour hostess'. Two days of coach excursions from Punta Arenas had been arranged but after the first one Peter and I decided to be anti-establishment and organize a bird-watching outing. With the help of the Spanish-speaking tour administrator, Jaime McMahon, who had now joined the party, we hired seven taxis and with twenty-six people set off for some of the places we had visited previously. We had not quite realised how difficult it is to control a large party of birdwatchers, who tend to be individuals. It was difficult to dissuade one small group from going on ahead and frightening all the birds before the rest of us arrived there. However, we clocked up thirty-five species during the day and everyone in our multinational party seemed happy. For me the most memorable sight was a group of thirty-five Black-necked Swans bobbing about in the sea in the Fitzroy Channel. They were evidently busy feeding, but on what we had no idea.

Next day in the late afternoon we set sail for Antarctica. The Straits of Magellan were beautiful, with distant huge cloud formations and sea birds all around us, including Magellan Penguins and Black-browed Albatross. Most exciting of all perhaps were the Comerson's Dolphins, small, black and white, which we saw porpoising ahead of us in the narrows of the Straits. Our passengers, so wary of each other before, were happier now as we embarked on our great adventure. There had been some dramas before we actually departed, including the mad pianist who had tried to stow away, and an English trio who found they had an extra person – an Argentinian journalist – in their cabin. We had learned about the problem on the previous trip when the steering had broken down in the Drake Passage and the ship had had to be steered manually by its large wooden rudder. We were assured that all that had been sorted out.

There was a day at sea when the sun shone and those who cared enjoyed the albatrosses, shearwaters and petrels and the anticipation of more to come. There were also many – mostly Americans I regret to say – who never ventured on deck. On board with us was Sheila Burnford, author of *The Incredible Journey*. She was enjoying every minute, as was Len Hill, the founder and director of Birdland at Bourton-on-the Water. Also with us was Jeffrey Boswell from the BBC who was making a film about tourists in Antarctica.

Port Stanley, our first port of call, was as special and enchanting then as I have found it on subsequent visits. The houses are bright and cheerful, the flowers in their gardens bigger and better than you would see in most places in England and the people, largely of Scottish origin, kind and friendly. It has an atmosphere of genuine Scottish hospitality. Our lunch at Government House was pleasantly informal, and after lunch the Governor's wife, Lady Haskard, took me in the official car, a brand new London taxi, to photograph Steamer Ducks. Back on board the *Navarino* a battle was raging. Half the passengers (the European group) wanted two days in the Falkland Islands, which would have taken in Carcass Island and West Point Island and we would have seen colonies of penguins, breeding albatrosses, Elephant Seals and Fur Seals. The American group said that the trip was not scheduled and that the important thing was to be able to say we had been inside the Antarctic Circle. This would probably mean steaming south for six hours at a later stage without necessarily seeing anything. There was a two-hour conference among the expedition leaders and the ship's captain and it was decided that we should make an early start and visit both Carcass and West Point Islands on one day.

Waking up at 5am and going ashore at 7am we fitted in both islands, each one a wildlife photographer's paradise. The scenery is spectacular, the wind blows all the time, the air is clear and sharp. Peter recorded twenty-nine species of birds as well as Elephant Seals and Fur Seals. On Carcass Island I used a great deal of film but on West Point Island I was overcome by the basic urge to go to the highest point, called Mount Misery. This was not just my mountaineering instinct but a need to get away from the other passengers. I set off with just a couple of companions, one of whom kindly offered to carry my camera bag. My excuse was that I had been told that there was a colony of breeding Black-browed Albatrosses near the top.

My companions disappeared and I saw nothing but dramatic cliffs beyond the summit. There was no sign of anything breeding and a fearsome gale was blowing, so I headed down towards the cleft in the hills where the main party had gone to look at a colony of Rockhopper Penguins. Here there were Black-browed Albatrosses, in their wonderfully symmetrical cone-shaped nests, and hundreds of Rockhopper Penguins nesting among the tussock grass mounds. But it was five o'clock, the light was going and my light meter was in my camera bag which had disappeared over the hill with my kind helper. Peter was not very pleased with me. He was disappointed that I had missed a good photographic opportunity. On both islands we had been treated by the farmer/owners, the Bertrands and Napiers, to home-made scones and cakes in their homesteads – this for nearly a hundred visitors. They even seemed sorry to see us go.

Two days at sea and the dreaded Drake Passage lay ahead. On the first morning we stopped the ship and put out a jar on the end of a long line in order to sample the water. We looked at the brown soupy liquid under a microscope. It was almost entirely blue-green algae. At that stage the air temperature was 7°C, the water 8°C. Soon we would be crossing the line of the Antarctic convergence where the sea temperature suddenly drops 5°C.

On the whole the day was peaceful, and people started hatching plans. Very few passengers, including ourselves, had been on a package tour before and we all found it rather difficult submitting to mass orders. The first result of this, the following morning, was a notice on the board saying that everyone should present themselves in their underwear at 9am for inspection. The joke went down very well on the whole, though one young American lady did not think it at all funny. The culprits were three Brits, including Sheila Burnford who is, alas, now dead.

The Drake Passage started to live up to its reputation that night. Peter and I had a very large bare cabin. We managed to acquire a table so that Peter could paint and this was cleared on going to bed. But as the ship began to roll it fell over and hit me We got up and lashed our cases to the beds, then wedged ourselves in our bunks with pillows. The gale blew all that night and the following day and night. I spent most of the day on deck watching the sea and the birds. Giant Petrels were following us; there were a few Light Mantled Sooty Albatrosses and flocks of beautiful Antarctic Petrels – small dark birds with a white bar all along the back edge of their wing: my favourite I think. A surprising number of people went on deck to look at the birds, indicating that sea-sick pills or patches were being effective. Meals were hilarious, with the ship heaving, rolling and judder-ing and chairs flying all over the place. It all helped to induce a feeling of solidarity among the group.

On the third day we sighted a rocky island and our first iceberg which was brown on top with volcanic dust from Deception Island. The storm had blown us a hundred miles off course to the east but the sky now cleared and the Captain was able to get a sighting. We steamed along to the south of King George Island through a blue, foam-flecked, wind-streaked sea. Our first landing was at Potters Cove on King George Island. One side of the bay was icecap, with nunataks (rocky peaks) and blue-green ice cliffs which were calving into the sea. On the other was a great sugarloaf type of rock mountain.

This was before the days of Zodiacs and we were taken ashore in two lifeboats, dressed in our red parkas and life jackets. The landings were not easy, and on the first one it took two hours to get everyone ashore. Once on land we left our life jackets by the landing place and picked them up on returning to the ship. This was the method of checking that no one had been left behind.

There were Elephant Seals with long noses and obnoxious breath. Like everything else they were unconcerned about visitors. There were Gentoo Penguins and a few Chinstraps – for me the most elegant penguins. There was a breeding colony of Giant Petrels high up on a bluff, with their swans-down babies the size of a bath sponge. We had now seen Giant Petrels in their much more handsome white form as well as the rather boring untidy looking brown ones. There were lots of engaging little Cape Petrels (or Cape Pigeons or Pintado). They seem to be flock birds and tend to peck around ships for surface food.

A day later we arrived at Deception Island, a tipped-up volcanic crater five miles long and two and a half miles wide. It had erupted the previous November and we were one of the first ships allowed in. The entrance, known as 'Neptune's Bellows', is very narrow and only navigable at certain tide times. There had been an Argentinian base here which was bombed by the British in World War I. The Chilean station had only been evacuated the day before we arrived and was half buried in lava dust.

We awoke the following morning anchored off the old whaling station. It was bright and sunny: a nice change from the preceding grey days. Twenty-six of us set off in the big orange motor-boat to do a tour of the crater. The whole island was brown except for a few patches of snow low down, and on the higher peaks of the crater along the rim there were big-gish ice masses with red rock beneath. In a bay not far from the Chilean station steam was rising from rocks near the water. The sea was steaming too. We recorded the temperature of the water as 36°C. Round the newly created island of about one hundred acres, just two months old, gulls were eating dead fish. Our boat broke down here and we watched bubbles coming up through the water. There was a strong sulphurous smell. The lava dust kept choking the pump on our boat so by the time we got back to the ship we were quite cold from the wind.

In the afternoon we landed at the old whaling station which had most recently been a British base. The whole place had a desolate, forbidding air. The Chilean, Argentine and British scientists working there at the time of the eruption had left in a hurry and it was very untidy. We were saddened by the trail of ugliness that man leaves behind him. We climbed up to the rim of the crater near Neptune's Bellows where there is a window in the rock known as 'Neptune's Window'. We were confronted by a startling view: a sheer cliff fell beneath us, with dark, smooth concave cliffs on either side rising far above the gap where we stood. On the inner side, down on the beach, lay a Leopard Seal and on either side, high in the rocks, Pintados and Sheathbills were nesting. We also found the nest of a Wilson's Petrel under a rock.

A few days later, at Paradise Bay, we met a Chilean Airforce officer who described the eruption. It had begun with earthquakes, sometimes several tremors a day, all through November. On 4 December the eruption began with a huge explosion and a vast black mushroom cloud. When the tremors ceased it became quite dark, although in that season it was normally light all night. Then ash began to fall and there was lightning and thunder. The centre of the eruption was the new island which we had visited in the morning and which had developed in 100 metres of water. Fireworks followed in the bay where we had seen steam. The scientists at the Chilean station decided to walk the two-and-a-half miles to the British base. The following day everyone was evacuated by a helicopter from a Chilean ship outside the bay. The Argentinians, based on the far side of the crater, walked over the hill and were picked up by boat. It was impossible for any ships to enter through Neptune's Bellows because during the eruption the water level rose and fell three metres or more and the currents in and out were enormous.

Paradise Bay, on the mainland of Antarctica, lived up to expectations. Passing through the Gerlache Strait we saw our first big castellated icebergs. The sun shone, the sea was calm and the scenery was incredibly beautiful. Penguins were porpoising in the sea and there were Crab-eater Seals lying on the sea ice. The bay is surrounded by high snowy peaks with huge glaciers coming down to the sea. The Chilean station, occupied at that time, was surrounded by a breeding colony of Gentoo Penguins. There was a mixed rookery of Chinstraps and Gentoos on a promontory close by and lovely blue ice caves with fringes of icicles under the glacier. The only problem that day was the American ladies in the party, who insisted on picking up the penguin chicks to cuddle them, aided and abetted by sailors from the ship.

That evening feelings ran high over our future plans, with the customary division between the Europeans and Americans. The Americans insisted that we must run to schedule (always difficult in Antarctic waters). They wanted at all costs to say that they had crossed the Antarctic Circle, which could mean missing out on landing somewhere. Nor were they pleased when they were asked by Peter not to handle or disturb the wildlife. Owing to a lot of pack ice on the sea the following day our progress to Palmer Station on Anders Island was rather slow but we passed through the spectacular, narrow Peltier Channel, with high peaks to starboard and snow mounds to port. There were two American stations at Palmer, an old and a new. Peter and John Cadwalader went ashore to meet the station commander to obtain permission to land the passengers.

Before going to bed that night Peter had put up a notice on the board asking people not to handle any penguins or other birds while ashore. He had also sent a note down for the crew to the same effect, since they too had been picking up birds and had also been seen throwing stones at a seal. On his return at noon from the shore he found big trouble: the crew were on strike, so no one could go ashore. The bosun, a big burly Chilean who was the seamen's union representative and in charge of all shore parties and landing operations, was so incensed by the note that he wanted to have a fight with Peter. He confronted Fred Berry, the biologist, whom he thought was Peter, and started to quarrel with him. Fred was a huge gorilla-like man who spoke not one word of Spanish. He had taken a lot of money off the crew at cards the night before and thought the bosun was arguing about that. Jaimé, our administrator, was sleeping off the night's crew party, which had gone on until 4am, but someone woke him up to deal with the situation and to explain that Fred was not Peter. It was all rather like a comic opera. Luckily the bosun laughed and accepted Peter's apology for sending a note rather than speaking personally to them. But in the meantime the passengers were becoming difficult since they had been sitting around for three hours waiting to go ashore. By then it was lunch time so I seized a bread roll and, with some medicinal Chilean brandy inside me, rushed to catch the small boat to the penguin island with nine other people. We were landed on the island in the bay amid a huge colony of about 5000 Adelie Penguins.

In the meantime the large boat had broken down so no more people could come and most of my companions went back to the ship so I had a whole hour with more than enough penguins and time to watch and photograph them without red parkas in the background. There were many half-grown birds with down still on them and pink krill on their white tummies (this happens when they are fed by the returning parents). Some of the young were in crèches with one adult looking after them. Many were chasing their parents for food. Skuas and gulls were flying overhead and there were a number of dead babies – victims of these predators. The clamour was continuous and the smell of the penguin rookery terrible. But for me it was all wonderful. Later Peter managed to join me and we shared this happy experience briefly before going over to the American station laboratory where they were mainly studying lichens.

The penguin island in the morning was good but even better was the afternoon expedition. Peter and I, with Len Hill from Birdland and Pamela Johnstone from Mole Hall, in Essex, were taken to Humble Island, a special study area and a sanctuary. At the centre was a freshwater lagoon with a wonderful variety of breeding birds including Arctic Terns, Skuas and Giant Petrels. Surprisingly there was a considerable amount of vegetation – moss, lichens and grass. Bergybits (tiny icebergs) were bobbing about near the shore and the Adelie Penguins were jumping out among them. This was certainly the best penguin rookery that we had seen.

Next day we were up at 4.45am to experience our entry into the Lemaire Channel. It is very narrow, with high mountains on either side, and is often blocked by icebergs. The *Navarino* was not strengthened for ice, so the Captain was understandably nervous and we proceeded very slowly. But we were lucky. On the port side are Una's Tits, two rounded mountains (it does not seem to be known who Una was). On the starboard side are steep cliffs where Snow Petrels nest and at the far end Mount Scott looms up, an impressive enough mountain to be named after Peter's father.

Soon after breakfast news came from the bridge that we had arrived at the British station on Argentine Island but that the Captain was anxious about the weather. He was not able to anchor and would only allow two people, Peter and me, to go ashore for a quarter of an hour. Rushing up on deck we found the keen passengers already queueing to get on the small boat lying alongside. There was always one particular couple at the front of the queue. They had without fail managed to be in the first boat ashore every time – they did not push, they just infiltrated like mercury and they always sat in the front for all the films. They were not very popular and I am sorry to say they were British. This time they were among the eight people fortunate to get into the boat. Also aboard were our administrator Jaimé, Jeffrey Boswell from the BBC and Len Hill. After the eighth person went down the gangway the crew would not allow any more on board, so a strangled cry went up from those waiting. But we were off through the pack ice and round the bergs into the channel leading to the station.

There were fourteen British Antarctic Survey people there, one of whom had been evacuated from Deception Island by the Chileans. There were nine dogs chained up behind the huts. Apparently they were sent there on retirement from stations further south where they had to work harder. One had had puppies (by mistake!) so there were more than there should have been. We were greatly impressed by the orderliness and tidiness of the station – much the best we had seen in the Antarctic. Everyone was delighted to see us and especially with our gifts of red meat and wine from the ship's stores. Unfortunately there was no time for the coffee and jam tarts that we were offered. The ship's horn was summoning us back. The weather was deteriorating and the forecast bad. We weaved our way through the thickening pack ice to be greeted by an angry mob who were asking why they could not all go ashore, and who wanted to have their letters franked with the station stamp. Peter and John Cadwalader, as expedition leaders, were of course the butt of their anger. The Captain was persuaded to allow one more trip across to the station to take the letters, but unfortunately he was seen taking not just Jaimé and the secretary, Doris, but nine Chilean seamen as well – which meant more trouble for Peter and me.

Eventually the boat came back and we immediately set off southwards under a grey sky. The pack ice was quite thick, there were some spectacular icebergs and the sea was flat calm. The light improved as we edged our way forward, and I went up into the bows to watch and photograph. There were little parties of Adelies playing on the ice, also Crab-eater Seals and an occasional Leopard Seal. It was eerily quiet; the only sound was the slopping of the water round the bigger bergs and the occasional crunch and grinding noise as the ship met one and rode over it. We were pleased that the fantastic beauty of the scene put everyone in a good mood again.

After reaching the open sea we had to steam south for six hours so that those who really minded could say that we had crossed the Antarctic Circle. We reached it finally about 9.30pm. Most of the passengers were playing cards in the lounge. Peter and I and a few others were on the foredeck. Jaimé came to ask me if I would break a bottle of champagne on the stem to celebrate. I was not going to let everyone in the lounge get away with bringing us all this way for nothing, so I persuaded Blanche, a black American teacher who was a friend of mine, to come out on deck. The sea was quite rough by now and we lurched down to Number 1 hatch and up the ladder to the bows again. A waiter brought a bottle of champagne and six glasses – not easy with the pitching of the ship – and we shared this second one in an icy wind on the heaving bows. Blanche was so happy she hugged me and I felt that it was perhaps worth all the extra time at sea.

I was able to sleep off all the excitements of the previous few days as we pounded our way north to Cape Horn. We landed on a small island (Grevy Island) near Woolaston Island which was memorable for a small bird sitting on the rock: a Babbler, which looks like a wren with white spots on its head. Memorable, too, because Jeffrey Boswell, our BBC friend, was stranded for some time on a rocky islet, and Jaimé sprained his ankle so badly that he became incapacitated for some days.

After Antarctica nothing could be quite so exciting, but I was unprepared for the passage through the Beagle Channel. We had a day 'of almost indescribable scenic splendour. Glaciers coming down from the heights to fall straight into the sea – blue and white cascading down in the changing light, hills with mauve/blue rock, green beeches near the shore; purple hills above and now and then glimpses of snow peaks with wind driven snow high above. The weather was unbelievably kind, with changing light all day. Sun and rain showers followed each other rapidly'. Wild beautiful country which made my heart sing.

We arrived at Puerto Natales further up the coast of Chile on 20 February and spent the following day in the Paine National Park. On a large lake with reeds round the edge there were about fifty Black-necked Swans with cygnets and a pair of Coscorobas. We also saw Yellow-billed Pintails, Crested Duck, Red Shoveler and Chile Teal. There was one spectacular waterfall from a river fed by the glaciers coming down from magnificent and dramatic peaks that rose close by. Luck was with us again – I have been to Paine since and not seen a mountain let alone its peaks. Rain is very frequent there and people have spent weeks without seeing the mountains. Sadly we came upon no Guanacos but I had seen one from the ship earlier. Peter recorded fifty species of birds, twelve more than Roger Tory Peterson on the previous trip.

That day was the last of the really good weather. We went on further north, stopping at Puerto Eden where a small colony of miserable looking Alacalufe Indians were living in corrugated iron sheds. There was one more stop in the Guaitecas Islands in the rain. The landing on Chiloe Island was impossible owing to the weather and we finally disembarked at Puerto Montt on 25 February. Here there were welcome letters from home, including two from Dafila, delivered by the Lindblad agent. We had three more days of group excursions and events on both the Chilean and the Argentinian side of the continent before leaving for home.

Our group had become much more well knit. There was a considerable spirit of bonhomie, probably due to the thought that we should soon be parting company and that we had shared a great experience. We were more mellow, more tolerant, not only amongst ourselves but of the organisers too. No one complained when Doris, the secretary, came round for the passports. We submitted to orders and smiled patiently when she snapped at us. It takes some getting used to but we had all learned how to cope with a package tour.

We thought we had returned to civilisation, but the hotel in Buenos Aires was brand new and still unfinished. Our bedroom on the eighteenth floor had no towels, no cold water, and a pile of plaster under the bed. Half the time the lifts did not work. We went up to our room around midnight after arriving late, and Peter refused to go to bed until our luggage came up. When it did finally arrive he was painting and had a watercolour wash on so he still could not go to bed. His ability to sit down and paint anywhere at any time was amazing – and sometimes frustrating for me. Delays at airports were opportunities for him to sit in the busy lounge with a glass of water from the bar, to paint in his diary. The flight would be called but Peter could not be hurried from his work. I envied him his capacity for concentration and ability to 'switch off'.

We arrived back in England on 2 March. Peter left for Argentina again on 22 March to attend an IUCN conference at Bariloche for a week.

CHAPTER NINE

Family Interludes

On Peter's return from Argentina at the end of March we left immediately, together with Dafila and Falcon, for Israel, where he was to be shown the nature reserves of which General Abraham Joffe was the Director. Not long before, General Joffe, or Avrahm, as we called him, had been taking his troops through the Sinai Desert in the Six Days War. He had halted his army on the march to make them mark out nature reserves. He was a wonderful avuncular figure, an enthusiastic naturalist and apparently known to everybody, Israelis and Arabs alike. Travelling with him in his open Jeep was like travelling with royalty: everybody waved and greeted him as a friend. He had a delightful sense of humour and a charming German wife.

The first day, we visited Professor Mendelsson's Zoo at Tel Aviv University's zoological department where they keep a number of birds and mammals. The following morning we were taken to the Maagan Mikhael Bird Reserve further north along the coast where there were some fish ponds with waders but no ducks. Peter and Avrahm walked about on a hill with their binoculars while Falcon explored an ancient burial cave. At fifteen Dafila was definitely into birds but thirteen-year-old Falcon was not keen. His particular interest was bones which he displayed in his museum at home. It was therefore inevitable that an excursion into a burial cave should prove very exciting for him. To my horror he emerged triumphantly bearing a skull and other bones. Avrahm did not appear quite as shocked as I feared; Falcon was allowed to keep one arm bone – a smooth shiny ulna

– but the others were put back. That night when I went to say goodnight, the bone was under his pillow.

Lunch that day was in Akker, an ancient fortress port where we had a delicious Arab meal before seeing the Crusaders' Palace. Avrahm was as well informed on the historical sites as he was in natural history and we enjoyed our visit to this old city. Wherever we went he was greeted by friends, mostly Arab. I suppose we were surprised by this in view of his high-ranking position in the Israeli army and their recent success in the Six Days War.

In the next two days we covered a great deal of ground. We visited the Hula Swamp and glided through the tall Papyrus in a flat-bottomed boat. We walked through wooded gardens to two separate sources of the Jordan, one of which had an altar to the God Pan. We went up to the Golan Heights, to Kuneitra, and on to look at a crater lake near the Syrian border. A fine view of the snow-clad slopes of Mount Herman excited Falcon and me but was not part of the itinerary. The road south to Kuneitra was littered with wrecked tanks, trucks and cars, and had suffered from the tracked vehicles which had traversed it in twenty-two hours of sudden warfare nine months before.

Next day we went back up onto the Golan Heights where we passed deserted Arab villages. It was a rather depressing scene. Peter and Avrahm kept stopping to check on the wheatears to the extent that Falcon and I were reduced to saying 'Not another wheatear'. I think six different kinds were identified. There was also a profusion of wild flowers to photograph, but because of the mine fields Avrahm was strict about where we walked.

After visiting the Golan Heights we ate St Peter's fishes by the Sea of Galilee, went to Capernicum, where Jesus fed the multitude on loaves and fishes, and also to the site of the sermon on the mount. Avrahm's knowledge of the Bible, both Old and New Testaments, was far greater than ours. We felt rather ashamed when he told us that his previous visitor, Juliette Huxley, had been much better informed. Possibly the most memorable event of the day was dinner with Zieky Sa'ad, the head man of the Druze mountain village of Beit Jahn. Situated on the plateau of Mount Meron, Beit Jahn is the highest village in Israel. Zieky Sa'ad was an old friend of Avrahm's and we were treated to a family feast. The atmosphere of cordial friendship was overwhelming, the people and the setting combining to make it a very special evening.

The pace hotted up the following day, which began with a visit to Nazareth, on to a gliding field at Megida, then an exciting visit to Hammadiya, near the Jordanian border, where we were provided with an armoured car as an escort while we drove through farmland to a hill site in search of gazelles. The armoured car which preceded us had a pole in front with a seat on it manned by a mine spotter. We saw thirty gazelles (*Gazella gazella*) but luckily no mines.

We travelled on to Sebastiya, with its old Hellenic Temple and Roman forum and in the evening arrived, tired and dusty, in Jerusalem. Then we were off to Jericho, by way of the Desert of Judea. We climbed down to a spring deep in a gorge in the bare white hills. From here a canal takes water down to Jericho. I felt that this must have been the place where Jesus spent his time in the wilderness: it had an atmosphere of isolated serenity. Down the hill we looked across to the blue-domed monestry of Der El Kelt, built into the hillside above the canal. Alpine swifts circled round it. Then we descended again to Jericho, to see the water channel that brings life to this oldest city in the world. Amazingly, we were still 1,000ft above the Jordan valley. We looked down on a riot of purple Bougainvillea and exquisite gardens. We visited the site of Old Jericho where, deep down, a tower dating from 6000BC had been unearthed. Passing Qumran, where the scrolls were found, we went to the Dead Sea, 1,200ft below sea level and 1,200ft deep. We lay on our backs in the incredibly salty water. It tasted very nasty and it was a relief to wash it off afterwards in a nearby pool.

One crowded day followed another and it concerns me now that we were probably too weary to appreciate fully the sights of Jerusalem. Perhaps it was the crowds of tourists, or perhaps my lack of religious enthusiasm, but my outstanding memories are the beauty of the Dome of the Rock, and a colourful Palm Sunday procession winding its way from the Garden of Gethsemane to the Church of the Holy Sepulchre. There was a little more religious atmosphere in Bethlehem. We liked the manger inside the church, but there were altars, ikons and crosses everywhere and little left of what had been the birthplace of Jesus Christ.

Driving through beautiful desert hills after a brief visit to Arad brought us to the amazing fortress of Masada, perched on top of a flat-topped hill overlooking the Dead Sea. Peter described it in his diary:

'Our first view of the fortress of Masada was from the Arad road. There it was atop its cliffgirt mountain overlooking the blue Dead Sea. The haze-softened red mountain faces across the Great Rift Valley in Jordan. At first sight it is fabulous and becomes progressively more so as you get closer and learn about its history. Avrahm, as usual was a marvellous guide. Masada is almost at sea level and therefore 1,300ft above the Dead Sea. From the road over the mountains of Judea we looked down on it – then across it and finally up at it from the foot of the Roman-built ramp used to storm it in the Great Revolt in AD72. Dead Sea Grackles with pink windows in their wings sang musically as we climbed the foot-path. At the top were Short-tailed Ravens. The building has been slightly rebuilt using the original stones, and a black line of mortar has been incorporated to distinguish the original untouched walls from the restored ones. On the whole the effect is good. The building, the ceremonial baths, the mosaics are all well shown and well preserved and there is a feeling of loving care in the way the archaeologists have left it which I found admirable. The original temple – perhaps the earliest synagogue known, dates from the 10th century BC. Herod built the main fortifications, storage rooms, bath houses and water storage system from 40-4BC. Herod's successors and Roman procurators lived there till 66AD, the year of the Great Revolt which was finally put down in 70AD except at Masada which was besieged in 72AD. Modern Zionism has built up the story of the 976 zealots who held out against the procurator Silva and his 10,000-15,000 ranged in eight camps (still clearly to be seen) round the foot of the cliffs. The capture of Masada from the Romans by Menachen Ben Yehude of Galilee had been the start of the Revolt.The Roman eagerness to recapture it can well be understood. The magnitude of the earthworks of the so-called "Dam"- a scree-type ramp built with wood reinforcements (still to be seen sticking out at various points) to bind the clay is absolutely astonishing.

'After two years – and still with adequate supplies of food and water, the Romans could finally breach the wall. On the night before they could break in El'azar made a great speech calling on all to be prepared to die rather than be slaves. They burned all their belongings (except for food – to demonstrate that they were not forced to surrender by lack of it) and Josephus Flavius records that they "chose ten men from amongst them by lot who would slaughter all... and the one who remained after them all examined the mass of those who lay on the ground, and when he had assured himself that all were dead he set fire to all corners of the royal palace and with his full strength he drove his sword into his body up to the hilt, and fell dead beside his kinsmen. Thus they all died believing that they had left no living soul behind to bear the Roman Yoke."

'Yet as Avrahm sat in the shade of the Byzantine church built 400 years later (with big Grey Gekkos on its walls) talking to us about whether humanity has evolved into a greater degree of "goodness" since then, there was little aura of grimness about the fortress.'

Our visit to Israel was to end with a week's holiday at Eilat in order to do some fish watching. Our hotel was on the Marine Nature Reserve side right out of town and close to the reserve. We were virtually in the desert, with bare yellowish rocky hills behind us which glowed red in the evening sun, and blue sea in front. We all spent most of the day fish watching with our masks and snorkels and while Peter painted the fishes in his diary in the evening, the children and I explored the hills and dry valleys. One evening we were thrilled to see an Ibex.

The day after we arrived Peter was struck down with 'flu and a temperature of 101° F. The chief doctor from the hospital in Eilat came out to see him and prescribed sixteen pills a day for two days which soon sorted him out. He was such a strong healthy person normally that I was always extremely worried when he became ill on a foreign trip and equally relieved when he bounced back. It was not easy to keep him away from a nearby coral reef for long.

It was an idyllic holiday interlude. We snorkelled twice a day, visited Moses Rock (a large underwater coral head) and the 'Japanese coral gardens' and were taken by the Park Warden by boat to the Coral Island, with its ruined castle. Dafila and Falcon became experts at finding Pterois (both *radiata* and *volilans* – the fireworks fish) and Peter had visits from various distinguished Israeli scientists at which he gave and received advice.

A letter from Mike Garside which reached us before we left Israel reflects our interests at that time: gliding, swans, Falcon's tame rats and our treasures in the Animal Room:

'*My dear Peter and Phil,*
'All is well at the New Grounds. Superb sunny days with tight little cu's

which suck people off the hill – but cold northerly winds. We've woken up to snow each morning this week – six inches on Monday!

'The Bewick's cygnet apparently left on Sunday morning and so they opened the Rushy Pen. However it came back in the afternoon with the pen full of people, and has been here since!

'The rats have produced young, although we don't know how many, of course. The frogs seem fine, although they don't do anything except eat, and the Dragon produced an egg on Monday morning which John doesn't think will be much use as it apppears to be going mouldy already.'

Twenty-three years later, in 1991, when Falcon's first marriage had broken up and I was a widow, I took him on holiday to Eilat to enable him to learn to scuba dive. On the third day, as we walked back to our rooms after breakfast, he said, 'You know, I think this is the hotel we stayed in in 1968.' He was right (we were able to identify the actual bedrooms that we had had) though the character of the place was so changed that it was hardly recognisable. In 1968 the complex was three or four kilometres out of town; now the surrounding area was built up.

One night a group of some 200 teenage students invaded the hotel. At 1am I rang reception to complain of the noise – they were tearing up and down the corridors shouting and banging on the bedroom doors. I was told that the police had been called. With the aid of earplugs I eventually went to sleep but awoke at 5am to see the figure of a young man sitting at my dressing-table. I shouted at him and he disappeared through the terrace doors. He had taken my gold chain, a gift from Peter, some cash and my camera bag. The worst loss was the gold chain, which was of particular sentimental value. The hotel authorities were not much help but said they would call the police and tell the students that their rooms would be searched. When Falcon and I went to breakfast I looked at the lines of students seated at the tables. Nearly all of them wore gold chains round their necks; there was no hope of identifying mine. But on returning to my room I did find my camera bag, complete with its contents, on the basin.

In August 1969 we went to Zambia, again taking Dafila and Falcon. We were fortunate in that Peter and I were sponsored by the Wildlife

Conservation Society of Zambia (WLCSZ) and Zambian Airways, and the children by the Zambian National Tourist Board. We rather liked calling the Conservation Society Wiliconsox, because it sounds funny. The officials were not amused.

Our first excursion after arrival in Lusaka was to Lochinvar on the edge of the Kafue Flats where the water birds were numerous and wonderful. We found very young Lechwe lying in the grass where their mothers had left them and saw large flocks of Pelicans using thermals high up in the sky on migration. They fascinated Peter, his mind on gliding.

Our next adventure took us to Livingstone on the north side of the Victoria Falls. First we flew over the Falls, then we walked to the middle of the bridge, which is the border with Zimbabwe. We climbed down the bank on the north side to have a close look at the Devil's Cauldron. Mesmerised, we stayed to watch the sun dip over the lip of the falls.

Peter was giving a talk that night so after an early meal at our hotel, which was only 300 yards from the Falls, Dafila, Falcon and I went for a walk. There was a moon, but even so I was not too keen on walking in the dark in the wilderness area between the hotel and the Falls. However, Falcon insisted that he would look after us. Holding our hands, he led us to the edge of the slope down to the Devil's Cauldron. In the moonlight the sparkling curtains of water were entrancing. Still slightly fearful, but elated, we returned to the hotel before Peter arrived back.

A drive through the Game Park the following day was photographically rewarding when an obliging White Rhino with a baby allowed us to creep up on foot and take pictures from behind a bush. We flew to Ngoma in the Kafue National Park where Peter spent some time talking politics with the distinguished mammal man, Frank Ansell, who was completing the *Smithsonian Mammal Atlas*. Our game drivers produced many 'firsts', such as Lichtenstein's Hartebeeste, Puku, Grysbok, Spring Hares at night, and a nice view of a Serval cat. We spent one night at the beautiful tented camp by a river listening to lions roaring close by.

We left Ngoma in a Charter Aztec that flew low over the Kafue Flats so that we could see the wildlife – mostly large herds of Lechwe. Apart from the antelope and the birds it is a vast area of water and swampy vegetation. At 11am we landed at Blue Lagoon. We taxied up to the front lawn of Ronnie and Erica Critchley's house, which stands on a slight rise in the flood plain, to be greeted with glasses of champagne – I had been feeling

tired and it was just what I needed. The Critchleys were staunch support-
ers of conservation in Zambia.Their knowledge of the wildlife and also of
the people and politics involved was extensive and entertaining. Both were
great 'characters' and became lifelong friends. From the house we could
see Lechwe and Bushbuck and three kinds of plover on the lawn, also a
Secretary Bird to remind me of my old home.

After a day in the city we left at 4pm for Mfue in the Luangwa Game
Reserve. As Peter was sponsored by 'Wiliconsoxz' he was on business as
much as pleasure. Elephant culling was a big issue at that time, as it is even
today, but nowhere more so then than in the Luangwa Valley. Elephants
were already being cropped in that area and there was an abattoir close to
the Lodge in the Reserve, which did not seem a good thing from the
tourists' point of view. It appeared that no one knew whether there were
15,000 or 3,000 elephants in the reserve, so there was plenty of room
for discussion.

If our visit to Luangwa had political overtones for Peter to wrestle with,
it also provided wonderful and rewarding possibilities for photography for
me, always aided and encouraged by Peter. The camp where we stayed on
the edge of the river was looked after by Norman Carr. It was Norman who
quietly rescued, reared and released successfully into the wild two lion cubs
at about the same time that Joy Adamson was having such trouble with
the famous Elsa. He wrote a delightful book about them called *Return to the
Wild*. We were lucky to have him as guide. Memorable things were the
Carmine Bee Eaters nesting in the sandy cliffs above the river and watching
a herd of elephants mourning over a dead youngster.

Back in Lusaka a few days later Peter and I were invited to have Sunday
lunch with Kenneth Kaunda and his family in State House. KK was very
friendly and we had a relaxed and cheerful meal. It was of course
an opportunity for Peter to discuss wildlife conservation with the Head
of State.

We could not leave Africa without a visit to the sea to explore the coral
reefs. We went first to Watamu in Kenya to snorkel in the Marine Park just
south of Malindi where we had stayed in 1961. The point where the
Ritchies' house stood had been washed away. Unfortunately the weather
was not good and the sea was rather rough and murky. The children were
disappointed that it was forbidden to pick up shells, even dead ones, on the

beach. That is now the order of things wherever there is a Marine Park: leave them for other people to see.

We were joined here by Leslie Brown, who became a legend because of his exploits while studying flamingos. He went on a famous walk across one of the big Flamingo nesting salt lakes and nearly died of heat exposure. A skilled ornithologist, he kindly gave up time to take us out birding.

From Watamu we went south to stay at the Two Fishes Hotel at Jadini. We had the good luck there to be looked after by Phil Glover from the Kenya National Parks Service. Peter had met him before and found him 'gentle and charming'. On the day after our arrival at Jadini Phil took us to the Shimba Hill's Forestry Reserve for the day. Here we were able to see for the first time Sable Antelope, first a herd of thirty-one at a distance and then a magnificent bull who came quite close before disappearing at speed when he saw us. The bulls are black and the females a rich chestnut with long swept-back horns.

After days by the sea, snorkelling and making some attempts at surfing, we were fit enough for the next leg of our wonderful African holiday. This time it was a private visit to stay with John Savidge in Ruaha, in Tanzania. He and his wife kept a tame Hyrax, a most enchanting pet which came to dinner at night.We had our first view of Go Away Birds, said to be Prince Philip's favourite birds, and also Ground Hornbills which hop about, behaving like clowns.

Although all the places we visited during this six-week holiday provided us with new and exciting adventures, nothing was quite as spectacular as the Masai Mara Game Reserve. We stayed at the lodge at Keekerok and, because Peter was there, were always given VIP treatment. The Mara Reserve is the northern part of the Serengeti plain, and the large herds of gnus, wildebeeste, etc migrate from one area to the other. We had two and a half days based at the Lodge. I can do no better than quote from Peter's diary:

'But the most unforgettable part of our Mara days, to be savoured and enjoyed at the time (and in retrospect for the rest of our lives), was the thrilling profusion of Gnus and Zebra (and Topi). Nature was being rarely prodigal. Here were numbers and diversity in a magnificent display under a dappled sky on the rolling plains of the Mara. It was a sight to take the breath away. It is not always that we recognise the golden moments of life, but this time I believe we all did.'

It was not always sunlit – but it was just as impressive when one day the black thunder clouds edged up, the tracks ran with water and the animals' hides glistened in the wet.

Our travels were still not ended. We were to be the guests of a wonderful family called Hopcraft, first by the lake at Naivasha and then at John and Sandy's farm on the shores of Lake Nakuru.We established a life-long friendship with them. John took us on safari north to Lake Baringo where we camped below Johnathan Leakey's house. We visited Teddy Bear Island and cooked eggs on the hot rocks beside the springs.

When at last we flew back to England it was not easy to squeeze ourselves into our tourist-class seats. Falcon's most precious bone was an enormous elephant's femur which was nearly as big as he was. Also tucked away in his night bag was a complete skeleton of a Dik Dik.

Back at Slimbridge life was always an extraordinary mixture of office and home. In the 1970s Peter was kept very busy by his work for WWF, and the Wildfowl Trust struggled on. In 1970 there was the excitement of opening Welney, followed in 1971 by Caerlaverock and in 1975 by Martin Mere, Washington and Arundel.

Our social life was hectic, too. Visitors came and went and I was glad to have help in the house with the entertaining. Our guests included Prince Bernhard, the Duke and Duchess of Kent, Douglas Bader and his wife, Miriam Rothschild, and our old friend James Robertson Justice. Perhaps our most frequent visitor was Max Williams, who still kept and bred the more difficult waterfowl in Hertfordshire. His unfailing sense of humour, his sound advice on all sorts of matters and his interest in birds made him a special friend.

As Chancellor of Birmingham University Peter visited the campus several times a year. I enjoyed these visits almost as much as he did, though on one occasion our reception at a dinner to which we had been invited seemed rather hesitant and disorganised. On returning to Slimbridge we were greeted by Mike Garside who asked what had happened to us the previous night. 'Why?' we asked. 'Why didn't you turn up at the dinner party?' It transpired that we had gone to the wrong one!

In the summer of 1973 we were invited to dine at Windsor Castle. Dougie Eccleston, who was working for us at the time, asked me jokingly whether I had taken my tiara out of the attic. We booked into a hotel in

Windsor, went to have a drink in the bar and found the press lying in wait. I cheerfully told one tabloid journalist that I had found my tiara in the attic and dusted it down. I think Peter was faintly shocked when I was quoted next day in a gossip column.

When the time came to dress for dinner we discovered to our horror that Peter had no black socks – only the red woollen ones he was wearing. I always packed for him, so it was my fault. Although red socks might be suitable for some occasions, they certainly would not do with white tie and tails at Windsor Castle. We rang the hotel desk to ask if by any chance there were any black socks in lost property, but we were out of luck. It was the chef who came to our rescue – he was prepared to lend Peter his thick black woollen ones provided he could have them back early next morning because he was going fishing.

At home there was always the pleasure of the children's visits. Dafila, who was up at Oxford, used to come down with her friends. When Falcon, who was working in Liverpool, finished the construction of his famous tower in 1974 we had a great celebration.

Our swimming pool, built in 1970 with a legacy left to me by an aunt, was a great asset and made us very popular with the young. Peter said that his morning swim gave him an extra ten years of life. Nowadays, sadly, I can no longer jusitfy the cost of keeping it in working order.

CHAPTER TEN

The Lindblad Explorer

It was not our usual form to be late, but on our way to Nairobi en route to join the ship the *Lindblad Explorer* for the first time, we caught the aircraft at London Airport with ten minutes to spare before take-off. The list had closed, but somehow (Peter's charm I expect) they got us on board . It was April 1971 and Peter had been invited to be a guest lecturer on the ship. Nairobi at that time was particularly good for buying camera equipment that was not obtainable in the UK, and at reasonable prices. On arrival I spent part of the day finding and buying a Novaflex 400mm lens. It was one of the best and most useful lenses I ever had and has travelled many miles with me in the following years.

Buying the lens made us late for joining the Lindblad excursion into Nairobi National Park, but luck was with us again. One other passenger had also missed the bus. Mrs Wilma Brown was a splendid elderly Australian with much previous Lindblad Travel experience and the three of us had a minibus to ourselves. The park was as good as ever and the driver most willing and helpful as I tried to get good photographs. Unfortunately our, and his, enthusiasm took us off the main track and we became stuck in the mud with no other vehicles in sight – all this for a Secretary Bird. Luckily Wilma was no small stripling and thought nothing of casting off her shoes to lend her not inconsiderable weight to help us push. Our driver was overjoyed when we got out without too much difficulty. We went down to the hippo pool and walked through the Acacia grove by the river Athi. There were Weaver Birds building nests, giraffes just across the river and hundreds of 'woolly bear' caterpillars in the bushes. Later we saw a lion with two young which stalked some Wart Hogs and bounced them.

The next day we flew to Mombasa and that afternoon boarded the *Lindblad Explorer*. Cabin No 144 almost became our home from home, though we did later sample all the decks. No 144 was next to the reception area, on the middle deck not far from the dining-room. People queueing to go to early breakfast used to lean on the door and shout greetings to each other. If it became too noisy, I used to open the door suddenly and watch their expressions of surprise as they fell backwards into our cabin. This wonderful 'little red ship' as she became known to us is still sailing the seas in far away places such as Antarctica, under different management and known now just as the *Explorer*.

Our Cruise Director was Dr Lyall Watson, author of the bestseller *Supernature*. As well as organising our lives on board, Lyall was a very good lecturer, his subjects ranging from Oceanography to The Dangers of the Deep. Peter and I were rather sorry about the latter as we planned to have everybody snorkelling when we reached the Seychelles. We certainly managed to persuade Penny Skelton into the sea, and that was the beginning of another era of my later life. Others may well have been put off by tales of Stone Fish, Scorpion Fish, Echinids, Jelly Fish, poisonous shells, etc.What a lot people miss if they never look under the surface of the sea! Fortunately Peter was able to lecture on fishes with slides of some of his paintings.

The airstrip on Mahe, the main island of the Seychelles,was still under construction, so the islands were wonderfully unsophisticated and free from tourist developments. Snorkelling was a delight in the warm, clear sea and the green Phelsuma Day Geckos in the palm trees were enchanting. On the first evening at Mahe we went up the hill to see if we could find the rare Scops Owl. We started off in a car, then collected a Seychellois guide and set off walking on a uneven track in the dark. Down and down we went, then across a stream where the track was very wet. Frogs croaked and huge snails abounded; I trod right on one and heard the shell crunch sickeningly. Then up and up, round sharp, steep bends until at last we stopped to listen at what was said to be one of the places where the owl could be heard. Not a sound. So on and up we went to listen once more. This time someone thought they heard something, but it was not a Scops Owl. Then the track began to go downhill.At this point Peter, thinking of the return journey, dug his toes in and refused to go further. Our guide went on for another quarter of an hour while we sat listening. He came back and said that the only sounds he had heard were a dog barking and distant hymn singing.

Our island the next day was Frigate. My objective here was to photograph the rare Magpie Robin which was flitting around in the trees near the house of Harry Savory, who owned the island. It is a quite handsome black glossy bird about the size of a starling, with a white patch on the outside of its wing. There were certainly ten of them in the vicinity of the buildings but they tended to keep in the shade and were not easy to photograph. The numbers had apparently increased since Mr Savory eliminated around a hundred cats, an introduced species.

The islands of the Seychelles are wonderful for birds. One of the most exciting was Cousin Island which belonged to ICBP, now Birdlife International. We were in the first boat ashore and were greeted by our old friends Malcolm and Mary Penny, the wardens, who, with their three small sons and four or five Seychellois wardens, were the only inhabitants. Fairy Terns wheeled and chattered about us and a baby was perched precariously on a ridiculously small branch stump above the path. It seemed incredible that the mother could perch there and feed it, or that she could ever have kept the egg there in the first place (there is no nest – just the egg then the chick).

There was a small brown bird – the Brush Warbler – which is unique to the island and also the Toctoc, or Fody, which has been practically exterminated by the introduced Madagascar Fody, a much brighter bird with a red head and breast like a Cardinal. There were lots of warblers hopping about – very difficult to photograph as they move so quickly. We found a lovely big Black Gecko in the hollow of a tree and lots of inquisitive Skinks and also the Green Gecko. So many birds to see and so little time. Then there were the fishes. We swam out to where the waves were breaking at the edge of the reef. The water was clear, the coral very good and the fishes marvellous.

The Seychelles are partly granite and partly coraline. Bird Island, which we visited next day, is coraline and very flat. It is indeed a wonderful island for birds. There were enormous numbers of terns. We recorded six different kinds and many waders, including the delightful Crab Plover. Peter recorded 101 species in our first three days in the islands.

On the island of La Digue the passengers were greeted by flower-decked bullock carts which took us along sandy trails, first to see the Black Paradise Flycatcher (only four of which existed at that time) with the female sitting on a nest. Then there followed what was to be one of many visits in our lives to see copra being processed. We watched the coconuts being hacked open and some of the fruit being ground by a bullock going round in a circle to turn the huge wooden handle. Some of the coconut kernel was stacked on shelves, dried and bagged, then exported, mostly to India where the oil is extracted and used for making such products as margarine. La Digue is one of the most beautiful of the Seychelles Islands, with impressive rocks on the shore, a small settlement and a good coral reef offshore.

Praslin, our next island was different again (Gordon of Khartoum reckoned that it was the original garden of Eden). It is here that the famous Coco de Mer palm tree grows, in the Vallée de Mai. The vast leaves of the Coco de Mer make the winding pathways through the dense forest look like vaulting in a cathedral. The atmosphere caused a hush to fall on our group and Peter, Penny and I lingered behind. The silence was awesome. There is a rare black parrot found only in this valley on this island. We heard it several times but saw it only briefly, which was sad because I wanted to photograph it. We did, however, see the Blue Pigeon, Sunbirds and Bulbuls. Just before leaving we also saw a Tenrec – a funny little hedgehog-like animal – scuttling quickly away from us among the dead leaves. Later we bought a Coco de Mer coconut – the largest seed in the world.

Des Roches, a flat island with another copra factory, provided us with the opportunity to introduce the passengers to snorkelling. Conditions were ideal: the reef came up to the shore on the far side, the pools were shallow and there was a good diversity of colourful coral fish.

There followed a day at sea with moderately rough seas and a heavy rain storm: a day for nursing our colds – acquired as a result of the air conditioning – and for gossip about the passengers, known as 'pax' in tourist agents' jargon. One American has been seen putting sardines on his prunes for breakfast; another regularly drinks a half-and-half mixture of beer and tomato juice. Yet another and his wife drink a bottle of champagne in the bar every day at 11am. Today he was not there and his wife had him paged on the intercom because she thought he had gone overboard. He was actually in the library only feet away from her. And

Penny was having problems with her English cabin companion so she brought her whisky to drink in our cabin.

The remote island of Aldabra, beyond the Seychelles, was worth waiting for. It is a coral island twenty-one miles long with a large lagoon in the centre accessible through various narrow channels. The shore has a few sandy coves but mostly lava-like coral edging, with strange mushroom shapes or 'champignons' as they are known. I embarked on a long, hot trek to an inland pool through prickly shrub to see the Upside-down Jelly Fish, but we never saw the famous Aldabra Tortoise. Peter visited the Royal Society Research Station, the only settlement on the island. Landing and returning to the ship were hazardous in the rubber boats. We all got very wet but luckily had no accidents. It was not a very successful visit.

On returning to the ship we had our moment of drama. Lyall Watson called us all to the lecture room (later to become known as the 'Penguin Room' after Keith Shackleton had painted a splendid mural there) and solemnly announced that the generator had failed and there was no water, lighting or air conditioning. Later we learned that a piece of piping had burst and sprayed the generator with salt water. It had burned out completely. We had no option but to return to Mombasa on the remaining spare generator which could not take the full load so the journey was rather uncomfortable, with minimal air conditioning; but at least we had water and light. We also had a lot of disgruntled passengers. Lindblad kindly laid on some extra excursions to make up for the loss of part of our ship time. We escorted a group to the Shimba Hills above the coast, and also to Jadini where we had been the previous year. Most interesting was a day trip by Fokker Friendship to Zanzibar. This was outside the normal tourist itinerary and we were warned that with the Chinese Communists in evidence, we must be very careful how we behaved. There were a few problems at the airport, where anti-malaria pills were handed out and where Peter worryingly disappeared through a door marked 'No admission' and could not be found by our tour leader from the office when wanted. In spite of being off the beaten track tourist cars were laid on and we visited the spice-growing area and various 'sights' in the town. Penny and I went walking in search of shops and found ourselves in a dark alley with some Chinamen huddled together in what we thought a rather sinister way. Later we learned they were our Chinese laundrymen from the *Explorer*.

Phil Glover, who had been so kind to us and the children the previous year, came to rescue us in Mombasa and drove us to Voi in Tsavo Park East. Here we had a happy two days, meeting David and Daphne Sheldrick and viewing game with Phil. From there we had one long day in Tsavo West, where we visited Mzima Springs and saw the hippos in the wonderful clear water. In the distance I saw the top of Kilimanjaro in all its glory: a wonderful sight. I would have liked to have climbed it. We drove back to Phil's house in the dark seeing nightjars, coursers, owls, a Dikkop and a Honey Badger as well as a Taita wild cat. We had a 6.30 start next morning for a photographic drive to see the Lesser Kudu and Gerenuk before setting off on the 200-mile journey to Nairobi, where we met up with the British members of the *Lindblad Explorer* group for our flight back to England the following day.

The Seychelles were so lovely that we were determined to go back, and we managed to persuade Lars Lindblad to invite Peter as a lecturer again in June 1971. Dafila, now nineteen, came with us. The itinerary was much the same as the previous year but this time the ship did not break down and we visited the lovely Comoros Islands. Ylang Ylang is grown here for a scent factory and the smell wafts over the island. It is also where the thought-to-be-extinct Coelocanth had been recently discovered. We only had snorkels and the Coelocanth lives deep down, but that did not stop Peter from spending an hour and a half both morning and afternoon swimming over the coral reef off Grand Comoro in the hope of finding one. That day he recorded eighty-two species of fish.

This time Lars had asked us to do two back-to-back trips of two weeks each, which gave us the great advantage of knowing what to look for. On the second trip Keith Shackleton was with us. Our first day at Mahe started off with an invitation to join the Governor-General, Sir Bruce Greatbatch, for a Sunday curry lunch at the Rest House on Prison Island in a bay not far from Port Victoria. The area is a marine park and in spite of eating a large lunch and talking conservation politics with our colourful host, Peter recorded ninety-eight species of fish. We visited Aride Island, which now has wardens living on it year round but which at that time had not been bought by Christopher Cadbury and passed on to the Royal Society for Nature Conservation. The bird life there is outstanding.

Near the Amirante Islands we were involved in a rescue drama. It was

8.55pm and we had not long left Poivre Island when we received an SOS from a ship aground on the reef south of Alphonse Island. It was a cloudy night with a strong south wind. As the nearest ship, we were bound by law to go to the rescue. A light was visible at twelve miles and we had learned from the original signal that this was a Taiwanese long-line fishing vessel called the *Chin Fu*. She had driven onto the windward side of the reef and it was clearly impossible to effect a rescue from seaward.

At about 9.30 we sent out three Zodiacs but they ran aground and had to be refloated. At 2am it was decided to abandon the operation until daylight when the tide would be rising. Leaving at 6.30am, three Zodiacs made it and anchored off the fishing boat, which was driving further onto the reef all the time. At 9.45 we saw the boats returning with only three passengers – the crew had apparently preferred to stay on board, hopefully waiting for the arrival of another Chinese ship. Because the Captain, one of the three passengers, had a badly damaged hand he could not swim and had to be helped the fifty yards through the rough seas to the Zodiac by two of his sailors. After medical treatment to the hand, the three insisted on being taken back to their ship but her condition had deteriorated and it seemed that the chances of refloating her were negligible. Plans were immediately made to send out all our Zodiacs equipped with life belts. Keith Shackleton was one of the Zodiac drivers. The tide was falling, making the lagoon difficult to cross.

From the top deck we could see the boat only as a speck in the distance, with the white waves crashing round her. The Zodiacs were anchored on the reef in eighteen inches of water forty yards from the stern of the *Chin Fu*. Most of the men in the stranded ship could not swim and our people had to rescue them from the sea as they jumped in. The whole operation was extremely hairy. In the meantime two British naval survey ships arrived on the scene and the rescued men were put aboard one of them. The whole operation had taken eighteen and a half hours. Three huge glass fishing floats and one or two Chinese life jackets were our only souvenirs after a very exciting and dangerous operation.

We disembarked from the *Lindblad Explorer* on 6 July, leaving Dafila on board to act as assistant hostess. She was to translate announcements, daily programmes and so on for the benefit of the French-speaking Swiss tourists. On our return Peter and I stopped off in Kenya and had a happy visit to John Hopcraft's farm at Baharini on the edge of Lake Nakuru.

Peter's bird list for the two days came to ninety species. It is a place of which I have particularly happy memories, going back to the time in 1961 when Peter opened the Nakuru National Park.

CHAPTER ELEVEN

Wild Goose Chases in Romania

Our three expeditions to Romania in the 1970s have been well covered by Peter in his *Travel Diaries of a Naturalist Volume II*. I was too tired every day to write a diary. The primary object of these expeditions was to establish the numbers of Red-breasted Geese wintering in the area near the Danube Delta and to get good photographs of them. Little was known then of their movements after their migration from their breeding grounds in the far north of Russia. It was not easy to obtain permits to travel to the wilds of the country in the communist era. Luckily Peter had contacts with Professor Valerius Puscariu, whose influence helped us.

On our first visit we were accompanied by Sir Max Williams and Christopher Marler. Much of our travel arrangements had been booked through the good offices of Max. On arrival at Bucharest airport I was separated from the others and escorted to a cubicle where I was searched and had my camera equipment taken away. There was concern about my light meter and I had visions of being kept indefinitely in the nasty little cubicle. When I finally escaped I was greeted by a welcoming committee with bunches of flowers, arranged of course by Max. To his amusement it was not long before Peter had become Sir Walter Scott!

Each of our three visits, in 1971, 1973 and 1977, lasted for about two weeks at the end of November or early December. Each time we stayed in a large hotel in Tulcea on the banks of the Danube. This part of the exercise was known to us as 'torture' because so many things in the hotel did not work, in particular the plumbing. When you are out all day from 5am until after dark in very cold weather little things such as toilets which do not work and lack of hot water matter a good deal. Evening meals were a bit dicey, too, though at least the Romanian red wine was good. Meat and vegetables were scarce and the local fish, described on the menu as *Crap* (that, we understood, was Romanian for carp), was a frequent main dish. Shopping for our picnic meals had to be fitted in with goose movements and could only be done in Tulcea or a village on the forty-mile drive to the goose fields. There were queues for most things. The bread was good but butter (*unt* in Romanian) was hard to get.

I did a lot of the driving so that Peter could look for the geese. There were very few other cars but quite a few lorries carrying agricultural produce from the big communes, and also farm carts with no lights. The roads were narrow and the early morning and late evening drives in the dark were definitely hazardous.

On our second and third visits we had the advantage of knowing the country better, but the geese remained as difficult as ever to approach. The fields were vast, mostly wheat but some maize, and with no cover for would-be photographers. I had with me my Novaflex 400mm lens and also another camera with a 1000mm lens which Peter sometimes used. The photographic results of these expeditions were not impressive but the sight and sound of the flocks of Redbreasts flying with the White-fronted Geese will remain with me for ever. Not only was there the thrill of the chase but also on each occasion we had extraordinarily agreeable companions. These had varied over the years but the one hardy, brave constant was Sir Max Williams. The first trip must have been something of a shock as he had never been looking for geese with Peter before and Peter's single-mindedness of purpose in the fields was new to him. He arrived almost straight from a job in the USA, in a suit, and seemingly unprepared for the cold outdoor life that we were to lead. He appointed himself Tour Leader and took on all sorts of mundane jobs such as cleaning the cars' headlights every morning, checking the petrol, cleaning the windscreens, carrying camera equipment and generally keeping us all in good spirits. Memorably, he organised a meal one evening in Bucharest on our way back, where we listened to the most wonderful gypsy fiddler. Those trips would not have been the same without him.

CHAPTER TWELVE

The Lure of the Antarctic

There is something so special about the Antarctic that it acts like a magnet. Unfortunately, or perhaps fortunately, it is not easy to get there. It is the beauty, the wildness and the size of the place which grabs you. It is awesome: there is no other word for it.

The *Lindblad Explorer* never had more than a hundred passengers and they were nearly always wildlife enthusiasts. In 1971 we were invited to join the ship for an expedition to the Ross Sea area, leaving from New Zealand and returning via Australia. We were to take Dafila with us. Just three weeks before we were due to fly she had appendicitis, but luckily the operation went off smoothly and she was pronounced fit to travel.

We broke our journey in the USA to see Mike Lubbock, who was looking after a large collection of wildfowl on Long Island. Mike had moved there after working for some years as Curator at Slimbridge and it was good to see him. From New York it was a long journey to Auckland in New Zealand where the Lindblad passengers were gathering. We had already met some of them at an overnight stop in Los Angeles and went on with them as far as Fiji before changing aeroplanes.

We had problems at Nandi airport, at that time quite a small place. There were five people with the surname Scott and only two boarding cards. None of us could afford to be left behind because it would upset our cruise schedule. Peter found out that the plane was not in fact full but the authorities still would not issue boarding cards for us. In the end we just walked to the aircraft without anyone stopping us. It was one of those journeys when luggage kept getting lost, too.

We also managed to lose one of the English passengers in Auckland. A certain Miss Morgan, aged eighty, checked into the hotel for the night but was nowhere to be found the next morning when we were to leave for Christchurch. We were greatly concerned for her as she was travelling alone and no one knew her. We left Auckland without her but she mysteriously turned up later in time to take the train journey from Christchurch to Invercargill. She had no intention of telling anyone what she had been up to during her absence.

We sailed on the evening of 5 February under a bright moon, which was being circled by Apollo 14. The Scott family had cabins on what was variously known as 'millionaires row' or 'seasick alley'. They were on the highest cabin deck and extremely comfortable, with windows. We fixed maps and charts on the walls. Peter had a large orange-box taped to the table by his bed, specially cut out on one side so that he could keep his 'toys' (pencils, notebooks, paintbrushes, etc) in the bottom, and the far side of the box acted as a light shield between the bunks. We fixed temporary hooks to the walls for extra hanging space and made ourselves thoroughly at home.

Our first anchorages were in the Auckland Islands, where we found a sheltered cove called 'Sarah's Bosom' off Enderby Island. Most of the island was covered in scrub and low windswept trees with bright flowers called Rata. There was a large open grassy space where we landed in the Zodiacs. We nicknamed it 'the golf course' because of the short, smooth turf. The mowing machines were the amazing population of multicoloured rabbits. In the trees were flocks of brilliant green parakeets (Red-Crowned Parakeet). There were Sea Lions on the shore, Yellow-eyed Penguins all over the place and innumerable species of other sea and land birds. Most exciting for the Scott family was seeing the strange little Auckland Island Flightless Teal swimming about in the kelp under some rocks. Roger Tory Peterson, the distinguished American ornithologist who was with us, was as enthusiastic as we were.

If Enderby was good, then Campbell Island further south had to prove itself. There we were less fortunate with the weather but in spite of the rain we set off on a long trek up a mountain side, guided by the residents of the Research Station, in order to see Royal Albatrosses on their nests. The vegetation on the island is mostly heathland which grows quite high, and the boggy track up the hill was hard work. Dafila, with her recent appendix scar, was obviously suffering and I stayed with her. She also had a young researcher from the station keeping an eye on her, as well as carrying Roger's spare camera equipment in his rucksack. There came a moment when it was obvious that she was not going to make it. I was not prepared to let her go down the long peaty trail on her own but nor did I want to miss the Royal Albatrosses. The scientist, however, was only too delighted to escort a damsel in distress. So I continued, with Roger's cameras plus my own. Luckily the worst of the climb was over and eventually I caught up with the advance party. I do not think Roger was particularly appreciative of what had been a considerable effort for me. In any event, we were overcome by the enchanting great bird sitting on its nest, waiting in the drizzle and mist to be photographed, and to my delight Peter finally arrived there too.

There followed four days at sea, which I enjoyed in spite of some rough weather. We were kept busy with lectures and talks – if we wanted them – but there were always the sea birds to watch and the first iceberg to be sighted. We were hove to for some time off Cape Hallet in a force 9 gale but had a short excursion ashore where we saw pancake ice forming in the shallow bays where we landed. The ice is fantastic, like water-lily pads with turned up edges. Then there was the first sight of Beaufort Island and Ross Island with Mount Erebus in a clear blue sky. But there was still a force 9 gale blowing so we steamed slowly past Cape Royds, noting that it was too dangerous to land with such a strong wind, and went on to anchor off Cape Evans. Here we were able to launch the Zodiacs and go ashore.

The hut at Cape Evans was used by Peter's father for the 1909 expedition. This was where they spent the long winter preparing for the trek to the Pole. There is a famous photograph of Captain Scott sitting at his table in his den in the hut, with photographs of his wife Kathleen and baby Peter on the wall behind him; a large framed copy hangs in my sitting-room at Slimbridge. Peter, Dafila and I were allowed to go ahead of the other tourists, and I can only say that it was a breathtaking experience (our frozen breath, incidentally, was like blue smoke). There were the pony harnesses, the long table, the shelves with tins of biscuits and other food, as in the photographs – but this was real and, as Peter said, there was a happy atmosphere about the place. We went into my father-in-law's den and saw the table, the Emperor Penguin skin and the bare shelves behind, where the photographs had been. The three of us posed for George Holton, our American photographer friend. It was very cold. The whole visit to Cape Evans was moving and unforgettable, one of the very special experiences in my life.

We had not been ashore long when a white-out threatened to envelop us. It was snowing and the wind had got up. The Captain blew the ship's horn to summon us back. The ship then steamed slowly along, very close to the impressive 60ft ice wall of the Barne Glacier. It was decided to make another attempt to land at Cape Royds. There was no chance of anchoring, but the ship lay a little way off shore just south of the Cape. Two Zodiacs got away into a violent sea and we made a rough landing on ice-coated rocks. We walked back to the Shackleton Hut, used by the great explorer on his 1907-09 expedition. The aura of the past was there too: the feeling that the past was the present. We could not linger long but Peter wanted Dafila and me to see the little modern hut in which he had stayed when he had gone with the BBC in 1966. As we returned to the ship the sea was really big and the wind strong. We took a huge green one right over the bows, which drenched us, and I shall never forget the sight of Dafila with icicles hanging from the hood of her parka. We were lucky to get into McMurdo through pancake ice that evening and berth opposite the Discovery Hut in Winter Quarters Bay.

There was to be one more special experience that day. The passengers were going up Observation Hill in the evening in groups. The Scott family waited until 11pm and, accompanied by Keith and George Holton, set off up the steep little pointed hill from which members of Captain Scott's expedition to the South Pole had gazed southwards in the hope of seeing the returning party. On the summit is a large wooden cross with an inscription from Tennyson's *Ulysses*: 'To strive, to seek, to find and not to yield'. On top of the hill, which is 800ft high, the wind was so strong it was hard to stand still and it was bitterly cold. The view south was amazing, with Mount Discovery in the low evening light and the wind-blown snow on the ice plateau. The cold, the loneliness, the desolation, the beauty and the enormity of it all was awesome. Down below us to the north were the lights of the American base at McMurdo, but they seemed far away. Peter was very cold and not happy to stand still by the cross to be photographed. But for me, in spite of the cold and discomfort, this was perhaps the most moving experience of all. I was haunted by the thought of the party waiting there in vain and the three dead bodies lying in the tent to the south.

Dining with the New Zealanders at Scott base the next day was a happy occasion. It was good to see the lamp still burning in memory of Captain Scott under the portrait photograph. While we were there the weather deteriorated once again and we were summoned back to the ship. Next morning we woke to find that we were iced in: quite an exciting prospect, though not for the Captain of the *Explorer*. It took some clever manoeuvres to get us free and we moved off through the ice to look at nine Emperor Penguins on an ice floe and at the same time became the first passenger ship to go that far south (77° 54').

Before leaving Antarctica we went ashore once more at Cape Adare. Here we had a beautiful calm sea, though a swell made landing a bit tricky on the steep shingly beach and I managed to miss my footing while trying to hold a Zodiac, and got rather wet. It was here that Borchgrevink, the first person to over-winter in Antarctica, had stayed in 1899. His hut is still standing, though at that time it was not in good condition and mostly occupied by Adelie Penguins and snow. This was also the place where Captain Scott's northern party over-wintered. Victor Campbell's hut was in ruins.

Sadly, the weather decreed that we could not land on Macquarie Island until late one evening in the pouring rain. A long walk to the Royal Penguin colony was not on for the Scotts, and we did little more than visit the Australian research station. There were a further two days at sea before we had a brief stop at Hobart.

My next visit to Antarctica was in January 1978 with Prince Bernhard of the Netherlands and the 1001 Club. Among the many VIPs on board were Tenzing of Everest and his wife. Our departure was, as usual, fraught with problems. By this time in our lecture travels Peter's luggage always included a hat-box-sized case full of books. It was his reference library and was of great importance to him. To our horror the excess baggage charge was £124. Then we discovered that we had left his binoculars behind. Luckily a friend in Buenos Aires lent me some and Peter used mine. Not long after our arrival I developed a streaming cold which got me out of going to the welcome dinner in the Sheraton Hotel. The departure next morning was scheduled for 5.15 and Lars Lindblad took pity on me and offered me a lift by air from Rio Grande to Ushuaia in Tierra del Fuego. So I ended up flying in the Governor's light aircraft while Peter went on the long bus ride. At Ushuaia there was a great reception committee awaiting Prince Bernhard, including armed soldiers with machine guns – there were always soldiers with machine guns at any airport in Argentina. The runway at that time was not very long and ended in the sea. On one of the Lindblad trips a few years later the incoming plane overshot and ended up in the water. There is now a new airport with a longer runway.

Our first port of call was on the Falkland Islands, which were duty free and I became quite excited about buying an Olympus OM2 camera as recommended by Eric Hosking. An Olympus was considerably lighter than a Nikon and for some years I used Olympus equipment. In marvellous weather we visited Carcass and West Point Islands again – this time without the responsibility of passengers – and were as enchanted by their wildlife as on previous visits. I climbed Mount Misery with Keith Shackleton and Cary Lindblad, and managed to photograph the Black-browed Albatrosses and Rockhopper Penguins.

Our route along the west side of the Antarctic Peninsula was very much the same as the one we had taken in the *Navarino*. This time the weather was amazingly kind to us. We visited Deception Island, where Peter went swimming with other passengers while I walked with Keith a long way up the high bluff, from which we had a good view of the old lava-dust-covered Chilean station and looked down into the crater with a hanging glacier and lake at the bottom.

Paradise Bay was brilliant in the sunshine and Peter went diving in the hope of seeing penguins underwater. We entered the Lemaire Channel with a glass-like sea and not a cloud in the sky. Halfway along there was ice right across from one side to another. The ship stopped and we all landed on the ice and drank hot Swedish punch. Ice prevented us from going further south than Peterman Island, where we all went ashore. The views from here were spectacular, with Mount Scott dominating the background to the east. We attempted a landing at Palmer Station but this time the ice defeated us and we went back to Port Lockroy, where there are good opportunities for photographing Gentoo Penguins and Blue-eyed Shags. The hut here, a British station which had been occupied during World War II, was deserted but has since been restored by the British Antarctic Heritage Fund. While we were ashore the ice moved in and we had to be ferried back to the ship by life boats while one Zodiac with two staff members had to be man-hauled over the ice.

We had a magical afternoon steaming slowly past incredible icebergs, some of which were adorned with fringes of icicles sparkling in the sun. I spent the afternoon on the fo'c'sle as we went north towards the Neumeyer Channel. The pack ice was thick but we made it into the channel. By the time we had had dinner it seemed that the best was over but suddenly on the glass-calm sea there were Killer Whales everywhere, icebergs in the distance and, to crown it all, Humpback Whales disporting themselves.

Arriving in Hope Bay next day was rather an anticlimax. The Argentinians had entrenched themselves there; they were dressed in army uniform and there were huts to accommodate wives and families. Peter and Prince Bernhard were required to admire a baby who had been born in Antarctica. There is an Adelie Penguin colony there and the Argentinians had their line of husky dogs stretched across the space between the sea and the young birds so that the dogs picked off the penguins one by one as they came in from the sea. I found it all very depressing. We went to see the remains of the British hut which had burned down when our friend Bill Sladen was there.

In the afternoon the ship moved further into the bay and I went ashore at the foot of Mount Flora and walked about with Keith looking at fossils on a huge rock fall. Feeling rather tired, I found myself lagging behind and wondered whether to go back alone but it did not seem a good idea so I pressed on, overtook two passengers and headed up to Tenzing, who was sitting on a rock. The top of Mount Flora was shrouded in mist so I had no idea how high it was [it is 1750ft]. I did not really mean to go to the top but Tenzing said 'Let's go – we'll go slowly and see.' So then I had to. There were eight of us: Tenzing, Keith, Miguel Renal, a Canadian and his daughter, Tom Bata, Dick Ivey and me.

At one place a waterfall gushed out of a hole in the hillside and disappeared again into the rock-strewn slope a few feet below and there was a small lake at the bottom. Ridge after ridge appeared out of the mist. Sometimes we were on the snowy glacier, but as it was slippery we stuck to the rocks. It became a real rock climb, quite frightening in places, but I felt completely safe and happy behind Tenzing. At 5pm we stopped on a rocky shelf and decided there just was not time to reach the top and get back for the last Zodiac at 6.30. On our left was a great snow slope ending in a bowl half way up the mountain, on our right a rocky drop. We climbed back down the rocks – some quite tricky – then Tenzing and I, arm in arm, glissaded down the snow, then along the rocky ridge and back to another snow field with water running under it. A little stream of snow melt ran along the bottom of the bowl and we all drank there. Some further glissading took us down by the largish lake above the Argentinian base where there was a huge flock of skuas. We walked through the base and then to the jetty where a Zodiac came in. That evening I had dinner alone with Peter, followed by dancing – what a happy day!

The last excitement of special note was when I stood at the wheel and steered the ship round Cape Horn. We had hoped to land there but we did not have permission and at that time the Chileans and Argentinians were practically at war over several islands in the area. We despatched a boat ashore but our emissaries were sent packing by men with guns. So we decided to sail round the island. There was a slight swell and a popply sea. As we left, the bridge was crowded with passengers but no one was at the wheel. I offered to take over and our Captain (Hasse Nilsson) said, 'Go ahead'. All was well until I steered too far to port, turned the ship to starboard and over-corrected. The ship lurched to port and everybody on the bridge skidded wildly. Lars Lindblad, perched in the corner said loudly, 'Oh, my God,' and then, 'Who's steering?' The Second Officer appeared and took over but it was all taken in very good part and everybody laughed. Hasse Nilsson was to become a great friend over the years. He and I were able to share reading-spectacles when necessary in order to read the menu at dinner, and there were many good parties at his table with Swedish toasts.

By 1979 Peter and I were totally hooked on travel with the *Lindblad Explorer*. It was not just the ship, it was the exciting places she visited. Each trip was an expedition, with wild life as the core interest and the places off the beaten track. There was no doubt that Peter was a great asset as lecturer and it was my job to be nice to the passengers. That was, in fact, very good for me as I am not by nature a tolerant person.

Peter no longer had any inhibitions about Antarctica and I was especially enthusiastic when we were once more invited by Lars to join the ship for what was advertised as a circumnavigation of that continent. This time we went by New York and Rio de Janeiro.

So it was that we visited the Falkland Islands for the third time and found it all as entrancing as ever. Carcass Island once again was the favourite; Peter and I managed to escape on our own and had a whole day ashore. We climbed to the top of the hill and found a Red-backed Buzzard's nest. A Peregrine dive-bombed us and put on an amazing display of speed flying, causing me to use up a lot of film. As a final 'bon bouche' for the day I was allowed to take the wheel on the bridge for a few minutes when we left. I managed rather better than on the previous occasion.

While bobbing about in a rough sea off the Antarctic Peninsula, unable to anchor near the Polish station called Artowski, we came upon a small Dutch ketch with two men on board. We invited the skipper, Willi de Roos, on board the *Explorer*. He kindly agreed to give a talk to our passengers which turned out to be extremely interesting. He had been through the North West Passage (only the second sailing boat to do so since Amundsen), down through the Bering Straits and on to Vancouver where he had stopped and written a book. From there he had gone to Tahiti, Punta Arenas and on down south. He was considering circumnavigating the Antarctic continent but had still not made up his mind – his aim was to circumnavigate both American continents. He had us all entranced. He spoke of fear, and the fear of fear, and of approaching it step by step. He was remarkably articulate. He described how his boat had been iced in in the North West Passage and how he thought it would crack like the *Endurance*.

We were able to land at Artowski station later that evening. They were doing an interesting study of krill which they told us about and we saw several dead ones on the beach. They look like a large prawn and if you find them on the beach at Deception Island they are pink as they have been 'cooked' in the hot volcanic water.

There was rather more pack ice than on previous trips. On one particularly spectacular evening as we nosed our way through, the low light on the ice and icebergs, with the snowy peaks above us, kept me on deck with my camera until at least 11pm. It took us three hours to cover four miles that night. Sadly there was too much ice to go through the Lemaire Channel so we headed off to Palmer station, weaving our way at walking pace round the icebergs. On such occasions it was impossible to leave the deck. The scenery was spellbinding and there were skuas, Dominican Gulls, Gentoo and Adelie Penguins and Crabeater and Leopard Seals. There was a large colony of breeding Adelie Penguins there and the smell was very strong.

We left the Peninsula that day, 28 January, and after crossing the Antarctic Circle set off for the Ross Sea. It was at this point that Hasse came to a 'recap' meeting and told us that McMurdo had refused us bunkering and that we might not be able to go there. We therefore had to save fuel by proceeding on one engine, which meant ten days at sea. To keep people busy we organised a whale watch in shifts and even Peter and I took to exercising by walking round the decks. Ten times round made a mile.

On the fifth day a Russian whaler and a number of Minke Whales were sighted ahead of us. We all gathered on the observation deck to watch the hunt. The ship closed in on a whale and fired. Minutes later the whale blew, and blood mixed with water. We closed in on the whaler. Two small Minkes were hanging by their tails from the port side and within minutes the new one was winched up and strung alongside them. The harpoon was immediately re-set and they moved off. Twice they hooted at us but otherwise they seemed unmoved by the presence of hundreds of people photographing them. Our Captain tried unsuccessfully to speak to them. The parent ship had apparently been sighted earlier and we understood there were thirty-five whalers to one parent ship. The whole episode was rather like a nightmare.

On the eighth day at sea we crossed the International Date Line and lost a day. By rights it should have been the Sunday, but Hasse took pity on our parson friend, the Reverend C. Weed (known as the Rev Kelp) and we lost Monday instead. Then things started to happen. We were heading south west for the Ross Sea, both engines were running, it was 10° C and snowing, the ship was rolling and it seemed good and Antarctic. But then fog came down, we were hemmed in by huge icebergs and the wind was blowing in the ice behind us. So the Captain turned the ship in her own length and back we headed north east. We were able to turn south again a few hours later but we had a rough night, with the ship pitching. The barometer made an all-time low for the Ross Sea at 937.5 millibars and the barograph went off the bottom of the paper. The next day the barometer rose slightly – and so did the waves and wind. The passengers started falling as the ship rolled and pitched. The waves breaking over the lounge made it feel like being in an aquarium, so solid green did the water look outside.

On the tenth day the wind, which at 2am had reached force 10, had dropped a little. But we were now two days late and running at reduced speed due to the weather. Time for a lot of sleep, in between watching the petrels and Light Mantled Sooty Albatross.

On day twelve, still with a force 8 blowing, we sighted the Ross Ice Shelf. We arrived in calm water but a dramatic wind was blowing the snow off the 150ft cliff. Mist swirled round and shafts of sunlight disappeared into the mist behind us. Cape Crozier came into view. There were penguins, but not many – all Adelies and no Emperors. There were huge areas of dirty penguin rookery, with Mount Terror rising behind, way above the clouds. The sound of the sea breaking under the ice shelf with a shushing roar enhanced this almost mystic scene.

We steamed slowly round Cape Bird. Cape Royds came into view at about 7pm and Mount Erebus finally revealed its summit with a plume of smoke above the mist. There was sea ice south of Cape Royds but the ice was not fast enough to anchor alongside so we went by Zodiac, landing on the ice with a two-mile walk to the hut over soft lava. The helicopter which was meant to bring someone to open the hut never came. It was disappointing not getting to see inside again, but with Keith and Jacq Shackleton we went down to the water's edge and jumped about on the floating ice floes. A Leopard Seal lying on the ice was unco-operative about being photographed. It was a long walk back over the lava dust to the ship but we were rewarded by a splendid sunrise (or was it sunset?) over Mount Discovery at 1am.

After a three-and-a-half hour sleep we were up and off to land at the Cape Evans hut again. It was a relief to find everything we remembered still there: the dead dog, the pony harness and snow shoes, the stuffed penguin, the reindeer-skin boots and gloves, the canvas clothes worn by Shackleton's party overwintering in 1916. Outside there were penguin eggs in the shelter of the hut among the bleached pieces of wood, hay for the ponies and maize. Peter and I climbed the hill and from the top could see Hut Point, the Discovery hut and the smoke rising from McMurdo. We could also see the red American ice-breaker that was stationed there. After three hours ashore we headed south for the ice but the ice-breaker barred our way in the only channel of open water. It was obvious that we were not wanted at McMurdo base. The American passengers were not at all pleased. We turned north again. Next day the fo'c'sle was covered with snow and icicles. As ever the scenery was spectacular. Five miles off the coast on our port side sheer, mountainous cliffs rose to a height of 5000ft and there were great tabular ice bergs in the Hallett Bay area.

By late afternoon next day we were approaching Cape Adare. Snow petrels were flying round the icebergs, there were Giant Petrels and a mass of Antarctic Skuas. We went ashore at 8pm in the same place as our previous visit. As before, it was a tricky landing on the steep shingle beach with a big swell. This time Peter got very wet and someone fell very heavily in the Zodiac. We walked slowly along the beach to the huts, seeing a few moulting Adelie Penguins en route. The hut belonging to Scott's northern party was a wreck now, but we went through the half open door of Borchgrevink's hut. Snow blocked the entrance but I managed to take a flash photograph of the interior.

At 11 pm we were summoned back on board by the ship's siren because of a freshening breeze. There followed the most amazing night. The Zodiac drivers, including Keith, had been launching boats from the shore in rough conditions, aided by a bottle of rum to keep them warm, but they were all soaked and must have been very cold. Keith had to go out again to tow in a broken-down Zodiac. But at last all were safely in and the 'Little Red Ship' sailed away, with a vast full moon showing off the high top of Cape Adare. The last of Antarctica! We felt quite emotional about saying goodbye.

Soon we were dancing in the bar. A wild evening followed, with all the staff, lecturers and a few staunch passengers. Our friend John Smith (from Smith Square, London) appeared in his dressing gown and rolled-up bala-clava hat looking like Genghis Kahn and danced with one finger on the light in the centre of the ceiling. Finally Mike McDowell, a Zodiac driver at that time, played Handel's Water Music followed by the Fireworks Music, which was conducted in turn by Alan Gurney, Pete Puleston, Peter and Keith while we all gathered round, playing imaginary instruments. At about 4am a friendly American judge (one of the passengers) entered the lounge in his dressing gown and immediately took up an imaginary instrument. As an impromptu happening it was an unforgettable way to end our last day in Antarctica.

The next day the sea took its revenge with a force 10 gale on our starboard side so that we rolled all day and slid from one end of our bunks to the other the following night. A few days at sea meant that the passengers had to be kept busy and happy so the inevitable fancy dress evening was a laid on as soon as the weather quietened down. The theme was

'Masquerade on Ice'. Peter dressed up as 'The Belle of the *Lindblad Explorer*', with a blonde wig and a dress borrowed from a passenger. I went as a tabular iceberg in a box covered with white paper and plastic bags. We were both unrecognisable and unfortunately (we were staff) both won prizes.

It is sad to leave the beautiful Antarctic, but the Sub Antarctic islands are immensely interesting from a wildlife point of view. Bad weather prevented us from seeing the King Penguins on Macquarie Island but Campbell Island was just as good as we remembered from the earlier visit. Peter and I enjoyed a scramble up the hill to look down on a Sooty Albatross's fluffy baby on its nest and then walked a long way and made friends with a nesting Royal Albatross. After watching a spectacular rain storm sweep across the hills we found our young albatrosses performing their courtship display, and the sun came out. This was a glorious day. It was a good day for Kodak, too, considering that it rains 325 days a year on Campell Island. We were lucky.

The return home from the Antipodes was prolonged by a short visit to Auckland and an ornithological outing to see Wrybills with our good friend Ronald Lockley, followed by a much longer visit to Hawaii. On arrival at Honolulu on Saturday 24 February we changed aeroplanes and flew straight to Maui. We were to stay in the Pioneer Hotel at Lahaina, an old whaling port on the island that liked to keep its character. The hotel, right by the harbour, had retained its old-fashioned appearance. This is where all the whale research people were based. At that time it included an IMAX camera crew and the distinguished marine biologist Sylvia Earle. It was she who had invited us to join her here in order to see Humpback Whales.

The morning after our arrival we were ready with our hired flippers and all the rest of our swimming gear in a state of excited anticipation. We boarded a large fishing vessel called *Sports Diver*, along with about ten other people, including Sylvia and her daughter 'Mouse', and the huge IMAX movie camera. As we went out to sea we saw several whale spouts in the flat calm water, but as we approached, the whales sounded. Later the sea got up a bit and as we neared a whale-shaped island a friendly whale was sighted.

Peter and I were told that in the event of getting close to a whale we must let the camera and crew go in first. As we were not in the script, we must keep out of its way. The divers went in and, finally, Peter and I with our snorkels. I found my breath completely taken away by the chilly water (72° F) and excitement. We dropped into bottomless clear blue depths. That time I saw Peter and the divers way below but no whale. But the next encounter was the real thing. From the boat we saw some whales splashing with their flippers and porpoising. Peter, Sylvia and I followed the camera. Determined to see something this time, I held Peter's hand. Suddenly, beneath us, way down in the blue, I saw something white – the flipper of a whale. Then two whales materialised. They came up slowly to have a look at us while we lay there. I let go of Peter to get my little Nikonos camera ready. Peter swam off and we watched two whales watching us. Peter was so close to one that he saw its eye moving from him to me. Then they slowly moved off. I can only describe the experience as awesome. People still on the boat shouted and pointed so that we should know where to look. We swam over to some other whales and found two more, and then three more. I had no sensation of fear, but the first two were so close that they made more impression than the next ones. Peter and I were in a state of euphoria. Later he painted a picture of this event.

The next day we went out in another boat where Peter Tyack and Bernie Krause had a microphone in the water so that we could listen to the whales singing. It was another magical day which included swimming with a large pod of Spinner Dolphins. Inevitably it ended with yet another dinner, this time with 300 people and Peter receiving a standing ovation for his after-dinner speech. We came home after that trip with memories which were to last a lifetime.

CHAPTER THIRTEEN

The High Arctic

Peter had always said that there was more wildlife in the Arctic than the Antarctic, so it was exciting when we were invited to join the *Lindblad Explorer* for a trip to Spitzbergen and Greenland in August 1972. Because the ship was having problems with its variable pitch propeller we had two days in Bergen before boarding at Kristiansund. It was fun to celebrate our twenty-first wedding anniversary in Arctic climes with such special friends.

We found that we already knew many of the passengers and it was particularly good to have Keith Shackleton and Roger Tory Petersen with us as lecturers, and Rod Salm as a Zodiac driver. Even more special, we had Falcon with us as well. He had finished school and was able to get away before starting work.

But our problems with the propeller were not over. It had been manufactured in Ålesund so we put in there for further repairs. It is a very attractive little town with Kittiwakes nesting on a cliff in the main street. There were good photographic possibilities and I enjoyed the enforced stop. Peter, with Rod, Keith and one or two others, went out in a Zodiac and tried diving with rather inadequate gear. But at least they saw some fish and Peter painted them in his diary. When we finally got away we steamed up the beautiful Norwegian coast in lovely hot sunshine. I have been to Tromsø twice, the second time in 1995 with Tony Soper in a Russian ship. It has a very unusual modern church called the Arctic Cathedral. Built of stone, with a series of steep-pitched roofs, it is rather austere but has brilliant stained glass windows and seems to embody the spirit of the Arctic. It was not quite finished in 1972 so it was interesting to revisit in 1995 and find that I was still moved by its beauty.

Our arrival at Bear Island the following evening provided us with a dramatic view of the tops of the mountains appearing out of the mist over the sea. We were approaching the southern end, where the cliffs rise up to the 1600ft mountain Miseryfjellet. The cliffs are home to thousands of sea birds: Little Auks, Fulmars, Guillemots, Kittiwakes and Glaucous Gulls. It was questionable whether we could take Zodiac trips in the thick mist but it cleared for a while and we did go out, with Keith at the helm, under the dark sinister cliffs. The sound of the birds was tremendous. Some were having difficulty in getting back to their ledges in the wind. For Falcon the highlight of the little expedition was going through the Perlenporten cave in the Zodiac. This was the scene of the climax in Alistair Maclean's thriller novel *Bear Island*. The atmosphere, with the mist outside and the splashing water at dusk, made it all very spooky and exciting.

The next day we landed at North Haven, where there is a radio station. The week before we were there, Mr Bjorn, one of the staff, had been eaten by a Polar Bear while checking the meteorological instruments in a storm (Mr Bjorn had been eaten by a Bjorn on Bjornöya). We did not see any bears, but Falcon and I went for a long walk on our own and I was quite frightened of getting lost in the rather featureless landscape with the possibility of meeting a bear.

When I visited Bear Island again in 1995 the weather was so bad that we did not have good views of the bird cliffs to the south and made only one short landing halfway along. As a stopping-off place for the Barnacle Geese which come to Caerlaverock in Scotland from Spitzberg it is of special interest to the Wildfowl and Wetlands Trust.

Peter recorded our visit to Svalbard in his *Travel Diaries of a Naturalist*. It is memorable to me because of the near-loss of a passenger on the little island of Svensköya. We had landed on a steeply shelving shingle beach. Peter and I wandered quite far and nearly became lost as the mist thickened on our way back. With a few similar lagoons at the top of the shingle banks and other features it was not easy to find the Zodiac landing place. Even Peter was not sure. I was worried about Falcon, who had gone off on his own. We had seen Polar Bear droppings. It turned out that he had walked to the east and eventually come upon a hut. Inside were two men asleep.

The Lindblad voyages. *Above: left*, Keith Shackleton driving a Zodiac in the Antarctic; *right*, Lars Eric Lindblad in Greenland.
Below The Lindblad Explorer ice-bound in the Lemaire Channel. Peter and Lars Eric stand by.

Left The Lindblad Explorer fo'c'sle with an ice fringe on the bell after a stormy night in the Ross Sea .

Below Dafila at Cape Hallett, 1971.

Right Hot and cold.
Above Falcon standing on the rocks by Knut Rasmussen's Glacier in Greenland.
Below A heatwave on the way to Spitzbergen off the coast of Norway. Peter, Keith and a passenger sunbathing.

Philippa and her guardian Shau Liu at the top of the '51 steps' climb at Wolong Sichuan, China. *Right* The Victoria Falls at sunset from the Zambian side.

Above Welcoming party for Peter. Harassis tribesmen at Yalooni in the Omani desert.
Below Peter, Richard Leakey and Aubrey Buxton looking at fossils near Richard's
camp on the shores of Lake Turkana, Kenya.

Above One of so many sunlit hours. Philippa and Peter on Heron Island off the Great Barrier Reef.
Below Peter with a Shovel-nosed Shark in the channel at Heron Island.

Philippa swimming with a large Potato Cod in 'the cod hole' near Lizard Island, Great Barrier Reef.

Not wishing to disturb them he wrote in the sand, 'Falcon was here', with the time and date. On his way back he met Lars and a small group so he led them back through the fog to the hut.

The two men – twins – emerged from the hut explaining that they had gone to sleep after having been up half the night because of a Polar Bear which had been round the hut and had only left a couple of hours previously. Lucky Falcon! It turned out that the twins were manning the Decca station so we took them back to the ship for a meal. In the meantime it was discovered that one passenger tag was missing: someone had not returned to the ship. It was still very foggy and we now knew that there were Polar Bears on the island. Peter and Keith lead two search parties ashore, and it was Peter who finally heard a thin call of 'cooee' (a sound 'not attributable to any known bird'). And there was Miss Jenks walking towards them in the mist. Some months later she wrote to Peter from New York telling us that she had been mugged. When asked if any other terrible thing had ever happened to her she replied that she had been lost on an island off Svalbard. 'But couldn't you read the street names?' they said.

The danger of Polar Bears was very real. At an early briefing we had been told that if we came upon one while out walking, the answer was to curl up in a ball. Not long after, at an evening recap, one of the passengers described how she and her companion while walking along had seen what they took to be part of a Polar Bear showing above the top of some nearby rocks on top of a mound. They threw themselves on the turf, curled up into balls and waited. Nothing happened – until suddenly a passenger wearing a large white fluffy hat rose from where she had been sitting behind the rocks admiring the view.

We never did see a Polar Bear and even on my trip in 1995 the sightings were all very distant. But the wildlife was altogether wonderful, not just the birds – the Barnacle Geese and Ivory Gulls up on the pack ice north of Svalbard were the highlights – but the plants and flowers as well. Svalbard had provided us with a glimpse of its rich wildlife and we had had our excitements. From there we headed to the east coast of Greenland, which would be much more icy. In fact, it was so icy that although we were close inland and heading for Hold-with-Hope-Cape we were prevented by the pack ice from going into Young Sound and so on to land at the weather station on Clavering Island. That was a pity, but we had memorable views of skeins of Pinkfeet migrating south against the icy cliffs of Clavering

Island. And the evening light on the pack ice as we steered south again was spellbinding and infinitely photographic.

Before reaching Scoresbysund we had wonderful views of Minke and Fin whales. The town itself was described by Peter in his diary as 'one large midden' and he and I walked quickly through it to go botanising. I find it interesting that Peter had recorded thirty-nine plants in Svalbard, which shows how broad his interests were. We had learned the names of Arctic plants when we were in Iceland with Finnur Gudmundsson in 1951 and I still remember many of them now, pronounced with a distinct Icelandic accent.

A circumnavigation of a large island called Milne Land by way of a narrow fjord with some beautiful icebergs in it cheered us up after the rather depressing morning at Scoresbysund. We did not get very close to anything, but there were some Musk Ox on the slope of the mainland, the scenery was wild and wonderful and we recorded a few birds, including a Snowy Owl. From there a night's sailing brought us to Iceland where we became rather more ordinary tourists for two days. It was nostalgic to find wild Harlequin Ducks and to be able to point out to Falcon the house where we were married. Hofdi, which no longer belongs to the British Embassy, has the distinction of being the place where Ronald Reagan met with Kruschev. Peter and Falcon went to watch Spassky and Fischer playing chess in Reykjavik and were very much taken up with the drama of the game.

After Reykjavik we did not land again until we arrived in Angmassalik, in Greenland, a much more picturesque place than Scorsebysund. Finnur Gudmundsson had joined us at Reykjavik and his presence certainly enlivened things on board, though accommodating him was not easy since he was a very large man and the ship was already full. Lyall Watson found himself sharing his cabin with a very talkative and rather opinionated scientist. When at last we managed to go ashore again it was near the Knud Rasmussen glacier at the head of the Sermiligak Fjord, where we stretched our legs and looked at the plants. We left Greenland from a small airfield in among the mountains in Kulusuk Fjord. It was a spectacular place to end our expedition, with the ship lying out among the icebergs.

CHAPTER FOURTEEN

A Dog and a Corpse

When I look back I am amazed at how much time Peter and I spent travelling. It was only possible because we had such good people looking after the Wildlife Trust, while the efficient Mike Garside took care of Peter's other interests. As far as the Trust was concerned, the most important people during our Lindblad Travel years were Professor Geoffrey Matthews, Brigadier Tim Sparrow and Brigadier Stephen Goodall, who could be relied upon to deal with any crisis. As for the WWF, Peter was very often able to do good business for them on our travels, visiting Heads of State and lecturing on both WWF and WWT on the ship. We collected quite a number of American members that way.

In 1973 we fitted in two trips on the *Lindblad Explorer*. The first began in March and we were away for around six weeks. We joined Lars Lindblad and the cruise party at Lhao Lhao in Argentina. It was our first time on board the *Explorer* with a Swedish crew. It turned out to be an interesting voyage. The ship was not quite full, which was always agreeable, and we had our friend Rod Salm, the marine biologist from the Seychelles, on board as a lecturer.

After a day of very rough weather and big seas we arrived at Masa Tierra, or Robinson Crusoe Island, in the Juan Fernandez Archipelago. There was a small town and a high volcanic mountain with an airstrip near the top, from which Lars and his wife left us later that day. The population was 650, there was no doctor, midwife or nurse and, we were told, the mortality rate was high. It was rather a depressing place.

It was not long before we discovered that there was a large dog called Vodka on board ship. Vodka had short sandy-coloured hair, was obviously young and was very friendly. The Captain was not pleased to discover that one of the stewardesses had brought it on board at Puerto Montt. It excelled itself during the first full briefing by coming into the lounge and making a large puddle in the middle of the little round dance floor. Some of the passengers complained but there was nothing much we could do about it until we reached Easter Island a week later. Our two Cruise Directors, John and Marie Darby, kept it in their large cabin most of the time and it was exercised on deck first thing in the morning. It was up to me to go round afterwards with Kleenex and poop-scoop so that non-doggy people could not complain. The dog was not the only animal on board. There was also a charming male Coati-mundi, brought on board on a previous trip by a crew member, which had the run of the ship. It could be very friendly, although its teeth were a bit sharp and it tended to pester the poor dog. Its most spectacular performance was climbing along the ropes on the life boats on the top deck, hanging over a rough sea. It was really a very engaging animal. Not so popular was the occasion when it started to have a sexual affair with the electric leads to the hot plate in the dining room. What with the dog and one of the passengers having a heart attack during the first few days at sea, things were not going too well for the Captain. The heart attack was not fatal, but more problems were awaiting us.

Early on 17 March we arrived at a small volcanic-rock bird island called Sala y Gomez. For the bird enthusiasts this was going to be wonderful, but on the windward side the waves were breaking one-third of the way up the 98ft high island and passengers were warned of the difficulties of landing on rocks in a swell on the leeward side. Peter and I went ashore in the first Zodiac with the keen 'birders', picked our way over the sharp rocky terrain among juvenile shearwaters and headed for the nesting Frigate Birds and boobies. Looking back we saw an overturned Zodiac being towed by another which was collecting a floating fuel tank. We heard later that a Zodiac full of passengers had flipped on the rock at the landing place and turned over. Some people could not swim and had to be pulled out onto the rock while the Swedish boatman jumped in and rescued others who were floating away. One elderly Englishman had been caught in the Zodiac's ropes by his binoculars, which were round his neck, and had to be extricated from under the overturned boat. He was given artificial respiration by Rod Salm and taken back to the ship lying flat in the bottom of a boat. His wife, who had stayed on board, saw what she thought was his dead body being brought back. Luckily he was all right, but he spent the rest of the voyage telling everyone how he had seen his whole life go before his eyes as he was drowning. Rod and another diver later went back to the scene of the accident to collect all the missing cameras and other gear from the bottom of the sea. They were watched by some thirty sharks and I do not think Rod was very happy down there.

We were with our group of bird watchers at the far end of the island but heard the ship's siren summoning us for immediate return. As we approached the landing area to board the Zodiacs we were greeted by John Darby who directed us by a different route – in order, he said, to avoid walking past the dead body of one of the passengers. The wind had freshened and getting the people back to the ship had to be carried out in relays. Peter, who had his mask and snorkel with him, decided to take a look in the sea with Rod, but did not fancy the number of sharks and got out again quite quickly. The deceased passenger was an elderly Swiss gentleman who had simply gone ashore, sat down on a rocky ledge and had a heart attack. He did not appear to have left any instructions regarding burial, so they had to be sent for from Lindblad head office in New York.

We arrived next day at Easter Island, where the Captain planned to leave the corpse and the dog. We had a whole day ashore and visited all the historic sights. The statues were awe-inspiring in a curious way and seeing the quarry from which they were hewn was fascinating. At the end of the day we returned tired to the ship to find the Captain, Hasse Nilsson, sitting sadly in the bar by himself looking miserable. We asked him what was the matter. 'I have still got them both on board,' he said. The authorities would not accept the corpse because there were no refrigeration facilities on the island and no aircraft for a week. They were not prepared to keep the dog either. Next day we received a cable from New York and there was a moving burial at sea. The dog remained on board until Singapore.

Three days later we arrived at Pitcairn, the island of the Bounty mutineers. We were taken ashore by the local inhabitants in their long boats through the big swell and landed in Bounty Bay. At that time the population was eighty-six, mostly Seventh Day Adventists. They laid on a

vast lunch for us in the village. My photographic goal was the Pitcairn
Warbler, which is endemic, but warblers are difficult anywhere and in the
rain even more tiresome, so Peter's drawings and notes are more special
and informative. We met various members of the Christian and Young
families, whose histories go back to the mutineers. The Youngs are related
to Lord Kennet's family (Peter's step-father was a Young) and we bought a
beautiful shark carved by one of them in miro wood from neighbouring
Henderson Island.

After all these various adventures we had several peaceful days at sea
with blue skies, blue sea, and birds and flying fish to watch. Peter and the
Darbys set up a flying-fish watch in shifts for volunteers. This involved a
one-hour stint on the top deck or the bridge wing recording the number of
sightings of different species. Peter's drawings had been photocopied so
that we knew what to look for. He also painted a key to the Gadfly Petrels of
the South Pacific Tropics so that we could identify them.

After these islands it would be difficult to beat the totally unsophisticated Marquesas, our next port of call. I think we were the first cruise ship
ever to appear there. Our sixty passengers were treated to a great welcome,
with dancing girls on the beach under the coconut palms and a kava drinking ceremony. Knowing that Gaugin, who died in 1903, had been buried
in the Marquesas, we persuaded the Captain to put some of us ashore on
Hiva Oa. We landed in the evening and walked through the village of
Atuona and on up the hill in the dusk to the cemetery. We found the grave,
made with dark lava rock, with a frangipani tree growing at its head. A
fallen flower from it is pasted in my diary.

We visited two more islands in this group: Nuku Hiva and Faka Rava.
On Nuku Hiva we made a long excursion by boat and on foot through the
forest to Taipi Valley, where Herman Melville stayed and subsequently
wrote *Taipeh*. When he was there the locals were still cannibals. During the
next few days we visited Tahiti, Raiatea and Bora Bora, where we did all the
things tourists do – except that Peter, Rod Salm and I did more snorkelling
than most people and Peter drew and painted lots of fish in his diary.

The most interesting event in Tahiti was meeting Bengt Danielson of the
Kon Tiki expedition fame. We were to see much more of this likable man
and his wife later. Heavy rain storms delayed our arrival at Bora Bora
but in my diary I recorded that, 'We came into the lagoon of this most
beautiful of all islands as dusk fell with a wild clearing sky.' We felt rather

envious of the residents of Bora Bora Hotel at the water's edge whose rooms had platforms jutting out over the clear sea and coral beneath.

Two days later, our arrival at Rarotonga caused rather a stir. We were the first passenger ship to be able to enter the harbour and tie up alongside – the harbour mouth was only 16ft deep and the ship's draught was just 15ft. Peter and I remembered that this was where his mother first received the news of Captain Scott's death in the Antarctic. I could see that Peter was moved by the memory. There followed several days at sea, and some rough weather, too. On 6 April the day's programme announced that the Coati-mundi would give a lecture on 'Knots, Ropes and Splices'. But we lost that day, since it was when we crossed the international dateline.

We arrived at Tongatapu in the pouring rain, but in spite of the weather I enjoyed our time ashore. The Tongans lived up to their reputation for friendliness and we were treated to an excellent lunch of baked fish, pork, bread-fruit, sweet potatoes and fruit. We had eaten similar local food on other islands but undoubtedly this was the best. Peter spent the day snorkelling about a mile away from the ship. The piece of Tapa cloth (made from banana leaves) which I bought that day hangs above the studio door in my house. There was another day at sea before we arrived at Suva in Fiji.

Days at sea on the Pacific Ocean are very different from those in Antarctic waters. Peter was kept busy with his lectures and telling the passengers about the fishes which they might have seen, the Coati-mundi kept us all amused, the dog settled down, and the flying-fish watch proved popular with many of the passengers. Packing up and leaving the ship was always tiring and my third visit to the main island of Fiji was disappointing as it was raining. Our plan, however, was to go to Castaway Island with a delightful elderly American friend called Nancy Legendre, whom we had met before on the *Explorer*. In the hotel on Castaway we slept in a thatched *burre* by the beach, and spent most of our time face down in the sea. The coral and the fish life were good then, just straight out from the shore. After Peter died I went back there with Penny Skelton. The island was as delightful as ever but we had to go out on a half-hour speed-boat ride to get to good coral and fish life. The coral around most of the resort islands was in a sorry state from pollution.

CHAPTER FIFTEEN

Indonesia: a Diver's Paradise

In October 1973 we were off again in the *Lindblad Explorer* on another great fish-watching expedition. It was our first visit to Indonesia. By this time international travel was becoming a little easier but Lars' arrangements for our flight by BOAC could still go wrong, as we were usually on stand-by. On this occasion we were off-loaded in Paris with the worry once again that we might, literally, miss the boat. We arrived in Djakarta a day late and caught up with the group in Bali. We had Nicola with us and also our friend Nancy Legendre.

We enjoyed our first introduction to Balinese dancing – a very special performance of the *Ramayana* dance at the hotel next door to ours. We loved the *Barong* dance, performed the following day; the *Barong* is a fabulous animal and the whole dance is full of colour, humour and clever mime. At night we watched an outdoor performance of the *Ketchak* dance. The dancers are dressed as monkeys and the acting shows a remarkable perception of animal behaviour. On this trip we were lucky to have so many friends. It was our first long voyage with Ron and Valerie Taylor, of shark-filming fame. Rod Salm was also with us, so there was great interest in the underwater world.

As mentioned earlier, the inhabitants of some of the islands where we called had not seen a cruise ship before. There appeared to be a population explosion – hundreds of children greeted us wherever we went. They clung to us, poked our skin with their fingers, seized our hands and followed us. It was a somewhat irritating distraction and made photography difficult.

We went snorkelling and bird watching around various small, uninhabited islands. In a crater lake on Satonda, a small island just off Sumbawa, we saw grebes and bee-eaters, but the most exciting wildlife on shore was on Komodo Island. Starting very early in the morning Nicky and I went on a long, hot walk to see the famous dragons (giant lizards). This involved climbing over a high ridge and down the other side: a two-and-a-half hour excursion which brought out the best – and worst – in our small group. We had an Indonesian guide who had arranged for a dead goat to be hung in a tree in the valley over the hill. (It was on this hilltop that four years later our guide was to lose a member of his group, a Swiss gentleman who had decided to wait at the top while the others went down into the valley. When they returned only his watch and binoculars remained. He was never found and it was assumed that he had been eaten by a dragon. By the time of our third visit in 1977 a cross had been erected at the spot. We had no idea that they could be really dangerous!)

As we approached the trees where the goat was hanging, out of reach, we were greeted by two big dragons. Their long, yellow, forked tongues flicked in and out. Weismar, our guide, chased them off with a big stick, the goat was lowered, and after a while they went off to feed on it. By this time several dragons were on the scene. A baby one was continuously driven off by the bigger ones – it ended up being fed the ham from our picnic lunch! Another goat was put out and two really big dragons got down to a feast, occasionally both feeding on the same animal. The bigger one finally swallowed half the second goat in one mouthful, horns and all. Even then it was not satisfied and went on feeding on the remaining meat. When the meat was finished they retreated to the shade and slept. One was obviously very hot and was gasping. Encouraged by Valerie and Ron, some of us stroked one of the big ones and Ron measured it with his tripod. It was about 11ft long.

I have been on two other occasions to see the dragons – once over that steep hill and once nearer the shore – but it was never quite as exciting and successful as that first time in 1973. There is now a viewing place not far from where people land on the beach, with warning signs about the danger of meeting a dragon as you walk through the trees.

The dragons were not the only interesting feature of Komodo Island.

We found a special place with very good coral and reef fishes which I have also visited more than once. For me there is nowhere to beat Indonesia for underwater scenery and coral fish. The sheer drop-off walls which go down vertically, with brilliant corals on them, are spectacular. There is just one problem for a diver and that is that the currents at different levels can change quite suddenly.

On the largest inhabited islands we were always given a warm welcome – informal, enthusiastic, and often with some dancing or singing laid on. The musical instruments were usually bamboo pipes, and some of the dances involved hopping over bamboo poles as in a sword dance; once there was a 'bewitched' bamboo which controlled the dancers.

Our second visit to Indonesia was in 1976. It was again with the *Lindblad Explorer*, but on this occasion we were travelling from east to west on our way back from a cruise which had started in Alaska, went on to Japan, the Japanese islands and the Carolines, and ended in Bali. We visited two remote islands before arriving at Bau Bau, on the island of Buton, to receive an extraordinary and rapturous welcome. I do not think anything like this could happen in those parts again. Although the people had been told of our expected arrival by Lorne Blair and his brother, who had been wandering round Indonesia for some time and with whom Lars had been in touch, the welcome was spontaneous and genuine. This was their first cruise ship.

We were greeted on the pier by a vast crowd of people in brightly coloured costume and walked down the avenue between them, shaking hands as we went. There was a formal reception in a government building near the jetty, where elegant dancers performed a colourful scarf dance. There was a welcome speech in Indonesian,which was translated while we were served tea and rice. We were taken to an old sultan's palace on top of a steep hill with dancers performing for us all the way. The girls wore black and silver or shot-silk pink skirts, and blouses of all colours decorated with gold. All the time people were saying 'welcome' and shaking hands. There were welcoming banners at the courtyard of the palace, where a great feast was laid on out of doors under the frangipani trees. The food was mostly rice-based and very sweet, and there were eggs baked without their shells. A woman attendant sat behind each tray of food, on which were several plates or saucers with huge, brightly coloured domed lids.

We took off our shoes and went into the palace, and found Captain Hasse Nilsson and his wife Amie being plied with yet more food. There was more dancing by more beautiful girls and finally we were taken down in open trucks to the market in the town. The jostling crowds had been rather unnerving but the spontaneity and magnificence of the welcome was over-whelming, a never-to-be-forgotten experience.

A completely different kind of welcome awaited us on our visits to the Asmat region of West Irian on the Indonesian coast of New Guinea. This is the notorious head-hunting area but the welcome was no less warm or spectacular. The ship had to anchor a long way out with only about a foot of water under her. That first time we set off very early in the morning in one life boat and six Zodiacs for a long ride to the low-lying coast.

We went to the Asmat region again in 1977. Each time we were greet-ed at the mouth of the river by naked warriors standing on canoes uttering war cries, and puffs of what looked like smoke (it was actually lime). Chanting and wailing and clamouring with long spears, they clung to our boats to help them get up the river. The way of life of these large, dark-skinned, striking people is very complex. It includes wife-swapping, head-hunting (males only), worship of the hornbill and fear of the crocodile god. On our second visit in 1977 to Agats, where there was a missionary presence, we were sad to see the men wearing dirty khaki shorts. Their symbolic 'Bis poles' had all gone.

Of the four villages we visited on the two trips, Owus in 1977 was perhaps the most interesting. The fact that it was raining added another dimension to the day. There was a delayed start from the ship because we were told that there was a battle going on between the village of Owus and the next one up the river. We finally set off in three life boats with their awnings up, and four Zodiacs.

It was an hour's ride to the mouth of the river and I was glad to have Peter's wet-suit top as well as my clothes underneath to keep me warm. Other people were wearing all sorts of things, such as black plastic bags and bath hats. At the river mouth half a dozen war canoes were waiting by a grass rain shelter in the forest. The Indonesian guide in our Zodiac gave the warriors presents and told them to wait until all our little fleet had arrived. The rain teemed down and it was surprisingly cold. At last everyone was present and out came the narrow, dug-out canoes, paddled by 8ft spears decorated with feathers or plumes. They came with great war cries and threatening postures and we were soon surrounded as more kept emerging from hidden creeks on every side. The river was quite narrow, with marvellous forest on either side and a number of birds – egrets, whimbrels, sandpipers and so on. And still it poured with rain as we set off upstream on a falling tide.

The warriors swarmed aboard our boats and we towed their canoes, thus reducing our speed. A splendid warrior with a painted face perched beside me on the stern. The blade of his knife, which was stuck in his arm-band, was perilously close to me but he kindly moved it. More or less naked except for some decorations, he was shivering yet his skin was warm to the touch of my hand. Suddenly the chief in our boat said that they must all go back because his people came from another village and the inhabitants of Owus would fight them if they appeared there.

We pushed on up river against the stream and the tide. As Owus came in sight, group after group of canoes came pouring out from the creeks and sides of the river, the warriors uttering war cries, splashing us in mock threat and throwing clouds of lime. Finally about fifty canoes lined up abreast behind our fleet. It was a stirring and moving experience. The five-hour ride was forgotten as we squelched ashore through the mud on to the prickly vegetation beyond.

At last the sun came out, and so did the cameras. The local women – the older ones looking strangely masculine – were dancing topless on the shore. Several of them had red hair and red skins. Many of the men wore shells through their noses. Outside the long house where we ate our picnic lunch 'Bis' poles had been erected and some very lively dancing was taking place. The performance related to the expected arrival of a wood spirit – which finally materialised wrapped up in grass with a mask. Then two more appeared, one from the river, and another two from the woods, all accompanied by chanting and howling. The interesting Asmat wood carvings relate to local culture. The hornbill and the crocodile feature in many and we acquired a very special one of a dug-out canoe containing the head of a rival chief which would have been an important feature of local history.

When we departed we were given a great send-off, but then the men looked almost sullen. What, we wondered, were they thinking? Were they mystified by this strangely dressed crowd of people who descended on them for two hours, looked at them, photographed them, gave them cigarettes and bought their carvings – then departed? Did they resent us? I do not think so. Envied us, perhaps. Money had not really touched them, but cigarettes *had*, and that is what they wanted above all. Their welcome had seemed genuine even if they had been paid for it. For us it was a brief glimpse of another world.

The lure of Indonesia was the fish life. The Islands were interesting but sometimes intimidating. Once, at Larantuka on Flores, we had stones thrown at us in our trucks and on Banda, while coming down the hill alone through the village, I was threatened by a young man with clenched fists making a cut-throat sign. Children tried to pull our watches off. These were isolated incidents but now there are major political troubles in Indonesia. Some of the worst riots have taken place in Banda.

Banda is one of the 'Spice Islands' and a visit to the nutmeg groves was part of the day's activities. Last time I went there in 1990 a local entrepreneur was planning to market nutmeg jelly to the west in a big way. We tasted it and would certainly recommend it, though I have never seen it outside Indonesia.

New, unvisited islands were always a special delight. Kasini, in the Moluccas, a day by boat from Banda, was such a one. We were not expected but a welcome ceremony was hastily arranged for us after we were given permission to land. The 'street' between the two rows of little grass houses was sand, swept clean, and outside each house were spices drying colourfully in the sun – nutmeg, mace and cloves. Soames Summerhayes, a delightful American girl called Pamela Schilt, and I decided to explore. We followed a path behind the village, up a river bed which became a clear stream among the sago palms, through the tall nutmeg trees with fruit hanging from them and finally to the big forest trees. High up on the steep hill we swung on hanging lianas, pushing each other way out over the forest floor. On the way back we passed coconut palms, rhododendrons, orchids and red flowering forest trees. Fantails, a Sunbird and Imperial Pigeons squawked away in the background above the canopy. Back at the foot of the hill I found Peter, who showed me a kingfisher by a waterfall.

Before setting off for the Trobriand Islands, Solomon Islands, Vanuatu and islands further east, we had a private excursion inland at Port Moresby to the Variarata National Park. Here we saw the Red Bird of Paradise displaying high up above us in the tops of tall trees. It had a striking call and looked spectacular with its red plumes, yellow head and green throat. From an observation point 833ft up we looked out over a small area of primary forest and the bare (burnt-out) hills beyond to Port Moresby itself. As we sat, a large green Bird-wing Butterfly flopped past us.

In 1984 on our fourth visit to Indonesia we boarded the *Lindblad Explorer* in Port Moresby and sailed west to Kota Kinabalu. On the Indonesian islands people were becoming more used to tourists and the children mobbed us, begged for sweets or tried to pull off our watches or gold chains. But in the sea, the reefs were still as rich with coral and fishes. I have a vivid memory of returning on my own to the Zodiac off a reef at Wangi Wangi when I hit a strong surface current going the wrong way. Luckily the edge of the reef was at no more than 12ft down and I was able to pull myself along on the outside edge until I reached the boat, where Valerie was hanging out on a line waiting to pull in any stragglers.

Banda was once more rather intimidating. Someone dropped a stone on Peter's foot and cut it and I acquired an Indonesian boy who held my hand to protect me from rather aggressive locals. But the dive site at the entrance to the harbour was as brilliant as ever and this time I was able to dive as Peter's buddy.

It was on this last cruise in 1984 that we visited the Toraja Province on Sulawesi, travelling by bus from Parepare on the coast. The Captain told us that the rats there were as big as dogs. 'I have seen one like a Pekinese,' he said. Driving inland we stopped to photograph the 'Erotic Mountain', so called because according to legend a couple had committed incest and been turned into a mountain. The cattle were small, pale chestnut or grey in colour, with large eyes and white backsides as though they had sat in whitewash. Higher up, there were a lot of buffalo. Apparently around eighty of these animals are slaughtered for one funeral ceremony. There was a spectacular rocky peak named 'The Ladder to Heaven': because man had sinned it never went any higher. At the village of Sigundu we were welcomed by a local guide and shown round the houses, each of which had a buffalo head on it. A splendid piebald buffalo was paraded through the village for us to see and photograph. Next day we visited other villages, walking everywhere along steep muddy paths. On a high cliff there were square holes for corpses, and rows of skulls. There were also effigies made of wood and clothed, including hats or turbans. The carved figures, made in the likeness of the deceased, were apparently only for upper-class people. Some bones and corpses were in caves. Peter and the ship's biologist disappeared into one cave for so long that I became worried. It was the bats that were interesting Peter.

The houses were all on stilts with U-shaped painted roofs. We went up the ladder into one. It had three rooms: two bedrooms and a central one with a square, built-in fireplace and huge cooking pot. The houses face north, where the ancestors come from, and cooking is done on the east side where life begins. Corpses are put in the central room on the west side until they become too decomposed and then in the 'spare' room on the south side.

In 1985 we were guests with Jacq and Keith Shackleton on board a catamaran-type boat built in Indonesia and sailing from Bali. She was called the *Asmara Lumba Lumba*, which means the 'loving dolphins', and was carrying about thirty passengers. By this time I was a qualified scuba diver, as was Jacq (she had learned to dive in our pool at Slimbridge), and since Peter had had a heart attack and was not allowed to dive, Jacq was now my diving buddy.

Peter and I were honoured with the owner's cabin which had the biggest, bounciest bed I have ever slept in. Unfortunately, it was so well sprung that it acted as a trampoline and the rough weather in the Straits of Lombok finally reduced us to sleeping on the floor, with the huge silk duvet flung over us to keep us warm in the cold air conditioning.

It was on this diving trip that Jacq and I had an interesting night dive together on a wall. The walls are incredibly colourful and spectacular and as we dived in we had the added excitement of seeing Flashlight Fish blinking all round us like fire flies. It was only my second night dive and Jacq's first. We each swam with a small torch and with our little fingers linked. We were especially pleased with ourselves for coming up to the right boat at the end of our forty minutes – there were three boats and not everyone found their own. So, the two grandmothers were on a great high. Later we celebrated in our cabin and Jacq photographed us in our huge, luxurious bed drinking Cointreau.

*   *   *

Our last trip to Indonesia in 1987 took in a lot of places on the way, including Hong Kong, where we had a delightful visit to the Mai Po Marshes, now established as a reserve, with Ken and Sue Searle. Ken Searle's zoo in the Hong Kong Botanical Gardens was excellent and of special appeal to us because of his interest in waterfowl and his contacts with the Wildfowl Trust.

Our ultimate destination was the Rowley Shoals off the west coast of Australia, opposite Broome, where we were joining an expedition in a cata-maran-type boat called the *Kimberley Explorer*, organised by Mike McDowell. This was essentially a fish-watchers' expedition. The islands, which are nothing more than a few sandy shoals surrounded by coral reefs, certainly provided us with all the interest and excitement that we had expected. There were sea snakes with various different patterns, frequent strong currents and a tide rise and fall of 5ft. We had many adventures and saw wonderful fish, including a Leopard Shark. Peter was snorkelling and I was diving, with Mike mostly, and sometimes with other old friends. There were fast drift dives into a lagoon, deep dives, shallow dives and sometimes three in a day. The cruise ended with a really rough sea on the way back to Broome. I was one of the few people not to be seasick although, unusually for me, I had been sick on the way out. Experiencing a rough sea in a three-deck catamaran boat is something out of the ordinary, but then that whole expedition was very much out of the ordinary – a 'one off'.

From Broome we made our way to Darwin, which I still remembered as the hottest place I had ever visited. It had changed a good deal since our visit in 1956. After our rather uncomfortable two weeks on a ship we enjoyed the luxury of dining in our bedroom with sandwiches and champagne and fruit supplied by the Sheraton Hotel. Now we were in the hands of Ian Morris, from the Australian Parks and Wildlife Service. From Darwin we headed east in the wonderful Kakadu National Park, not too far from Humpty Doo where we had been among Magpie Geese in 1956. Kakadu is undoubtedly a dream place for wetland wildlife (the aboriginies from that area talk of 'dream times' so those seem appropriate words). We stayed at the Holiday Village where one day we were delighted to welcome a wild Magpie Goose, which walked in through the open doorway of our bedroom.

The Park has so much to offer. We were taken out in a boat from which I could photograph, we visited the Nourlangie Rock where there were aboriginal paintings, saw thousands of Magpie Geese and had a fascinating flight over the whole area from Jabiru, where there is a small airfield belonging to the nearby uranium mine. Later we flew by helicopter over the Jim Jim falls.

Peter celebrated his seventy-eighth birthday at Kakadu. We had a dinner party with some of the wardens but for some reason we made a mistake about his age. We told them that he was seventy-nine – and went on thinking this until we arrived home in early October.

CHAPTER SIXTEEN

From Canada to Bali

Our next trip, in 1976, was the first of two *Lindblad Explorer* expeditions which started in Prince Rupert on the Canadian coast and ended in Bali. The twelve-hour flight to Vancouver over the Pole was in itself exciting, with splendid views of Greenland's icy mountains. Sailing out of Prince Rupert with Peter's 'library' suitcase missing was rather worrying – though with ten pieces of luggage I suppose it was not surprising that the airline did not lose more. All Peter's reference books for the far north, as well as the fish books were in this rather heavy hat-box type case. Ours was not the only piece missing – there were ten in all. We set off into a rough sea with a strong wind blowing and were in the middle of dinner when we heard a helicopter circling. Dinner was abandoned as we glued our noses to the windows to watch all the missing pieces of luggage being dropped one by one on to the net lying over the tiny swimming pool on the after deck. It was a hazardous manoeuvre but everything landed safely.

That was the year when Dafila was spending six weeks at the research base at Old Chevak to study the breeding behaviour of Tundra Swans. For her PhD she was studying the behaviour of Bewick's Swans, but at the time it was not possible to go to their breeding grounds in the north of Siberia. Tundra Swans are closely related, so they were the next best thing. With the help of Cal Lensink from the Fish and Wildlife Service we arranged to meet up. Nunivak Island was on our ship's itinerary and had a small airstrip, which was our chosen rendezvous.

The south coast of Alaska and offshore islands have spectacular quantities of sea birds and riots of strikingly beautiful wild flowers. We visited Glacier Bay, Dundas Bay, Middleton and many more islands, including the Barren Islands and the wild, rocky Semidi Islands. Each had its own special character; each was a photographer's paradise. There were whales, dolphins, sea-otters and sea lions. There were the frustrations, too, of rainy days and sometimes fog. At Sand Point, where the ship stopped to refuel, Peter and I went walking up a hillside and were delighted to find the *Dryas octopetela* in flower. This was 'our flower', bringing back memories of our time in Lapland in 1950 and our happy expeditions to Iceland in 1951.

The Pribilof Islands were shrouded in fog but the huge rookeries of Fur Seals are the great feature there. They are not nearly as attractive as the Stellers Sea Lions which we had been looking at earlier, but interesting to watch from the observation hide used by the scientists studying them. The males are very aggressive and can be quite dangerous and it is not pleasant seeing them tearing about among the females and newly born pups, often severely injuring, if not killing, the babies while they defend their harem.

Peter and I found the bird cliffs more appealing. From the top of the cliffs we could see Common Murres (guillemots), Thick-billed Murres and Black-legged and Red-legged Kittiwakes nesting. Quite close to us were Parakeet Auklets with their orange beaks, Least Auklets (or 'Choochkies' as the Americans call them) and, strangest of all, the Crested Auklet, with its bright orange wax-like bill with a curled feather hanging over it. The flowers on top of the hill on St Paul were profuse, especially deep purple lupins and yellow arctic poppies with the foggy dew glistening on them. There is still some controlled culling of the Fur Seals and I found that the culling business somehow pervaded the atmosphere.

We arrived at Nunivak Island in a strong wind and rough sea. Our Cruise Director decided to land us on the south side, thereby completely upsetting our rendezvous plans with Dafila since the airstrip and Mekoryuk, the Eskimo village, are on the north side of this fair sized island. Initially we were greeted by Eskimos with guns – they thought we were Russians. On learning that one of the Zodiac drivers was French, the Eskimo turned to him and said, 'Parlez-vous Français?'; they were fishermen from Mekoryuk who came to the south side every summer to fish for salmon and stayed several weeks catching and drying fish for the long winter. They were amazed to see tourists.

It was an extremely tricky, wet landing from our Zodiacs but well worth it. We saw Emperor Geese, Sandhill Cranes, Eider Ducks, Longtails and finally, after a long walk up and over a hill, we had a good view of two Musk Oxen. We had to crawl over the ridge to get to within 100 yards of these charming animals with their white socks under their brown, shaggy coats. There were twenty-four of us, all armed with binoculars, cameras and lenses of varying sizes. Two dozen tourists, some in bright red parkas, crawling in line over the tundra was an amazing sight in itself!

The following day the Captain took the ship in as close as he could to Mekoryuk. The approach to the village was over shallow water and Peter and I were taken on the two-mile ride by Tevita, one of our friendly Tongan Zodiac drivers. A lone elderly Eskimo stood on the beach and we enjoyed his friendly call across the water as we approached: 'The top of the morning to you.' We explained that we were looking for a rather small blonde girl who should have arrived by plane the day before. He took us through the deserted village, consisting of two rows of wooden houses with a narrow board-walk down the middle, to the place where he said we might find Dafila. We walked quite a long way in single file along the boards: the Eskimo, Peter, me, Tevita and a white dog that followed us. We stopped at a house, knocked and called 'Dafila'. No reply. We went in. There were three bedrooms, and the beds had been slept in, but there was no one there. 'There was an aeroplane yesterday,' the Eskimo said. 'She may have gone.' There was one more place to try. We walked back to another hut and banged and banged on the door. At last we heard the pattering of feet and a very sleepy Dafila opened the door. It transpired that she had arrived the day before and met up with three stranded archaeologists who were trying to get to another island. They had been playing bridge until three in the morning.

We took her back to the ship. The plan had been to keep her on board with us and put her ashore at Hooper Bay, only two hours off our route. The Captain was anxious to do it and Dafila had agreed to give a talk to the passengers. But Francisco, who was keen to get up north to the pack ice, had other ideas. He wanted a winter reindeer skin and asked Dafila to take him ashore with a few passengers to show him where to buy the skins. When they returned, the Captain and Francisco decided that they must put Dafila ashore again as there was only some 4ft of water beneath our keel, and we had to move. I went on the long ride back to the shore with her and watched the small, sad figure lug her bags up the path to the little Eskimo village while I returned to our warm ship. The Captain was very apologetic.

Next day we were beset by fog and had a few adventures with bird-watching parties nearly getting lost at sea. Later we reached Little Diomede Island in the Bering Strait, which is only two and a half miles across. There are the two islands, Big and Little Diomede. Big Diomede belongs to Russia, Little Diomede to the United States. Between them lies the International Dateline. We stood on Little Diomede looking at the other island, from today into tomorrow.

The Eskimo settlement on Little Diomede tumbles down a steep hill and we saw it in the not unusual swirling mist. Each house has a stack of walrus-tooth ivory under the floor, although there were said to be restrictions on the number of walrus that could be taken in a year. We saw walruses at sea, but sadly we never had a really good view of them. We ventured up into the pack ice but did not get far. It was very different from any pack ice I had seen before, broken up in weird shapes and sizes, with a lot of brown dirty pieces. There were some birds and three walruses on an ice floe, and the fog cleared briefly for us to see the midnight sun well above the horizon.

Four weeks after leaving Prince Rupert we reached Yokohama. Steaming south through the Japanese smaller islands was full of surprises. Most are volcanic and I achieved the doubtful distinction of being the first woman to climb to the rim of the crater on Tori Jima. This island is the home of the Steller's Albatross but there were none there at that time of the year. Tori Jima had last erupted twenty years earlier and was still spewing out sulphurous fumes. On another inhabited island, Haedijo Jima, we attended a bull-fight in which two bulls fought each other but no harm came to either. We had a lovely day on Chichi Jima, with snorkelling, an excellent local Japanese lunch and the excitement for Peter of finding a new fish book, which he spent the rest of the day reading, and arranging to have one sent to him at home.

We came to Iwo Jima, where the American soldier, Joe Rosenthal, had finally planted the Stars and Strips after five days of fighting. Despite the hill being 546ft above sea level, most of the passengers climbed to the top to see it. I stayed on the beach and photographed the coloured rocks round the fumeroles near the shore. Mud was sprouting two or three feet out of the ground and water running down into a pool below. Further along the beach were sprouts of pebbles coming up below the tide mark.

We loved the Mariana Islands: Mog Mog, Falalop, Map and Yap. The people were delightful and the fish watching was good. The Marianas, with their extensive coral reefs and excellent snorkelling and birds, led us on to Saipan, which was of special interest to our American friends. We were still in the theatre of World War II, with all its gruesome history. The Japanese inhabitants of Saipan, including women and children, all committed suicide either by drowning or by throwing themselves over the cliff rather than surrender to the Americans. This was also where the atom bombs were loaded for the drop on Japan. It was a depressing place. I went snorkelling.

Before arriving in Indonesian territory at Ternate we visited one of the most wonderful coral atolls I have ever seen: Helen's Reef. There was very little land showing as we arrived, just the breakers, a distant very small island with palm trees, two wrecks and a coast guard ship. A tropical rainstorm delayed our departure from the *Explorer* and finally there was just one snorkelling boat with seven of us aboard. We found a beautiful drop-off, lovely coral and hundreds of fishes – including crowds of Pyramid Butterfly Fish *(Hemitaurichthys polylepis)*, a small shark and Manta Rays deep below. A ray swam straight towards me with its mouth open, and an all-black one dived right under me. I recorded fourteen different butterfly fish.

CHAPTER SEVENTEEN

A Volcano and a Festival

In the 1970s we reached a stage when Lars Lindblad allowed us to choose in advance which Explorer cruises we would like to join. His only stipulation was that we must do two back to back. Peter was always popular with the passengers and could contribute so much with his knowledge of coral fishes as well as ornithology. (There were invariably more species underwater than above.) By this time we were accepted by both staff and crew and were invited to parties in the crew's quarters, which we took as a great honour. We enjoyed meeting the multi-national crew below decks; as well as the Swedish officers there were people from England, Spain, France, Finland, Austria, Argentina, Canada, Germany, Portugal and Tonga. It was noisy, cramped and hot down there but every-one was wonderfully relaxed and happy. Socializing in the lounge was often enjoyable too since the passengers had become rather like a club and we knew many of them from previous trips. If we were not too tired after an exhausting day, we loved to dance on the tiny round dance floor in the lounge. A rough sea covered up any foot faults and there were some handy pillars to hang on to when the ship rolled.

On the back of the Indonesian expedition, in 1977 we embarked on a cruise from Port Moresby to Fiji. This was still the era when there were very few small cruise ships. We were to visit the Trobriand Islands, the Solomon Islands and the New Hebrides, now known as Vanuatu. The Melanesian inhabitants of Kiriwina in the Trobriands, dressed in traditional grass skirts, greeted us warmly and provided a splendid meal of yams, sweet potatoes, taro, chicken and pork. The chief's house was elaborately carved and painted. We admired the imaginative carvings and bought some pigs (which figure profusely, in every conceivable posture) as well as crocodiles.

Still in the Trobriands, we visited a little island called Nasikuaba which had a tiny village at the foot of limestone cliffs – with only twenty-eight inhabitants, all the same family. They were shy and mostly sat around looking at us – topless Melanesian girls in grass skirts and men with woven G-strings. They did not mind being photographed and some were weaving lovely pandanus baskets. Two fine dug-out canoes with carved prows were used to take the children to school on a neighbouring island. There were pigs, dogs and chickens, sprouting coconuts hung on bars and the sweet smell of frangipani. The water was crystal clear and the fish watching excellent.

When we climbed up the path over the cliffs to the cultivated area at the top we passed a cave with human bones, and our suspicions of cannibalism were increased; they were further confirmed on our next visit!

We stopped for a day at Guadalcanal and then at the little island of Tevai, where we were treated to an amazing and unusual dance by men wearing long, flowing, grass costumes and coloured masks with a cross over the eye holes. They looked rather like Daleks.

On Tikopia in the Solomon Islands the people were Polynesian – larger, fatter and paler than the Melanesians. Westernisation appeared to be looming here. The men wore tappa cloth shirts and there was a New Zealand Peace Corps schoolmaster. The women, though topless, wore plain-coloured tappa cloth skirts.

After the Solomons we sailed to Vanuatu, where something very special and unusual awaited us on Tanna Island. Our visit had been timed to coincide with the Toka Festival, which only takes place every two years. The moon has to be in the right quarter and various other, unexplained, factors determine the date for this event. Tanna is a large island with an active volcano which was erupting with full force when we arrived.

About fifty of us were prepared to go to the Toka dance arena inland in the forest. We left the ship by Zodiac at midnight. Waiting for us on shore were Land Rovers, a car and a bus. Five of us piled into a Land Rover with a driver called Tom. It was dark, apart from a few stars, and so impossible to see what the island looked like. We drove for about three-quarters of an hour on dirt tracks through the forest, at one point through deep cuttings and then came out onto a flat lava-dust plateau. The cone of the volcano was visible on our left but its distance was incalculable in the dark. Cloud streamed away from it. Every three minutes or so it gave a thunderous roar and showers of fiery rocks could be seen rising high in the air, sometimes to the left, sometimes above the peak. The greater the thunderclap and roar the higher and better the fireworks display. Tom said that some of the rocks were as big as Land Rovers, and we were not allowed to go closer.

The track became narrower and steeper. We met a truck which shattered one of our windows as it scraped past us, but no one was hurt. Finally we stopped in a clearing. We were covered in dust from the volcano, and it started to rain. From there we had to walk single file up a steep path through the trees. At this point some of our party became lost after taking a wrong turning. The rain stopped and after one last very steep, slippery climb up a smooth path we emerged at the top to find sleeping bodies among the trees.

Before us was a huge natural amphitheatre in the forest. We sat down under a coconut palm on the packed lava dust at the top of a high bank overlooking the arena and were told by our guide to stay on the edge of it and not to go down to the centre among the performers. This feast is the occasion for tribes and communities from all over the island to celebrate with mock battles and dances. The activities, we were told, would culminate with the arrival of their spiritual Toka poles and a ritual slaughter of pigs. The arena was lit by a small string of electric lights and a few pressure lamps, so it was fairly dark and at first quite difficult to see what was happening. The whole place was crowded. Groups of girls were dancing in different places. They danced in two lines, stamping their feet and beating straw 'hand bags' full of grass. The effect was like drums. At the end of the dance they would bow and a group of men would go through the crowd to meet them, lead them out a little way, then chase them back. Many of the men had painted faces – red with white or black shading. Each dancing group acquired its own little crowd of spectators around it. The girls were wearing long grass skirts with an upper layer forming a sort of bustle. On their tops they had a piece of cloth and in their hair plaited grass bands threaded with Christmas tinsel which glittered at night but looked strangely out of place later in daylight.

Every now and then a rabble crowd of half-naked men carrying staves charged through between the groups. They came right up to us and threatened us and we wondered what would happen as things livened up. When there seemed to be a lull, four of us went down into the arena. It was fun to see the dancers close to, but rather frightening to be among the crowd. I had no flash with my camera so we had to wait for dawn before I could take photographs. At one point we were caught between a group of dancers and the rabble and were swept in towards the dancers. The men came charging through, stamping and shouting 'Wa – Wa – Wa'. One of my group took a flash photograph and the leader of the rabble flashed his torch on him. They turned and charged us, sending us scrambling up the slope. Accompanying the singing and drumming of the dancing women was the thunderous roar of Yasur as it erupted from time to time. The whole scene and atmosphere were strange and theatrical. I was reminded of crowd scenes in a Shakespeare play.

At the first signs of dawn there came a sudden hush, an air of great anticipation and excitement. In a breathtaking moment someone said, 'The Toka poles are coming – they come from the west.' And behind us we saw tall, feathered poles borne up with masses of sticks, with crooks on the end. Carried by half-naked warriors, they looked rather like primitive maypoles. Some of the men had grass skirts and they all wore head bands with long chicken tail feathers in them. There was a great surge from the crowd in the arena to greet them – and a great bang from Yasur. Down they came, two poles borne by perhaps eighty men. On the west side of the arena they stopped, the hooked staves were lowered and the tall poles planted in the ground. It was too dark and the crowds were too dense to see exactly what was going on. When the crowd moved back, six chiefs stood waiting. The warriors formed into lines and were inspected by runners. Then the mass dancing and singing began, with more rhythmic stamping and chanting; the stamping was so great that the ground shook under us and they made holes beneath their feet.

At this stage small boys appeared and danced at the rear, and the wives and children of the chiefs jumped with two feet together behind the warriors. There was then more formal dancing with women and warriors. Forays were made from time to time with bows and arrows or spears and cutlass-type weapons. Clown-like characters also appeared, teasing the warriors, to the amusement of the crowd. As the sun rose opposite us the dancers could be seen through a haze of lava-dust. All the time Yasur thundered behind us.

After about an hour the warriors retreated and the Toka poles were removed. But then came another group and the performance was repeated. By now it was light and we were getting hot and thirsty. The ship's staff had managed to carry up supplies of sandwiches, beer, Coke, tea and coffee. There was Val Taylor offering us tea with lemon and sugar: it was an amazing feat on the part of the staff.

Now that we were able to move about I tried to photograph some handsome warriors with painted faces. We became entangled with the third delegation of Toka poles, and I had just started to photograph when suddenly they were all pushing gently past us until we were swept towards the arena where they met head on with the warriors from the previous dance in a great mock battle. Two Toka poles were raised right beside us and we quickly took shelter behind a small balustrade at the edge of the clearing, watched by a group of children high up above our heads in a Banyan tree. Dotted among the trees were a few little thatched platforms where the women and children had sheltered overnight. We estimated that there must have been about 2000 people there. Down a path we found the pigs in a kraal, some still tied up on the sticks on which they had been carried.

It was hard to tear ourselves away, but after some indecision Peter and I decided to start back; I did not want to watch the pigs being slaughtered. It was fascinating to see by daylight the route by which we had come in the pitch dark. We found Tom and the Land Rover with the broken window and set off on the bumpy ride back. We passed a truck which had gone over the edge – luckily it was not one of ours – and stopped to look once more at Yasur. After each thunderous rumble, mushroom-shaped clouds of smoke rose up into the sky.

CHAPTER EIGHTEEN

Russia, China and Mongolia

By 1978 we had recorded 3790 individual Bewick's Swans at Slimbridge and we longed to know more about their breeding grounds in the north of Russia. The Cold War was still on and it was not easy to visit the USSR but luckily we had the advantage of Peter's connections with Russian scientists through the IUCN and WWF. At last, in the summer of 1978, it was arranged for the Scott family to be taken to the Jamal Peninsula in northern Siberia. Dafila, who was up at Cambridge finishing her thesis on Bewick's Swans, was to come with us. Unfortunately, a few days before our departure for Moscow she became ill with serious bronchitis and was not able to travel. It was a terrible blow. Telephones hummed (with difficulty) to Moscow and I decided to stay with her in the hope that she would be well enough to go a few days later, if the expedition could be postponed that long.

Peter left by air, as arranged, and Dafila and I followed a week later. There was a terrible moment at Moscow airport when Russian immigration found something wrong with our papers, but we were rescued by a kind person from the British Embassy – and Peter waiting for us with a big happy smile.

Two days later we were off by Aeroflot from Bikoro (the national airport) to Salekhard at the mouth of the river Ob. Our party consisted of the three Scotts, Vladimir Flint and our interpreter, Lena. On arrival at Salekhard we were given a splendid reception by the Lady Mayor, the party chairman and our fellow scientists, Sacha Soroikin, Valery Orlor and Edouard Nazarov. The reception included a breakfast party at which vodka flowed and the food was more like that of a Russian evening meal.

It was at Salekhard that we acquired an extra member of the expedition. The Mayor decided that we needed someone who could catch fish for us and who would stay at camp while we were all out. So we acquired Vladimir II, who spoke no English. In fact, he spoke very little at all. Secretly we thought he was KGB sent to spy on us – and indeed one day in camp as we sat round the packing cases eating our evening meal, Peter started drawing a map of the area in his note book. Vladimir I called him outside the tent and asked him not to draw maps because Vladimir II might tell the Mayor and the party chairman – that, he warned, would be bad news.

The helicopter flight north up the Jamal Peninsula was interesting, if uncomfortable. Peter recorded the swans' nests as we flew and we finally selected a camp site near the Yuribei River where we set the tents just a few yards from the edge of what may have been a tributary. We all had hats with nets because on still days the mosquitoes were terrible. Vladimir called them his 'little friends' and said they did not bite him because he drank so much vodka. We had taken some bottles of vodka, purchased in the hotel tourist shop in Moscow, but Vladimir had a whole jerry-can of a home-made brew. Vodka certainly flowed freely every night as we sat round the packing cases eating dinner. Our main food consisted of reindeer, from Salekhard, and fish caught locally by Vladimir II.

For each of eight days we walked out across the tundra looking for Bewick's swans. Sometimes we took the little rubber boat in order to cross one of the innumerable waterways. The Arctic birds were a delight and on the whole the weather was kind. We all became very fit, including Peter, who was sixty-nine at that time. All that was missing were the breeding Bewick's Swans. We did find one old used nest and we did see a number of swans in flight but it was evident that we were too late in the season and also that this was not the main breeding area. But it was a very happy expedition and we had sown fertile seeds of co-operation with our Russian scientific friends.

Our departure from the camp site was not without drama. We did not have radio communication but the helicopter pilot knew where he had dropped us, and the departure date and time had been fixed in advance.

By noon all was packed up and ready. We had been sitting on the river bank waiting for hours when at last we heard the distant hum of the chopper. Dark clouds were looming and rain threatened. It was warm and the mosquitoes were ferocious. The sound came, but nothing was in sight, and finally the noise faded away. We heard it once more, further west, quartering the river, but again the helicopter failed to arrive. The vodka was finished and most of the food had gone. Supper time arrived, we emptied the contents of some remaining cans into a frying pan, heated it up and ate from it with spoons in Vladimir's little tent. It began to rain. Not long afterwards we heard the sound of the helicopter again. We lit a flare but once more it went off to the west. It took two more flares before it finally spotted us and zoomed in to land. Peter and I never went back to the Russian Arctic, but Dafila did reach the breeding site of the Bewick's, further west, with our Russian research friends. The Wildfowl and Wetlands Trust have supported an expedition to the Nenetski National Nature Reserve, near the mouth of the Pechora River, ever since.

In 1978 Lars Lindblad invited us to join one of his first tours to China and Outer Mongolia. No obligations, no lectures – we were just numbers, the last two of a group of twenty-four people, including two old friends from the *Lindblad Explorer*. We joined the party at Hong Kong and went on to Kwangchow and Peking by rail and air. We had a delightful American courier, Edie Macausland, and an old friend, Dick Brush, who insisted on finding a public swimming pool in Peking as he needed exercise. He took a taxi there only to find that he needed a medical certificate. Undaunted, he went to a hospital, insisted he was an emergency, obtained a temporary certificate and enjoyed a swim before we all went to the theatre. He received full marks for enterprise.

Being a tourist at a time when they were rare in China meant that we drew crowds and were stared at in public places. But everywhere we went we were made to feel welcome and, memorably, the people smiled. Peter and I very much enjoyed the sightseeing: the Forbidden City, the Ming Tombs and the Great Wall.

After five days in China we went to Outer Mongolia by train. Even fewer westerners had been there and the journey itself was quite an adventure. At the border it was fascinating watching the bogeys on the carriages being changed from the narrow-gauge Chinese railway to the wider-gauge

Mongolian. It took two hours, during which some of our party were taken to see a propaganda film in the station. Once we had crossed the border into Mongolia the food and service were immediately less good. But from the train we were able to do some bird watching, and particularly enjoyed the little flocks of Demoiselle Cranes. In China we had hardly seen any birds.

Hua Hua, our guide in Ulan Bator, wore national costume and marshalled us around like a drum majorette. There were Russian soldiers in evidence, said to be defending the Mongolians from the Chinese. On Sunday Hua Hua took us to the Lamasery (seminary) on the hill, where we saw monks being called to prayer in the temples. We were allowed inside and found the service immensely impressive. Hua Hua did not come in. She made it very plain that she considered religion to be a thing of the past and did not subscribe to it. Not since my time in Belgrade had I felt the influence of Communism hovering all around. The British Chargé d'Affaires invited us for a picnic lunch out in the country but we needed a permit and it was refused. As we had, in fact, already visited that part of the country with our group and had marvelled at the gorgeous wild flowers, it all seemed very petty.

We particularly enjoyed seeing so much of the country on what was for us just holiday – even if it was somewhat marshalled. We stayed in a *Ger* in the Gobi Desert and visited the spectacular Flaming Red Cliffs, where Roy Chapman-Andrews had found eight different prehistoric animals while excavating in 1924. The *Gers* (plural = *Gerud*) are made of trellis covered in felt and white cloth tied down with rope and are much decorated inside. The locals have herds of sheep and horses and move their *Gerud* on average about once a month. We stayed in another camp on the edge of the Altai Mountains, rode camels and saw a number of birds, including the brilliant Rock Creeper, three kinds of wagtail, Lammergeier and Golden Eagle.

The food in China had been extremely good even for tourists but things were different in Mongolia. We tried fermented camel's and mare's milk and several other local delicacies but I noted in my diary that I was actually living on brown bread. Most of our days in Mongolia were spent getting up very early for a flight or a bus departure. It was a highly pressurised tour but the country was wonderful, as were the birds, the flowers and the country people we met.

Considering that history is not my subject it was surprising that the place which made the most impression on me was Karakorum in the north. It was the original capital of Mongolia, built by Ghengis Khan in the 13th century but burnt down a century later by the Chinese. A large and splendid stone turtle had been unearthed during excavations but apart from some pillars nothing much else had been dug up. Unfortunately, Hua Hua was in a bad mood that day and read rather badly from a guide book. But the whole place had a wonderful atmosphere, as though it was guarding amazing secrets of Ghengis Khan's era. Not far from the turtle was a huge, square, walled-in lamasery with white walls and little turrets. It was built in the 16th century for the first Lama of Mongolia. At one time there had been sixty temples but these were sacked by the Manchurians in the 18th century. Only five temples remain.

We spent one more cold night in a Ger at the horse people's camp. Peter rose at 6.30 to light the fire and we made coffee, presented by a fellow traveller, before setting off for the return flight from Khujert to Ulan Bator. Our departure from Ulan Bator the following day was not without incident. The bus which was supposed to take us and our luggage to the station by 8.30 was late. When we eventually arrived we learnt that the train was not due until 11am so the bus took us back to the hotel via the main square, where a military parade was taking place. Rows of soldiers stood before the mausoleum of Sukhe Bator, where a general was seated at a table with a red flag flying. We stopped the bus to watch while the general made a speech and the soldiers dutifully applauded. I took some photographs including one of Sukhe Bator on his horse, with Russian soldiers at his feet. Although I was being very cautious, a man in uniform emerged from the ranks and spoke to our friend Dick Brush, who was also using his camera. He was told that photographs were forbidden. I managed to melt away.

Returning to the station we found all our suitcases piled on the platform (we had our hand baggage with us). When the train arrived we were told to remain with the luggage while Edie and Hua Hua found our reserved berths. After a while they called for six people to go aboard and we all knew that 'Mr and Mrs Pushy' would be first. It then transpired that there were no more berths. Hua Hua told us to get onto the train anyway, but we were prevented by the compartment guards. Then the carriage door was locked. By this time our baggage had been loaded onto car number six and I was determined to board the train so I more or less forced my way on, followed by Peter. Immediately the guard put his arm across the door and pulled up the steps. Down on the platform Edie and the couple who shared our sleeping compartment were looking desperate. I was not sure how we would fare without Edie to look after us, so I seized her bags from her hand and addressing the guard as 'Friend and Comrade' I implored him for help. Finally we did somehow get them aboard but there were only three four-berth compartments available for twenty-four of us. Our baggage was strewn along the corridor. Edie and Peter went in search of further accommodation. Meanwhile the first six people aboard had spread them-selves and their luggage all over the only available seats and would not move for anyone else to sit down. Then Edie and Peter returned, having found berths further along the train. It was at this point that 'Mrs Pushy' exploded; she was fed up with being bossed around – this was *her* compartment. We were all embarrassed but Edie kept her cool and eventu-ally everything was sorted out. We were scattered all over the train but at least we all had somewhere to sleep.

Just after midnight we arrived at the Mongolian border where a huge customs officer took away our passports, demanded to see our cameras and insisted that we give him our film. Earlier a Chinese girl had begged us to take her hold-all into our compartment but we had refused. Now we watched as the customs officers searched the train, including the central heating units in the corridor. Our official searched everything in Peter's briefcase: his bird books, diary, gliding magazines, WWT literature and every single one of his forty-odd photographs of the Wildfowl Trust. We lay there silently, watching; but nothing else was taken away. Our passports were eventually returned, but not our film. Peter went to see how the other members of our party had fared and learned that Bob and I were the only ones not to be given our film back. I lost only the ten exposures I had taken that morning, but poor Bob lost everything he had taken at Karakorum.

Back in Peking there was one more sightseeing event. We were taken to see one of the city air-raid shelters, which was like a scene from a movie. We went into a clothing store where, at the touch of a button, an area of stone floor behind the counter slid open to reveal stairs. At a depth of about fif-teen metres was a damp tunnel with patterned plaster walls and ceiling. We passed a kitchen, dining-room, hospital and decontamination area and, after a long walk, arrived in a large chamber where we were served tea. The shelter was said to accommodate 10,000 people; there were others in the city, built with volunteer labour and in all providing accommodation for four million people.

Not content with three weeks in China and Outer Mongolia we went on to spend five hectic days in Tokyo. This was what I considered a 'business trip', with a one-day bird symposium and a lot of formal and social meetings and meals. There was also some camera shopping and then a delightful audience for both of us with Crown Prince Hitachi and the Crown Princess.

We were heading for another *Lindblad Explorer* trip. This time we joined the ship at Hong Kong and headed south. Peter suffered a setback on our first day at sea when he broke a front tooth – upsetting enough at the best of times but even more devastating when you have to lecture. Amazingly, he managed to make an appointment with a dentist on our arrival at Manila the next day – a Saturday. Even more amazing, the dentist had made a new tooth and a plate by six o'clock that same day. Peter did not seem very happy about it but I assured him that it looked infinitely better than the gap.

Apart from dentistry, Manila did not have much to offer us. There was a shopping excursion and a guided tour of the Fortress and a cemetery – Peter and I could never understand why cemeteries feature so often on coach excursions the world over. The island of Corregidor, not far from Manila, which is maintained as a Second World War Park or monument, turned out to be unlucky for me. I was not feeling well that day so instead of going ashore for a bus tour I went for a short walk with some of the crew. I saw a few birds, including the spectacular Golden Oriole, but was ready to go back in the first Zodiac. That year we had larger Zodiacs, with hard decking. There was a big swell, the beach was sloping, and the Filipino driver, Nevis, had difficulty holding the boat. The four of us managed to get in but before Nevis could start the engine a big wave caught us on the beam, flipping us all in the air and landing us down on the deck. The first engineer, who was a large man, landed heavily on top of me. My arm went numb all the way up and my shoulders and neck were painful.

The boat was half full of water but we got safely back to the ship. Peter was still out with passengers and there were very few people on board. The ship had no X-ray facilities so there was no way of discovering whether I had broken any bones. My back and neck remained painful but I was able to do some snorkelling. The coral and fish life round those Philippine islands were very good at that time.

A few days later we arrived at Sandakan on the coast of Sabah, in the East Malaysian part of Borneo. This was my chance to have an X-ray. After a morning visit to the Orang sanctuary at Sepilok, Peter and I and the ship's doctor, Ralph Wilson, were taken to a surgery in town. Without Ralph's guidance I might not have had the correct X-rays taken – it was the third oblique one which revealed a cracked rib near my spine. Some of my fingers were still numb or tingling because of a pinched nerve but there was nothing to be done except wait for it to wear off.

As I settled my bill, Peter – who had been waiting downstairs in the very hot, crowded waiting-room – said he felt ill. He looked terrible. Ralph took his pulse, turned to me and said, 'This is pretty bad.' He cleared the bench of people so that Peter could lie down. While the secretary went to fetch Dr Chu the other patients stood around gawping. But just as Dr Chu was coming downstairs the Jeep arrived to take us back to the ship and we managed to get Peter on his feet and out of the door. Back on board his pulse returned to normal, Ralph gave him some pills for his stomach cramps and after a good sleep he was fit again. Afterwards we wondered what the other patients thought of someone being taken ill in the waiting-room and being whisked away from the ministrations of Dr Chu. We hoped it would not affect his custom.

The following day we left the ship and spent five days being looked after by our Malaysian friend Mr da Silva, in Sandakan. Some of this time was spent on a tiny island called Little Bakkungaan which is part of the National Park and where Green Turtles breed. We saw them laying their eggs at night and being tagged. And we watched the eggs hatching in the wire cages from which the turtles were then collected and taken to the sea. Seeing them hatch was amazing. One emerged from the sand and then they came out so quickly that in less than a minute it was like watching water boiling in the little cage.

We were on our way to Ashkabad in Turkmenia for a Species Survival Committee meeting. Our round trip to Ashkabad was fraught with problems involving wrongly dated visas and delayed, uncomfortable Aeroflot aeroplanes. However, for me there was one special delight: the opportunity to meet Fitzroy McLean at dinner with Moscow Embassy staff.

Fitzroy's exploits in Yugoslavia are legendary and it was wonderful to talk about his time and my time there in 1946.

The Ashkabad conference had something to offer in the way of excursions, as well as plenty of vodka and caviar. I particularly liked the Bakharden cave where we went down concrete steps to find a large underground lake, and several of us swam in the 84° F sulphurous water thirty metres under the desert. There were bats flying around and I hoped I was not swallowing too many droppings. Another excursion took us further afield to the Badkhiz Reserve by plane and helicopter. There was plenty of wildlife around the oasis and we enjoyed seeing the wild donkeys (Kulan). As President of the SSC, Peter always received VIP treatment and our hosts for the conference laid on excellent meals, though at rather strange times and in strange places. On this excursion in the desert the meal was lavish, with wine, vodka, brandy, soup, rice pilau, shish kebabs, salad and bowls of huge pomegranates, all laid on a long table under some pistachio bushes.

The best part of our return journey to London via Moscow was buying ice creams in the big Gum Store – for which we had to queue.

CHAPTER NINETEEN

Taking the Plunge

Peter had learned to scuba dive during one of our visits to the Bahamas, at a time when certificates were not required. I had felt too nervous and was sure it was too claustrophobic for me. So for many years I had snorkelled while Peter dived. I know that he was disappointed that I could not join him underwater.

It was not until 1979, when we were staying on an island called Pulau Redang off the coast of Malaysia, that I made the big break-through. Peter had been on a hectic two-week lecture tour in Australia for WWF. I had not been able to accompany him and as he was in his seventieth year I was worried about him because of the pace of the tour. I was, however, to meet up with him in Kuala Lumpur and then go on to join a production company making an underwater film about the marvels of the reefs in Malaysia, with Peter in the cast.

The accommodation on Pulau Redang consisted of a disused wooden clove warehouse next to the shore. There were two small bedrooms, one for our friends Ron and Valerie Taylor, the Australian film makers, and one for us. The rest of the film crew, which amounted to about twenty people, slept in one big room or on the long verandah. Behind the big shed there was a little stream with pools in the forest so Valerie and I could escape and bathe in fresh water when we felt disposed. During the day I snorkelled, watched the filming and wandered about. One evening, after filming had finished, Valerie summoned me and George, the twelve-year-old son of the director, and announced that she had two tanks set up on the shore all ready for a diving lesson. There was no getting out of it, and of course I could not be beaten by young George. That was how I eventually overcame my inhibitions.

The opportunity to continue my dive lessons came when Valerie invited Peter and me to stay with them on Heron Island later that year. Peter was due to attend a conference in San Diego in the November so we decided to go on from there. The whole island is a nature reserve. It has one hotel and a research station, neither of them visible until you come in to land. It is covered in trees and there are birds everywhere: waders, gulls, herons, terns, rails, shearwaters and doves. Most numerous were the Noddy Terns, which breed in the trees.

We were there at the time when the flowers of the local pisonia trees were dead and sticky. The poor birds get their feathers so stuck up with these brown burr-like pieces that they cannot fly and can be found on the beach and on the paths through the trees, pathetically trying to preen. Perhaps it works as a form of population control. I am not sure, but it is very distressing to see them so helpless. Visitors to the hotel are asked not to try and clean them up but that first time we did clean and liberate a few.

The Taylors' 'research house' consisted of two bedrooms separated by a kitchen, all with big louvre windows at the back and large doors on the front opening onto a verandah where we ate our meals. Noddies were nesting all round us. There were rails on the doorstep, white egrets in the tree opposite, shearwaters nesting beneath the building and a very strong smell of Noddy guano. There had been a drought, and the research station did not have access to the hotel's desalinated water supply. The water in our taps came out dark grey and smelling strongly of guano. But staying there was bliss. We went out in Ron's boat when it was convenient to them, and if they were busy with the IMAX team which was involved in underwater photography, we went snorkelling on our own.

My diving lessons continued, not always smoothly but ultimately successfully enough for me to continue and to enjoy going down with Peter. One of my earliest dives involved going in over sand by the harbour. There were not many boats in those days and we set off down the channel towards the reef. Suddenly Valerie, just ahead of me, signalled for me to stop and pointed to some Shovel-nosed Sharks on the sand just ahead. Wearing borrowed gear, with my mask leaking and my limbs rather uncontrollable, I panicked. There were boats overhead so I threshed around, disturbing the friendly sharks, and surfaced quickly by the jetty. Valerie had apparently been signalling me to wait so that Peter, just behind us, could see the sharks. I got a stern rebuke and the lesson of the day was, 'Keep breathing'.

If you stay on Heron Island you have to get used to the noise at night. The shearwaters, or Mutton Birds as the locals call them, make the weirdest sounds. To begin with it sounds like baying hounds, then all manner of strange noises follow.

Had it not been for that blissful week I might never have finished learning to dive. Encouraged by Peter I was able later, as a member of staff on the *Lindblad Explorer*, to put in a few more shallow dives with him. But it became obvious that I should do a proper course and get my certificate. This I was able to do at home in our pool. The local Fire Brigade Inspector, who was Secretary of the Cotswold BSAC Club, kindly agreed to teach me in August 1983. Every Friday evening for six weeks we had an hour of theory and an hour in the pool followed by a couple of gins for him (I was high just on bottled air!). After a terrible dive at Stoney Cove and an interesting navigation test in one of the Cotswold Water Park lakes, I finally made the grade and gained my BSAC Certificate.

We visited Heron Island again in October 1981 in the middle of an amazing three weeks during which we spent some time in Hong Kong, Sydney and further north, and visited Christchurch, New Zealand, where Peter was honoured with the John C. Phillips medal, IUCN's highest award. The week on Heron Island was an oasis of relaxation among a schedule of VIP dinners and hectic travel. It would not be my last visit, for Penny Skelton and I spent Christmas 1996 in the hotel there.

CHAPTER TWENTY

Here and There

In 1974, when Peter was a director of the TV wildlife film company Survival, Aubrey Buxton invited us to go on a two-week 'mystery tour' to Zambia to explore the possibilities for his daughter Cindy to do some filming there. Cindy, who had a pilot's licence, met us off our flight from London to Nairobi. After half an hour in the transit lounge we found ourselves heading for Lusaka in a Cessna 310 with Cindy and a friend who was flying the aircraft. With no pressurisation and no food it was a decidedly headachy experience. Because of the headwind and the fact that we got a little lost on the way, it took six hours.

There was a great deal of VIP treatment wherever we went but always some bird watching thrown in. A helicopter flight took us to Lochinvar, where we had been with the children in 1969, and then on, flown by the famous Jack Uys, to Blue Lagoon. Here we were once again given a warm welcome by the Critchleys. The next day we were off again in the chopper to Lusaka for an onward flight to Luangwa. Staying with Norman Carr on the banks of the Luangwa river for two days was a highlight. The Carmine Bee-eater colony in the river bank was spectacular though not easy to photograph with so much movement. A chameleon sat in a tree over our dining-table outside and tree frogs joined us on the table. Norman took us on a wonderful Jeep drive during which we saw many animals: Kudu, Buffalo, Puku, Hippos, Crocodile, Monitor Lizards and of course Elephants. We came on a group of five, including a smallish baby, all bunched round a large dead female. Every now and then the baby elephant would lay its trunk over her and the others too touched her from time to time. By dusk they had left her and Norman reckoned the female had died of old age.

From Luangwa we flew in two separate aircraft to Bangweulu where we stayed as guests of the warden, Ian Manning. Bangweulu is a vast shallow water swamp covered in tall reeds. The object of our visit was to see Shoebills and discover if it would be possible for Cindy to make a film of them. They are extremely shy and not easy to approach. When we did finally find one, it was certainly impressive. It is an Alice-in-Wonderland type of bird with its huge improbable bill and large eyes. Cindy's film on Shoebills was, I think, the first to be made of this splendid animal.

We were to visit the President, Kenneth Kaunda, and when the great day came Peter, Aubrey, Cindy and I arrived at State House and were taken to the reception area overlooking the vast garden with its strutting peacocks. Sadly, the Minister said he had only announced two visitors, so Peter and Aubrey had twenty minutes with KK while Cindy and I were left gazing at a leopardskin on the floor with a silver plaque on its head. However, the visit to the President was a success: Cindy was assured of the necessary co-operation when she came back to film.

Having flown back to Nairobi we set off again on safari. We paid another visit to Lake Nakuru, staying with friends John and Sandy Hopcraft, before flying off in a Cessna 310 to stay with Richard Leakey at Koobifora on Lake Rudolf (now Lake Turkana). This was new territory to us and very exciting. Richard flew us in an even smaller plane – with Cindy and I sitting on the floor at the back – to his camp on a point of the lake. We saw a number of birds: Egyptian Geese, Wood Ibis, Pelicans, Glossy Ibis, Garganey and Shoveler, as well as many crocodiles. There were zebra, Topi, Grants Gazelles and an oryx. We were shown the area where human fossils were being discovered which, Richard said, were two million years old. There was no dig, they just quarter an area of about 600 square miles every year. It is a sort of moonscape, and one can imagine how easy it would be to become lost. Recently someone went missing for five days. They were eventually found but died in hospital.

We stayed in Richard's reed-thatched guest house with its low walls of local rock – four million years old and made up of fossilized snail shells. It was pleasantly cool inside. We were warned not to leave things lying around because of thieving crows.

*   *   *

In 1981 there was a mystery tour of a different kind, when we were invited to visit Zimbabwe on a promotional tour for Sun Hotels. There were of course obligations for Peter, in the form of speeches, dinners and lectures, but as far as he was concerned it was all useful promotion for WWF and conservation in general. We especially enjoyed staying in the Bumi Hills. From our room at the lodge 350ft up on the escarpment we looked out over the bush to Lake Kariba. One night Hercule, a very large wild elephant, walked so close beneath our balcony that I was able to spit on his back. On another night we feasted in a tree-house over the water and stopped in our boat to look at the buds of the water lily which only flowers at night. The water birds and wildlife generally were superb.

The Victoria Falls were no less impressive from the Zimbabwe side than from Zambia. The river was very full that year and I found it as breath-takingly beautiful as ever. Also memorable in a different way were the Zimbabwe Ruins, way out in the bush, with their 20ft-thick walls and narrow steps. Little archaeology has been done there so their history remains a mystery. They have a curiously eerie atmosphere. A week before we arrived a witch had been arrested there.

On our return to Harare (then known as Salisbury) we had an unex-pected meeting with Romolo Fiorini, the son of the Italian who used to cast the sculpture of Kathleen Scott, Peter's mother. As a boy he had posed for her (Peter had always insisted that he, Peter, was *not* the model for all Kathleen's little-boy statues). It was rather difficult to relate this tall, craggy looking man with the statue of the small boy standing on the wall at home or the statue at Oundle.

During the late 1970s and through the 1980s we did the most incredible amount of travelling, much of it inspired by Peter's growing obsession with coral fishes. He ended by knowing, or being able to identify and name, as many, if not more, fishes globally than birds. One of our *Explorer* trips, in 1982, started off very much as a bird expedition but ended with the fishes. The Antipodes are not normally on the tourist route and the rough seas and the difficult landings we experienced explain why. There were Erect-crested Penguins, Sooty Albatrosses, pippets and even some parakeets, all seen from a wobbly Zodiac in a big swell off the 1800ft cliffs of the first islands. The Bounty Islands, a series of very barren rocky islands, were literally covered in birds. We estimated that there were some

200,000 Erect-crested Penguins. Looking at Tunnel Island from the top deck of the ship I had never seen so many birds in one place. The noise and the smell of guano were tremendous.

There were wonderful sea birds to be seen all the way through the Chatham Islands and the Kermadecs as far as Tonga. On Tongatapu we had an audience arranged with the King but the wind got up and the ship's Captain had to move away from the dock just at the critical time. Peter had wanted to talk to the King about whaling, though the ADC had reassured us earlier in the day that Tonga was not whaling.

Fiji, where we were able to go snorkelling, was much more rewarding than Tonga, especially Dravuni Island, where we were the first-ever tourists. The Kava ceremony when we arrived was suitably solemn. The sand-oven cooked meal, with fish and taro, was delicious and the dancing delightfully spontaneous. With a little persuasion the band played, especially for Peter and me, the farewell song *Isa Lei* which Peter and I had found so moving on the big island of Korolevu so many years before.

Our first port of call after Fiji was the island of Tanna, where we had previously attended the all-night feast. This time we went ashore in daylight. After driving as far as we could up the hill, we walked to the rim of the crater which was about a mile and a half long by a mile wide. There were three fumeroles in the bottom, two of which were active, making bangs and throwing rocks in the air. Sometimes they emitted noises like waves breaking on the shore – shu-shu-shu – then came a great woomph. One of them produced clouds of white smoke followed by a little round black cauliflower 300 ft high. The smell of sulphur was quite strong on the wind.

There was one marvellous Pacific island after another as we sailed through the Solomon's, the Calvados, the Deboynes, the Trobriands, the Siassis and back to Madang on Papua New Guinea. The coral reefs and fishes were superb. The trip also included an excursion up the Sepik River from Wewak. We flew to Angoram and were taken from there in a flat-bottomed boat up river. It was extremely humid and hot but we enjoyed seeing a village on stilts where there were pigs in the water and tiny children paddling canoes with amazing dexterity. In another village on the bank of the river we came upon a sago-pulping operation All this took place on a platform in the river, starting with the trunk of the sago palm and ending up with a thin grey paste.

We checked in to Indonesia at Jayapura with some difficulty. In the absence of our Indonesian agent, who was supposed to join us there, we sailed north for Ternate not knowing whether we had clearance to land anywhere. But the Mapia group of islands provided us with wonderful reefs and fishes and we were able to provide medical help to the small community on a small island. One evening our Swedish doctor went ashore and lanced an ulcer full of pus on the breast of the mother of a small boy.

Without clearance we did not dare to land the next day but we were rewarded with the most wonderful sighting of Fin Whales. A whale-catcher boat of unidentified nationality moved off when it saw us. The sea was boiling with Tuna fish, whales were porpoising all round us and there was a pod of Spinner Dolphins.

Two days after leaving Indonesia we checked into the Philippines at Surigao. From then on we were in the hands of the Philippine Tourist Agency, who were theoretically protecting us from pirates. We did not see any, but the army, with guns, was in evidence at every port where we stopped.

One of the highlights of the Philippines was going into a subterranean river on the island of Palawan, which lies in a national park. Local dug-out canoes took three or four people in at a time; one, carrying three eighty-year-old passengers, turned over while in the cave. The cave walls were weird shapes, with huge stalactites and pillars of stalagmites like organ pipes. Some resembled draperies, some statues, others above our heads were like great chandeliers. Some were almost white, some brown. The river turned and wove through the caverns. The water was warm and clear and seldom more than three to six feet deep. In one place there were three kinds of bats and, very far in, the edible birds-nest-soup Swiftlet in fair quantities. It was a most unusual experience.

We saw bee-eaters and Brahaminy Kites on Bohal Island, with its unusual Chocolate Hills, a large number of plum-pudding shaped grassy hills with flat pasture land between. It is the number of hills and their evenness and similarity which makes them so extraordinary. They are said to have been caused by volcanic action under the sea millions of years ago.

One other notable event occurred before we left the Philippines. Peter managed, with some difficulty, to speak to the famous Mrs Marcos (whom he met in a hotel) about WWF and conservation – and then left his precious diary behind. There were some anxious moments while contact was made with the hotel manager, who sent a driver to the airport with the priceless book.

In 1974 and 1975 we revisited the Galapagos Islands, every naturalist's paradise. Much had changed but not, most importantly, the animals. If anything they had become more tame and, in some cases, had increased. These were *Lindblad Explorer* trips, two back to back each time. On the first one in 1974 our biggest discovery was while snorkelling in the Devil's Crown near Floreana. We were in current in deep water just outside the pinnacled crater when we found ourselves in the company of a shoal of Hammerhead Sharks. Two came quite close to us but the main group of about thirty-five were all swimming in one direction over the sand in about 40ft of water. They took no notice of us and it was fascinating to watch them.

When we returned in 1976 we anchored the Zodiac inside the crater in about 5ft of water, and because our fellow snorkellers were nervous, Peter and I got in. Almost immediately we saw a shark. I had my Nikonos camera with me and took a photograph. When I had it processed later I found to my surprise that there were three sharks in the picture. Outside the crater we found our friends doing the same thing and the passengers all enjoyed seeing the Hammerheads.

We called on the famous Mrs Wittmer, who was a suspect in the case of missing characters on Floreana in the early days. She was in fact a cosy-looking German Hausfrau who did teas for tourists but when we were in the islands in 1956 the story of possible murders and strange goings-on was very fresh in the minds of the people we met on Santa Cruz. It seemed quite odd to be having tea in Mrs Wittmer's house. I found I could not get out of the place quickly enough and, unusually for me, felt quite sick.

From Santa Cruz we went by minibus to a village up the hill called Santa Rosa to look for tortoises. We walked through semi-cultivated fields and on through long grass into the rain forest which is part of the tortoise reserve. By this time it had started to rain and it was cold. Eric Shipton, the mountaineer, bribed me with sugar to keep me going. He and his delightful partner, Phyllis Wint, were splendid people to be with on any trip. We did eventually see seven, not very large, tortoises. On the big island of Isabella I did the five-hour climb to the top of the volcanic crater of Alcedo and saw some really huge tortoises.

Among the breathtakingly beautiful places in the Galapagos Islands are

Punta Espinosa, on Fernandina, Tower Island and some of the places on Santiago Island, where the Fur Seals play in a grotto. Very memorable, too, on one of these trips was a large shoal of some seventy Golden Rays in the sea off Tower. They were swimming backwards and forwards about three or four feet below us, looking like a mass of autumn leaves. Peter sketched them in his diary and painted a big picture of them in oils on our return home.

Most nostalgic of all was the cry of the Fork-tailed Gulls, handsome birds with a bright red gape. The sound is as haunting as that of the Fish Eagle in Africa.

In 1980 we went on an expedition to the Panda Reserve at Wolong, in China. Some aspects of this trip were hilarious, though it was serious business because we were representing the World Wildlife Fund. The distinguished scientist George Schaller was with us, as well as Nancy Nash from Hong Kong. We started badly by arriving on the wrong day, thereby missing the flight to Chengdu in Sichuan. But Peter and I enjoyed the extra day and the chance to revisit the Forbidden City.

On arrival at Chengdu the next day we were greeted by a delegation of officials. The day ended with a large, formal dinner party which we had difficulty in locating. Across the room behind a screen there seemed to be another formal dinner party taking place. We heard a familiar voice and as our meal ended who should appear from behind the screen but Lars Lindblad and his wife Cary. Our hosts looked rather surprised as we all greeted each other effusively. It turned out that Lars was on his way to Lhasa with a group.

At Sang Wa in the Panda Reserve we stayed in a recently converted timber-extraction factory. The rooms were comfortable and the brand new bathrooms looked promising. The weather was cold and very damp, so hot baths before the banquet on the first night seemed a good idea. Unfortunately none of us discovered until it was too late that the outlets from the baths were not connected to the drains. The result was that all three bathroom floors and the passage outside were more or less under water. Going to the loo in the middle of the night involved putting on gum boots first.

Next day twenty-four of us set off to climb the path known as '51 steps' in search of pandas. Peter and I each had a 'minder' and there was even a doctor to make sure that Peter, at seventy-one, could cope with the height and exertion. It was certainly a very steep and rather rough path up 500 metres to a little hut where a ranger met us (we discovered that the doctor had not made the grade – the climb had been too much for her!).

I enjoyed the varieties of vegetation – many flowering plants, including azaleas and rhododendrons – but there were no pandas, just bits of bamboo shoots and fresh panda droppings. Although our minders were charming and translated well they did not like to let us out of their sight and seemed to disapprove of our need to have a pee. Photography was difficult, too, because it rained one whole day and it was always damp and misty. The clothes in our room were as damp as if we had washed them. Another walk, up Ing Shu Ga or 'Hero's Valley', took us to some pandas in captivity. They did not seem very happy but it at least gave me an opportunity to take a photograph of one.

We spent a day selecting a site for an ambitious research station at Walnut Terrace, which I understand is now in existence. George Schaller and Peter drew a design for it which is in Peter's diary. The last day was spent driving up to the mountain pass at the head of the valley. A Jeep went ahead in order to clear rock falls from the track so that our minibus could get through. It was so cold at 3300 metres that our drivers lent us vast, padded, army greatcoats and provided large straw hats to keep off the rain. Eventually we came to snow on the road, so we could go no further. It was during the journey back, when Peter got out of the bus to look at a bird, that the doctor at last came into her own. Peter had left a trail of blood which seemed inexplicable until he pulled up his trouser leg and revealed a hole left by a leech.

The expedition finished with endless meetings with officials from the Chinese EPO. They were nearly always held in someone's bedroom and were very difficult, with set rules. Even our charming friend Wang Meng Hu ('Dreaming with Tiger') was not being helpful. The first meeting took place in our bedroom at Chengdu, where I sat on the floor. One speech by Wang Meng Hu went on for so long that it was finally brought to an end by the Deputy Governor – who then made such a long farewell speech that we nearly missed our plane to Beijing. As we rushed to the airport the local people were flailing their corn on the road and we drove over the straw, sending clouds of it flying around. We raced through a mad confusion of carts, bicycles, peasants, buses and trucks. Back in Beijing we discovered that only one room had been booked for the four of us and we were glad of Nancy's help in sorting things out.

No one could have made more effort to save the panda than Peter, George Schaller and Nancy. The telephone line between WWF HQ in Switzerland and Peter in Beijing was red hot. There had to be a financial arrangement for the Chinese. Later there was a dispute about what had been agreed and it was good that Peter had George, Nancy and me as witnesses to these conversations with Morges. Only the four of us know how difficult those last acts of diplomacy were. That week the decision was made for George to go ahead with his fieldwork project and the Research Centre at Wolong was eventually built.

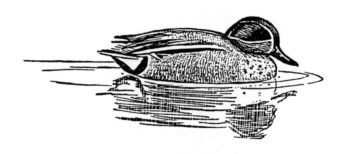

CHAPTER TWENTY-ONE

All at Sea

Peter and I had always wanted to swim with Dugongs, those lovely brown mermaids of the sea. Large gentle creatures, they are grazing animals. Peter had seen their first cousins, Manatees, in Florida but I had never seen a wild one of any sort. So it was that in March 1983 we found ourselves circling in a very small single-engine aircraft over Shark Bay in Western Australia. Below us we could see the long muddy trails left by the Dugongs in the shallow water. Attempting to swim with them from a boat was difficult. The water was altogether too murky but we did get very close to them and had good views of their broad, pale brown backs and heads as they came up to breathe. I wasted a lot of film on them. From the air the colours in the bay were spectacular: bright red soil on the shore, white sand beaches and brilliant blue/green sea.

Leaving Shark Bay in the heat of the day suddenly became problematical. Before returning to Perth we were fitting in a visit to Monkey Mia to see dolphins and to Coral Bay for the fishes. But the dirt airstrip near Shark Bay was very short, we had landed downhill and there was no wind. The pilot became very upset and said he had to shed 100lbs – just about my weight (though I was not sure I wanted to be left at a lonely station in the outback!). We were not prepared to leave our swimming gear, as we were looking forward to Coral Bay, so in the end we had rather a hairy take-off, having only discarded someone's camera box.

This little jaunt in Western Australia was a prelude to joining the

Lindblad Explorer group at Sydney and thence onward to find the ship in Townsville. Once again we were doing two back-to-back cruises, with a passenger change-over in Madang. This trip came after my diving lesson with Valerie Taylor and I had the fun of being allowed to dive with Peter. On board on this occasion were Christer and Kersten Salen whose company, Salen, would be taking over the ship from Lindblad. Peter and I were of course hoping that they would continue to take us as staff under the new management which, luckily, they seemed keen to do (we were invited to go on the North West Passage trip in 1984 but Peter said there was not much wildlife there so we did not go; the *Explorer* was the first passenger ship to achieve this).

The Philippine Islands were, as ever, delightful. The isolated reefs were still unspoiled but Peter became involved in a strange adventure off Zamboanga on April Fool's Day. One of the passengers, Ed Janss, had a special arrangement with the ship that he could have a Zodiac to go diving at each stop. He was a photographer with a particular interest in Nudibranchs (slug-like marine creatures). We were all ashore in the town when Peter and the two Jansses set off in a Zodiac with Mark Heighes, Valerie's young nephew, to dive off the nearby island of Little Santa Cruz. Peter came up early from his dive and heard a rifle shot. Mark was standing in the Zodiac having an altercation with two Philippinos in a canoe, one of whom had a rifle. The divers had no permit, they said, and they demanded that the visitors go ashore at once. But there were still two divers down. It was a tense situation: Mark said that three shots had already been fired into the air. He tried to contact the ship on his walkie-talkie but could get no answer.

When the Jansses surfaced the Philippinos continued to insist that they go ashore. The argument became heated, Mark became angry. Appeasement was necessary, so Peter and Ed agreed to go ashore. Once there Peter showed them his underwater board and Ed produced some specimens. There was more discussion and more fingering of the rifle. The bag of life jackets was opened and examined, with the rifle still being waved about. Then it was pointed at Ed's brand new dive bag. Ed opened it and took out his dive things. 'I'll take that,' said the man.

Just then the Cruise Director came up on the radio loud and clear, giving details of the ship's clearance. It was suggested that they took the man back to the ship but he said that he was in charge of security on the island and could not leave it. 'Don't give him anything,' advised the voice, but at that point the rifle was raised again. They were hostages and Ed agreed to leave his $75 bag as ransom.

In his diary Peter wrote: 'Bereras said, "I want you to confirm that you gave me the bag." "Yes," said Ed, "I gave it to you." "You gave it from the heart?" "Yes," said Ed, "from the heart." "Well, all right, you can go," and a few minutes later we were spinning across the three-mile channel to the ship, which had just been visible all the time. We sailed on time for Sandakan.'

Although we visited some places we had been to before, new on the list this time was Kota Kinabalu in Sabah, on the island of Borneo, and then Brunei, Kucheng and Sarawak. In all these places the heat was intense and we were sightseeing most of the time, not swimming. In Brunei Peter surprised the bus driver by stopping the vehicle as we passed the polo field in order to look at the large flocks of Golden and Ringed Plover. It was also surprising to find a Churchill Museum in the city, with a large statue of the great man outside. Churchill was apparently a great friend of the previous sultan.

It had been mind-blowing to swim with Humpbacked Whales in the 70s. Now it was also wonderful to swim with Spotted Dolphins off the north coast of Grand Bahama Island. At the invitation of Hardy Jones we spent five days on board a 72ft yacht called the *Cloudsley Shovell*, skippered by Bob Gascoigne. The dolphins were known to Hardy by name and it was sheer joy to swim with them and watch them playing. There was a mother with a baby and two large, very friendly adults, as well as a trio called 'the heavies'. I learned that it was a mistake to follow the latter – on one occasion when I put my head up I found I had a long swim back to the boat.

There is something very appealing about cetaceans (whales and dolphins). Perhaps it has to do with their being underwater mammals, and with their size and intelligence. Peter was deeply involved in a tremendous effort to save the great whales and felt strongly about seeing them whenever he could. One opportunity came in 1984 when we were invited by Brian Lourensz, a delightful Sri Lankan businessman, to join him at Trincomalee, where he kept a boat. He had a hut on Norway Island, a tiny island in the middle of the bay. Also in the party was a research team sponsored by WWF and the distinguished American photographer Flip Nicklin. They were aboard a yacht called *Tulip*.

The palm-thatch house on the island was a dream, with a friendly atmosphere. The only problem was that there had been tremendous rainstorms before we arrived. The whole bay was cloudy with the run-off from the hills, and the rain continued. Brian went off to work in his speed boat on the first day and by the afternoon Peter and I were building sand baffles to prevent water pouring through the house. Next morning it was still raining and there was quite a bit of drama, with *Tulip* first running aground and then being involved in a collision with another boat. Although the sun did come out briefly the next day, Brian decided that it would be best if we all went back to the town and stayed at the Anglers' Club, where we found our old friends Richard and Maisie Fitter, of Flora and Fauna International.

It was not until the third day that we managed to get out in Brian's small motor-cruiser to look for whales. Just as we came up to the *Tulip* out in the bay a Blue Whale was surfacing very close to the yacht. The back of the whale was clearly visible and seemed to go on for ever. The *Tulip* was 32ft long and I reckoned the whale was at least twice that length. We saw the fluke as it sounded – it looked small compared to a Humpback – and saw it blow five times more, but it was swimming too fast for us to catch up.

The following day we went out in the *Tulip*, but after three hours had found only Bryde's Whales. However, the next day our luck was in when we saw a Blue Whale, which surfaced and blew so close to our boat that it made me jump. The noise was fabulous. Peter was out in a small rubber boat from the *Tulip* with one of their crew. The two of them jumped in the water but even though Peter was within 30ft of the largest animal in the world there was not a chance of his seeing it, with visibility down to 12ft. He was, nevertheless, very excited by the experience.

The *Lindblad Explorer* trip that followed took us to many of the islands that we had visited before as well as to many new ones. It was a perfect opportunity for me to learn the Pacific fishes, to get to know them really well. Also, since I now had a diving certificate, I could see the deeper fishes. We passed and watched small volcanic islands erupting in the Trobriands, saw Bird-winged Butterflies on shore and visited some of the World War II historic sites. One morning, offshore from Tuam Island, Peter recorded 183 species of fish. There was an idyllic quality about that whole

expedition. Jacq Shackleton was with us and many of the passengers
were old friends so the atmosphere was relaxed. On 27 March I wrote in
my diary:

> 'After lunch we moored to Ginetu Island, the perfect South Pacific
> unhabited island. In the evening there was a barbecue ashore at 6pm. A
> perfect setting. No wind, no mosquitoes. A few drops of rain threatened
> us but no more and the sunset was beautiful. Pete and I came back to
> the ship in the last boat. Driving back in the Zodiac, the phosphores-
> cence sparkling in our wake, the warm air, warm sea and brilliant
> starlight right under the Southern Cross is surely very romantic and a
> memory to treasure.'

During the 1980s there were three other out-of-the-ordinary major excursions. In January 1986 we joined a Salen Lindblad cruise which started
from Colombo in Sri Lanka and took us south through the Maldives, the
Chagros Islands and on to Mauritius, all new places to us. This trip had a
memorable start – as we arrived to check in at Heathrow for our evening
flight to Delhi we had no Indian visas (our tour agent had forgotten to tell
us they were required and we were not allowed to fly without them). It was
particularly important for us to leave on time as Peter had an appointment
to see the Prime Minister, Rajiv Ghandi, the following day. If we had not, by
chance, met Jackie Fatesing, the former Maharajah of Baroda and
President of WWF India, we would have been in a bad way. With Jackie's
help we were allowed on board and managed to get everything fixed up in
Delhi. The interview with Rajiv, which I attended, was fascinating.
An attractive and delightful person, he appeared to have a very genuine
interest in conservation. Peter and I had met his mother, Indira Ghandi,
more than once and had found her equally charming.

We left Delhi the next day from an airport that must have ranked as one
of the most inefficient of its day, an experience which prompted me to
remark to Peter, 'Even if you have an appointment with God in India I am
not ever coming back to Delhi.'

The ship which was to take us south through the Indian Ocean was a
Yugoslav vessel called the *MS Ambassador*. Built for cruising in the
Mediterranean, she had an open deck close to sea level. This was where our
cabin was located, so we hoped for calm weather.

The diving in the Maldives was wonderful. The most memorable and unusual occurrence was when one day we found ourselves swimming in about 12ft of water under the boat with a whole shoal of Remoras, some of which were up to 3ft long. Valerie Taylor was feeding them, Ron was filming and they were very tame. It was so strange and unusual to find them unattached. Being sucker fish they are usually found clinging to dolphins or larger fish.

We were joined at Reunion by Robin Brown and his team from Central TV, who were making a film about Peter's life, to be called *Make the Boy Interested in Natural History*. Our brief visit to Mauritius thereafter was very much angled towards the endangered species. This was, after all, the home of the extinct Dodo so it was encouraging to find the two endangered species, the Pink Pigeon and the Mauritius Kestrel, being successfully re-introduced to the wild.

By this time we had acquired new passengers and Peter and I had been moved to a cabin on the bottom deck – a dark little box without even a port-hole. After a rough night at sea we were due back in Reunion for one day. Having been into town to get some money, we returned by the coastal road to the harbour along the dual carriageway. The waves looked frighteningly big and were breaking over the road. Suddenly an extra large one swept over the road, blew a hole in the door panel, filled the front of the bus with sea water and knocked us sideways. Luckily, apart from getting rather wet, we were unscathed.

Back on board there was much talk of a cyclone north of Reunion which might, or might not, sweep round between Madagascar and us. The Captain, however, was determined to risk it and we set off into very stormy seas. As the night wore on the weather worsened. In our little box in the bowels of the ship it was very claustrophobic. The cold tap in the shower turned itself on, the door fell off our wardrobe and there was a continuous banging. Later I discovered that this was caused by the anchor – which had broken loose – banging on the side of the ship. At 3am the rolling lessened and Peter said, with relief, 'She's turned round to go back.' We were lucky to get into the harbour: there was only one small mooring space left behind a vast tanker. We were stranded for six days in Reunion, where the local authorities were anxious to evacuate us from the ship. The waves, even inside the harbour, were breaking on the lower deck and the cabin we had occupied on the earlier part of the voyage was flooded. But thanks to the

Captain and Tom Richie, our expedition leader, we were allowed to remain on board. The alternative would have been to split us all up into several different hotels.

The cyclone, *Erinesta*, was reported to be the worst in the area for thirty years. The lamp posts on the jetty were blown over like broken reeds and on the Point the waves were breaking higher than the lighthouse. Entertainment had to be provided for the unhappy passengers, and Peter performed well with talks and games. We had been able to go ashore for the first three days, but the wind and rain were violent, the ship was rocking and some of the lines broke. Later we were forbidden to land and there was an 8pm curfew on the island. Jacq and Valerie bought all the plain white T shirts from the ship's shop and painted a logo on them with the wording: 'I survived Erinesta', which they then sold in aid of the Wildfowl Trust. In twenty-four hours 19cm of rain fell.

Eventually we did manage to go all round Madagascar. The large number of chameleons we found were of special interest since I had so much enjoyed keeping them at home; but we did not take any back with us on this occasion. The lemurs were fascinating but the Ringed-tails at Berenty were the most endearing of them all. More striking perhaps, but less easy to see, were the Sifakas up in the trees. Almost as memorable as the amazing animals and strange experiences ashore was getting up in the middle of the night to see Haley's Comet. I had been reluctant to be woken but it was well worth it.

We were away from home for two months. The tour ended in the Seychelles. On the way north from Madagascar we stopped at Aldabra, which we had visited in 1971. This time I was one of only five people with a scuba-diving certificate. Our Dive Master on the trip was Mike Messick and with him and the others I enjoyed one of the most amazing dives I have ever had. We started a drift dive a long way up-current from one of the channels which rush out from the lagoon. Mike carried the Zodiac anchor and we all drifted along together. It became better and better as we went: a turtle, thirteen different butterfly fish, Bat Fish which followed us, huge Jacks and Humphead Wrasse, then as we came to a patch of cold water a huge shoal of Yellow-lined Snappers. We were entirely surrounded by them and could hardly see each other. It was definitely a five-star dive.

CHAPTER TWENTY-TWO

The Unrelenting Eighties

The expedition in the *Ambassador* was Peter's last sea-borne lecture commitment. His health had not been good since he had prostate cancer in 1980, and underwent various treatments for it. In May 1984 he had another minor operation connected with his waterworks and frightened us all badly. In the middle of the night in hospital he had become very ill indeed. It it was not until the morning that his problem was diagnosed as water intoxification. After that episode he seemed a little fragile. Pressure of work was building up at home, including proof reading his book *Travel Diaries of a Naturalist Volume II*. I was worried about his health and undertook to attend and speak in his place at the opening ceremony of the Peter Scott Visitor Center at our WWT Centre, Washington.

On the way I stayed overnight with Falcon and his family north of Leeds, in Yorkshire. As Falcon was leaving the house for work in the morning the telephone rang. Peter had had a heart attack. Falcon drove me home in three hours and I found Peter in bed in the studio. The doctor said it was a minor attack but he must take it easy for a month. Full mobility would be restored in three months. From that time on Peter's health was a constant worry to me. How could we stop him doing too much? Everyone wanted him, and he was not very good at saying 'No'. However, in spite of everything we continued to lead a very full life. By September that year he was fit enough to cope with a one-man show of his paintings at Ackermans in London. By that time both Dafila and Falcon were married and we were enjoying our grandchildren. Life was good when we did not have to rush around all the time. It was a special delight to have Dafila's children Amber and Peter learning to swim in our pool.

Our first venture abroad after Peter's heart attack was to stay with our friends David and Herta Ogilvy at their lovely Château de Toufou in France. In this quiet setting we were allowed to relax and do as we pleased. David is a splended raconteur and we enjoyed his entertaining company as well as that of our charming hostess Herta. It was a peaceful little interlude in a life which continued to be hectic.

Later that year we went together to Madrid for Peter to attend WWF/IUCN meetings. We were to fly down to the Coto Doñana the following morning with Prince Philip. In the meantime I was desperate to see the El Greco paintings in the Prado, but I had no money, I spoke no Spanish and Peter was in a meeting at the Palacio de Congressos. The only thing to do was to walk to the Palacio, which I did, and to send in a note to him asking for some cash. The officials at the Palacio were very formal and security was tight because of the presence of Princes Bernhard and Philip. It did not look as if I would succeed. After a lot of persistence on my part they sent for a charming lady, a volunteer helper who spoke English. She had worked at the Prado and knew her way around so she took me on a bus and was able to show me all the paintings I wanted to see. Peter was rather envious when he came out of what had been rather a boring meeting but we managed to visit the Prado together the following morning.

After the heart attack we were never really quite sure what he ought to undertake, but there were certain opportunities which were too good to miss. In 1986, with his doctor's blessing, we joined a very unusual and interesting expedition to Cooper's Creek in the centre of Australia. Our good friend Dick Smith, who must be one of the most well known and liked people in the whole of Australia, was concerned about an area round Cooper's Creek and the Coongie Lakes adjacent to Sturt's Stony Desert. He organised a kind of workshop to meet at a tented site on the banks of the Creek. The 'delegates' to this party in the desert consisted of about thirty people, including zoologists, botanists, geologists, geographers and Ron and Valerie Taylor as fish experts. The threat of oil-prospecting in the area was very real as we could see from the shot lines on the Stony Desert. We were to explore the possibilities of establishing a national park or wetland reserve.

Above In New Guinea, on the boat ride up the river: Jacq Shackleton with the head man from the village of Pirien in the Asmat Region.
Below The reception at the Sultan's palace at Bau Bau on the island of Butong, Indonesia. No reception was ever quite like this again.

Above Asmat, New Guinea. The wood spirit, elaborately dressed in palm leaf costume, arrives at the village of Owus for a formal celebration.

Below Warrior canoes seeing us off from Owus for the long journey downriver.

Above Yasur Volcano in action on the island of Tanna in the New Hebrides. Rocks as big as Land Rovers were being thrown into the air.
Below Part of the vast crowd of tribesmen with their spirit Toka Poles at the Toka Festival on Tanna Island. The poles arrived after a long night of dancing in the woodland clearing.

Kakadu National Park, Northern Territory Australia. *Above* A flock of Magpie Geese, just some of the many thousands. *Below* A Glossy Ibis in a lily pool.

Right Peter painting a fish on board the Kimberley Explorer on the the way back from Rowley shoals off the west coast of Australia.

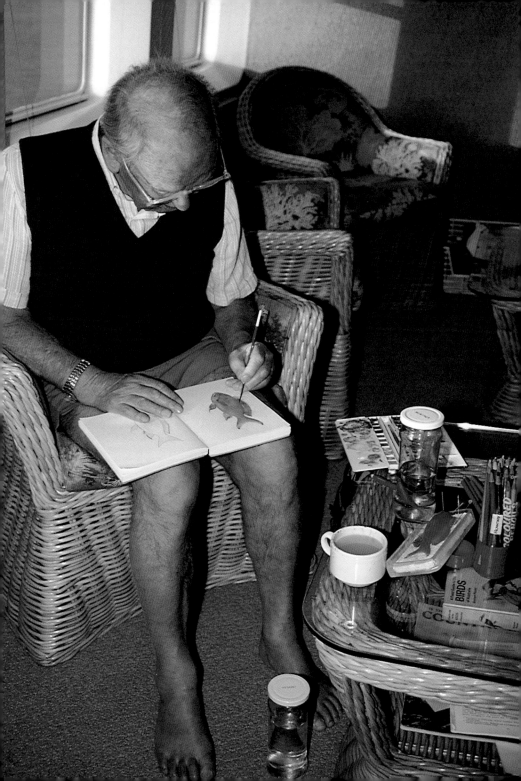

Above The *MS Ambasador* seen from the shore at Nosy Mangabe, Madagascar. Built for the Mediterranean, she lay very low in the water.
Below Canoes at the entrance to the St. Paul subterranean river on Palawan Island, Philippines.

Above Outer Mongolia. Horseman riding by the Lamassery at Khara Korin.
Below The Mai Po Marshes, New Territories, Hong Kong. Peter was involved with
the initial setting up of this wonderful wetland reserve, now looked after by
WWF Hong Kong.

Above Peter sitting on a deserted beach at Miranda, New Zealand, drawing a Wrybill while Ronald Lockley (left) and friends watch.
Below Peter with his friend and mentor Konrad Lorenz at Grunau, Austria, 1985. A happy reunion as Konrad died not long afterwards.

The Coongie Lakes system linked to Cooper's Creek provides a wetland habitat for a great profusion of waterfowl, including significant proportions of the total world population of such birds as the Freckled Duck and the Australian Avocet. From the base camp under the eucalyptus trees by the creek Dick drove us the three-hour trek over sandy tracks to the lakes. Here a small group of us camped for two nights and overflew the lakes as well as going out in a boat. It was very exciting to have our first view of Freckled Ducks. As a result of this expedition the area has now been declared a reserve, which is very satisfactory.

For a 75-year-old Peter did very well on a camping expedition. But one night he gave me a fright when he woke me up to tell me from the depths of his sleeping bag that his pulse was racing and he could hear strange irregular noises which he thought were in his heart. I listened and then reassured him that the sound was coming from the Taylors' tent next to ours and must be Ron snoring. His pulse rate promptly went down and we all had a good laugh the next day.

One of the highlights of 1985 was a visit arranged by Central TV to the Konrad Lorenz Institute Center at Grunau, in Austria. Robin Brown, the film producer, was anxious to film Peter and Konrad together. The last time we had seen Konrad was when Peter, as Chancellor of Birmingham University, had conferred an honorary degree on him eleven years before. He had stayed with us in the cottage more than once in the early days and was there at the time when we were talking about getting married. It was sheer pleasure to be with him again. He was eighty-one at that time, but his delightful sense of humour, his twinkling blue eyes, and his stimulating ideas about conservation and animal behaviour were as lively as ever. That visit was one of the happiest interludes during those last few years. Konrad was so generous in his praise for Peter and obviously felt responsible in some way for our marriage. With him I felt I was a person, not just Peter Scott's wife.

Peter always insisted that I should accompany him on his trips and in the 1980s we were seldom apart and hated it if we were. However, there was an International Whaling Commission in Sweden in June 1986 and it would have been difficult for me to get away, so Peter went off on his own. He evidently over-extended himself, and on his return had another heart attack. This time he was in hospital in Bristol for a week. There followed a pleasant interlude at home where we could be like an ordinary family. Peter was also busy thinking of plans for a new visitor centre at Slimbridge. But by September we were on the move again.

First there was a short visit to the United States for Peter to receive the Getty Wildlife Conservation Prize. A kind friend presented us with tickets on Concorde for the flight to Washington DC. Peter and I got every ounce of pleasure out of this treat as we sat among all the solemn-faced business people. We were invited onto the flight deck, which was surprisingly small. It was exciting to see the curvature of the earth from a height of 56,000 ft.

For some years Peter had been on the jury for the Getty Prize so he had had to be persuaded to retire before he could be awarded it himself. In fact, he was largely responsible for its very existence in that fifteen years previously he had gone to see John Paul Getty at his home in Sutton Place and asked him if he would be prepared to endow an annual prize of $50,000 for conservation. Peter suggested that it would be comparable to the Nobel Prize. Mr Getty replied, 'They tell me that the Romans used to compete for laurel leaves.' The $50,000 which Peter received went to the Wildfowl Trust.

The ceremony took place in the Baird Auditorium of the National Museum of Natural History in the Smithsonian and was very special for Peter because his old and distinguished friend, Dillon Ripley, made the presentation. It was a very prestigious event, lightened by the fact that all the other distinguished speakers were old friends of Peter's.

Having survived all that, there were more awards awaiting Peter for which we needed to travel. It was an inspired idea on the part of the WWF to have its 25th Anniversary Congress in 1986 in Assisi, the home of St Francis but there was a problem for us because Assisi is on a hill and I was worried about Peter's heart condition. However, he managed very well and our hotel was conveniently close to the Basilica, where a very moving and inspiring interfaith ceremony entitled 'Religion and Nature' was held. Peter was awarded the WWF Gold Medal and appointed a Member of Honour, and we were thoroughly spoilt throughout the whole visit. We had been flown out by Prince Philip in his aeroplane, which was a good start. He had frequently made seats available to us on flights to various places for WWF events, for which we were extremely grateful.

Pilgrims from all over the world gathered in Assisi and Peter and I greeted a deputation from Wildfowl and Wetlands Trust, led by a volunteer on our education staff, Val Hicken. It was exciting to see so many people from all faiths gathered in this famous ancient city. It certainly gave a great lift to the spirit and, one hopes, in the long run may have done some good for the wildlife cause.

In spite of Peter's health problems we continued with our fish-watching adventures throughout the eighties. In 1984 we were invited by the Marchioness of Hertford to join her and her daughter on board the *Lady Jenny III*, a small dive boat, in the Red Sea. I think it was on this trip that Peter and I discovered we had each looked back on our home as we left with the feeling that we might never see it again.

We left from Sharm el Sheikh on 19 November and were on board for ten days. At this time Peter was not allowed to dive, and Jacq Shackleton, who was also with us, had not yet learned, so I benefited from having the dive master to myself. The reefs were marvellous. Forever pictured in my mind is the scene on the wall of Jackson's Reef. Above is a mass of little golden Anthias, the water is clear and there is a riot of colour in the coral up near the edge of the reef. (That is what I think of when I lie in the dentist's chair!) To discover that I was expected to jump from the deck into the water 8ft below was rather frightening but I soon got used to it.

The big day was at Ras Mohammed, on the southern tip of the Sinai Peninsula. It has a spectacular reef where sharks circle the great round coral pinnacle. I swam twice round it and saw only three White-tipped Sharks and three Black-tipped the following day. Nearby, in the lagoon, we were followed by the huge Humphead Wrasse, one of which had a Remora on it. People used to feed them on boiled eggs, but happily that is now discouraged. We swam over the wreck of the *Yolanda* and duly noted the lavatory basin which some divers find it amusing to sit on. We were lucky, as in later years we were unable to dive there due to bad weather.

My first-ever night dive was from the *Lady Jenny III* on a site called 'The Temple'. We saw sleeping Parrot Fish in their cocoons and the little Flashlight Fish, *Photo blepheron*, darting round us like fireflies. It was a thoroughly enjoyable trip and Peter was wonderfully relaxed. On arrival at Eilat he had frightened us by fainting in a chair while we were collecting the luggage, but a charming Israeli doctor said that it was nothing serious. There was one hilarious day when we were all snorkelling and Peter was so happy that he wrote on his board: 'I love you' and without looking up put it in front of what he thought was my mask beside him. Louise Hertford sprang up with amazement and Peter had to explain!

In 1985 there was another fish-watching tour in the *Lumba Lumba* with Keith and Jacq in the Banda Sea. But in 1987 we decided we would call the tune and have our own expedition. With Ron and Valerie Taylor's blessing we chartered their boat, based at Cairns. I then had to organise our fellow divers and snorkellers. In the end they were all divers except Peter. I was so worried about him snorkelling on his own that I made him wear a red cotton hat which meant that I could more easily spot him in the water. It also prevented him getting his bald head sunburnt.

Organising our fellow travellers was not all that easy. Fom the cost point of view it was essential to have the full complement of twelve and this was finally achieved by Valerie bringing a niece, who shared a cabin with Jacq. We ended up having the internationally distinguished coral fish expert Jack Randall from Honolulu, and several other old friends from our Lindblad days. We also took, for my peace of mind regarding Peter, an Australian doctor.

Our first dive was close to Lizard Island on the Great Barrier Reef in the now famous 'Cod Hole'. Valerie had managed to have these wonderful fish protected. The idea of swimming among these huge creatures was rather frightening. As well as taking her camera, Valerie also took fish to feed to them. There were four really big 'Potato Cod' (*Epinephelus tukula*) – the largest was longer than I am – as well as a number of smaller ones and some large Maori Wrasse about 3ft long. To be accepted among these great sea animals was a wonderful experience – one I likened to feeding the wild Bewick's Swans in the Rushy Pen. We were among them for about an hour while Peter watched from above with his snorkel.

Heading south, we stopped to swim at 'Silver Tip City' on the Ferguson Reef. Silver Tip Sharks are notorious but Valerie was unafraid and the rest of us agreed to watch as she fed chum (bits of fish) to them while we stayed with our backs to the wall at a distance of about 50ft. In no time she had several sharks coming to her bait a couple of yards away from us. After a while Jacq and I decided to swim up-current along the wall but we had not been going for long when I became aware that sharks were taking an interest in us and circling round rather too closely. I wrote on my board for Jacq, 'I don't like this much', to which she replied, 'Nor do I' and we signalled to go back. But first we had to collect a buddy who had gone on. When we arrived back at the place where Valerie had been feeding we found that she had gone. Naturally, the sharks came looking for more food from us. From there we had quite a long swim in deep water back to the boat. I have to admit I was not too happy about those sharks.

We headed north to Raine Island, famous for the enormous Green Turtle nesting sites and sea bird colonies. We spent some time righting turtles which had fallen over a small ledge and landed on their backs. They were big and heavy. I photographed a Tropic Bird nesting under the ledge.

Going south again Peter was allowed to have one dive to 30ft using my gear. Valerie went with him and he was positively ecstatic about being down with the fishes and able to see them close up again. He wrote on his board for Valerie, 'It's so beautiful I can't bear to go.' They were down for an hour and a quarter. We paid a brief visit to Cooktown, the northern-most town in Queensland where Captain Cook landed in 1873. It was 45°C in the shade and a ten-minute walk into town from the jetty, so we did not spend much time there.

The most wonderful reef of all was the huge Osprey Reef in the Coral Sea outside the Barrier Reef, where we dived in more than one place. It was here that I went deeper than I have ever done before or since. The boat was anchored in the Pelagic Gully and the water was clearer than I had ever seen it. Jacq and I went down to 80ft and, after swimming round to the other side of the gully from the one where the boat was anchored, found ourselves on the edge of a bottomless cliff with beautiful corals and sea fans growing on it. Although it was awe-inspiring, the top was largely dead coral, so we went down further. I levelled off at 130ft and decided that that was deep enough, especially as I always had a small tank. Jacq, who had a big one, was at least 10ft below me and I wondered if I would know if she was 'narked' (had narcosis, 'raptures of the deep'). We swam along until the ridge ended in a round dome of rubble. To my relief, Jacq came up and we looked over the top and saw a mass of small White-tipped Sharks on the other side. When we started back along the ridge I began to float and had to pick up bits of rubble to keep me down. With Jacq's help we put some rocks in my pouch and headed out into the deep blue to cross the gully heading for the anchor chain. I was planning to decompress on the chain but I saw Jacq heading across to the other side so I decided we might as well decompress looking at something over there. We had five minutes at 40ft and another five at 15ft. We ended up with a little air still in our tanks after a 40-minute dive. Talking to Jacq afterwards I felt sure that she was slightly 'narked'. She said it was as though she had had a couple of gins down deep and it was marvellous. It was a wonderful, and memorable dive, all the details of which are vividly imprinted on my mind.

The North Horn of Osprey Reef also provided fantastic diving in clear water, with masses of fish. There were a number of sharks, many big groupers and other pelagic fish. Once again Valerie entertained us with a shark-feeding frenzy. She set up some bait on top of a coral bommie and in no time there were six White Tips and two Grey Reef Sharks as well as a large Potato Cod. Jack Randall was standing by with a spear gun, Ron was filming right among the sharks, Valerie was taking stills, and the rest of us were perched on a wall. They are very beautiful animals and on this occasion were not frightening. Osprey Reef provided us with the best diving of the whole trip. It was here that Jack Randall collected an unknown wrasse, which Peter painted and which was subsequently named *Cirrilabrus scottorum* after Peter and me.

On the way home from this trip we stopped off in Muscat for a week's stay at the magnificent Al Bustan Palace Hotel. The object of our visit was the presentation of the IUCN/WWF Report on Conservation in the Sultanate of Oman. There were representatives of both organizations attending, and in no time at all we were going from one engagement to another, business and social, including two opportunities to scuba dive or snorkel with Rod Salm.

The day after we arrived we were summoned to tea with HM the Sultan at his summer palace at Sohar. I had not expected to be included in this party so this was a bonus. We were flown by helicopter and welcomed to tea outside on the lawn by the Sultan. With us were Ralph Daly, who was based in Muscat and was the wildlife adviser to the Sultan, and Hartmut Jungius, from WWF. All went well except that Peter had his brief case, containing all his notes and a gift for the Sultan, taken away from him at the guard house and I was shivering with cold as dusk fell. Servants had to be sent flying down the avenue of casuarinas to fetch the brief case and my shawl. There were further complications later as no one had thought we might need to have a pee at some stage. The helicopter flight took over an hour and Peter had to use a palm tree before we left. On arrival they could not find anywhere for me so I was sent to the gents in the army loo.

Before Peter's heart attack in 1984 we had visited the Sultanate as guests of the government to attend a conference on the Oman environment organized by Ralph Daly and held at Salalah on the south coast. Conferences were affairs which I normally avoided if I could, but this one, which was really a 'workshop', was attended by a very interesting collection of scientists from all over the world as well as the relevant Omani specialists.

Situated on the dry strip by the coast between the sea and the tree-clad escarpment, Salalah provided us with a variety of extremely interesting excursions by bus and four-wheel drive vehicles. The meetings started early because of the heat and re-convened in the evening after an afternoon break. It was fascinating to leave the dry, flat area by the sea and drive up through palm trees, a waterfall and even tropical forest to the high desert area at the top. We learned about life in those parts, the vegetation, the climate and much else. It was quite different from anywhere I had been before. Wherever there was water there were a number of birds as well as a small bird sanctuary near the town. The social life became a little hectic. We got up every morning at 6.30 and if there was not a dinner engagement we often went to bed without an evening meal or ate it in our room. One evening Prince Bernhard turned up rather unexpectedly on his way to catch up with the Sultan, on whom he was bestowing the Order of the Golden Ark. Peter and I were invited to meet him in his VIP guest house and I think he was pleased to see old friends.

The most exciting part of the visit was a day trip to Yalooni where the captive-bred Arabian Oryx were released. It was laid on for us and four other delegates by Ralph Daly, who organized a helicopter to take us in from Muscat after the conference. The Arabian Oryx project was the first successful reintroduction of a species extinct in the wild made possible through the help of many international organizations and in particular by the Fauna and Flora Preservation Society (now Flora and Fauna International), and especially by HM the Sultan, who had detailed the Harassis desert tribe of Bedouin to guard them. When we were there Mark Stanley-Price and his wife Karen were wardens and lived *in situ*.

On arrival at the camp we were immediately whisked away to the area where the team of twelve local wardens were lined up and waiting in the shade of a small bush. Armed with guns, they were an impressive sight, dressed all in white and wearing leather belts with ammunition pouches.

We shook hands all along the line and with the local Sheikh. The heat was such that my Olympus camera started to play up. The mirror stuck every third shot which was frustrating. We were driven a little further to see the herd of eleven Oryx; three of them had been born in the desert and so were truly wild – a wonderful thought! With an ailing camera and the heat haze, photography was difficult but David Western kindly lent me a 300m lens and I managed a few reasonable shots.

My memories of the 1980s are kaleidoscopic. There were so many things, so many places, so many people. Of particular interest, though nothing much has been written about it anywhere, was a visit to Andy Warhol's studio in New York – which happened in 1983 during a WWT/WWF fundraising tour in the United States. Although it was all arranged, our host did not appear until we had more or less finished the excellent buffet lunch laid out on an enormous table. With his shock of white hair and rather gaunt face he looked exactly as in photographs. He was not with us for long but he did take an interest in the sketches in Peter's notebook and listened to Peter telling him about our Bewick's Swans. He offered to send some prints to England for our two organisations but I am not quite sure what happened about them. The whole episode had a surreal quality about it and I came out wondering if it had really happened.

There were other memorable occasions too. In November 1982 we were invited to a dinner party at Hampton Court given by Queen Beatrix of the Netherlands and her husband Prince Claus. It was an extraordinary sight to see Dutch soldiers holding staves with flaming torches as we arrived at the door. Everything had been brought over from Holland: the crockery, the wine, the food, the flowers, the footmen and the flunkeys. The entire British Royal Family was there. Peter and I enjoyed the occasion very much and found ourselves in a small reception room before dinner with all the Royals. It was the only time I ever spoke to Diana Princess of Wales. She immediately asked me if I had been going to ask when she would be bringing the young Princes to Slimbridge. I had not been going to ask her that but might indeed have followed it up if we had not been summoned to dinner at that moment.

In 1987 we attended another grand dinner at Hampton Court, again held in the 16th-century Great Hall. This was for members of the WWF 1001 Club, in the presence of Prince Charles. It was a lovely occasion but perhaps almost the most exciting event that evening was a telephone call from June White (Peter's PA) when we arrived back in our hotel room. She rang to say that a letter had arrived informing him that the Prime Minister was recommending him to the Queen as a Companion of Honour. We were on our way to the United States for a short visit and set off next day with a very happy and rather overwhelmed Peter. That was the same year in which he was appointed a Fellow of the Royal Society, an honour which deeply impressed him.

In 1953-54, when we built our house, people from the village had come to look over the site. They were amazed that our spare room had its own bathroom. 'Oh, that is for the Queen,' some worthy explained. We heard this story and the room has been known as 'The Queen's Room' ever since. It came into its own at last in February 1988 when the Queen lunched with us in the house at Slimbridge and then went on to open the Yuen Peng McNeice Observatory. She did not actually stay in the room but she did see it and I was able to tell her that Prince Philip and Prince Charles had each slept there. My then cook/secretary Nicky Little cooked the lunch and the whole meal was prepared 'in house', with June White waiting at table. Our guests included Sir John and Lady Harvey-Jones and Sir Percy and Lady McNeice. The occasion was very light hearted and the formal opening in the afternoon went off equally smoothly.

We enjoyed another royal occasion in April 1988 when we were invited to a State dinner in honour of the King of Norway in the Banqueting Hall at Windsor Castle. Once again we were on our way to the USA, this time to join a Lindblad Intrepids Club cruise in the *Illyria*. Later when we saw the terrible pictures of the great fire at Windsor Castle we remembered the breathtaking scene at the dinner for King Olaf. It is a huge room with a great vaulted ceiling; the dining table, about 12ft wide, runs the length of it. That night it seated 160 people. Decorated with flowers in gold chalices, candlesticks with small hooded candles and gleaming glass and silver, it was an arresting and very beautiful sight. Peter and I unashamedly enjoyed such occasions and always found all the members of our Royal family to be very friendly.

Peter's diary records: 'Then came one of the loveliest parts of the evening. Phil and I had decided to walk through the courtyards to the Castle back to our hotel in the High Street. It was a cold clear night, and we walked arm in arm down the hill – not too fast because of Phil's thin party shoes.' That says it all.

The Intrepids Club cruise was pleasant but more geared to the wealth than the intrepids. Compared with the other expeditions we did not feel quite at home, and although Belize has some of the best coral reefs in that part of the Caribbean our ship failed to find them.

CHAPTER TWENTY-THREE

Sunlight and Shadow

The Bitter End Yacht Club is situated on the easternmost end of the British Virgin Islands. A pleasant place in which to stay, with a coral reef just offshore, it was recommended to us by Richard Branson, whose Necker Island is close by. Peter had been invited to open a Waterfowl Exhibit and to receive the Zoo Medal at Washington National Zoo in May 1989. This event was to be followed by a fundraising reception for WWT at the British Embassy in Washington. It seemed a nice idea to have a short, quiet holiday together in the Caribbean before these formal events, and the doctors approved.

The yacht club looked rather like a small town. Our chalet, at the top of forty-nine steps, was reached by shuttle boat from the reception area, or a four-minute walk along the shore path among the trees. The steps were a severe blow – not good for Peter's dicky heart. The following day I managed to change our room to one which had only twenty-two steps. But on our first night Peter was taken ill and was in such pain that I decided to call a doctor. I had been told that there was a doctor on the island but at reception I learned that the nearest one was on another island and could only come if a boat was sent for him. This was duly arranged and the kind receptionist carried oxygen along to our chalet. Later a reassuring doctor arrived and diagnosed a viral infection of the intestine. The blame was put on a cheese-burger at an airport and we hoped for a speedy recovery after a day in bed.

Peter sat and sketched the view from our room, and the Bananaquits and Pearly Eyed Threshers which came to share our meals were charming. But Peter's temperature did not drop and the second night was almost as bad as the first. By this time he was suffering badly from angina. On the third day he seemed a little better but by the evening he was in continuous pain again. It was not a good place in which to be ill. The telephone in reception was the only one available and visitors were often queueing for it. I decided that I must somehow get Peter to Washington, but the journey would have been daunting. Then that night a message came through from Richard Branson to say that we could use his helicopter for a visit to his island or to go to Puerto Rico or wherever. Help was at hand! I called him back and explained the situation.

I still had to organise accommodation in Washington using the difficult telephone. The only people I knew there were the Ripleys (Dillon Ripley, Secretary of the Smithsonian Institute, was a long-time friend of Peter's) but they were in Connecticut. Eventually I traced them and was put in touch with David Challinor, a scientific adviser to the Smithsonian who would book us in somewhere. Another day was spent with telephone calls to Washington and to doctors, and much walking with food from the restaurant to our room.

Inevitably Peter was feeling much better on the fourth day and was determined to snorkel in the bay below our chalet before we left. I was tired and worried about the whole situation but there was no stopping him. It did seem a pity to leave but I decided that there were four points which made my decision the right one – first, I was having to carry two meals a day along to our room, and did not really know what to feed him; second, there was the long walk and the twenty-two steps; third, Peter did not like the walk in the dark even if he felt well enough; fourth, there was the difficulty of getting medical advice. Finally, after much to-ing and fro-ing and telephoning, we were lifted off in Richard Branson's little helicopter and taken to San Juan in the American Virgin Islands from where we were able to fly direct to Washington. We were both miserable, but I knew that I had made the right decision. We were met by Dillon Ripley's car and Irish driver, and taken to the Jefferson Hotel for the night. With our half bottle of gin and country clothes we felt rather out of place so it was a relief when David Challinor collected us for Peter's doctor's appointment and then whisked us off to stay in his lovely house in Hawthorne Street not far from the zoo.

It was comforting to have the various opinions on Peter's health and for four days we were thoroughly spoilt by David and Joan Challinor. Peter was still unwell but there had not been any further damage to his heart and rest was what was needed. From there we moved to stay with the Ripleys in their impressive town house. Peter was just well enough to make a speech at the zoo and to receive his medal but there was no doubt that he was still frail.

By the day of the Embassy reception life had caught up with me and I had a real stinker of a cold. There were a hundred guests and several speakers, including some of our WWT staff, who spoke about our conservation work. We stood for nearly three hours and then attended a dinner with the Ambassador, Sir Anthony Akeley, and fourteen people at which Peter and I were the chief guests.

The following day our diving friend Robby Pyle collected us in his car and took us out to his house in Greenville, Delaware, a two-hour drive in the rain. We had visited his lovely old family home before, and loved the beautiful garden and countryside around it. It was a relief to be there, but neither of us was feeling all that well. The following afternoon Peter was taken quite seriously ill. Robby and Brian Bertram, who was also staying, had gone out and I was alone in the house with Peter who was in great distress. He had severe chest pains and a temperature of 102.5°. On Robby's return I learned that in the USA you cannot get a doctor to come out. The only solution was an ambulance. In the meantime preparations were going on for a cocktail party to be held in our honour in the garden. As we left the house in the ambulance, the caterers were laying out the food.

The ambulance took us to the Christiana Hospital in Wilmington about thirty minutes away. Apart from the surprising hour-long wait on a trolley, the medical attention was wonderfully comprehensive and efficient. Pneumonia, anaemia, severe angina and other problems were diagnosed. And Peter was filled with pills and kept there for five anxious days. Robby was wonderful. He drove me to the hospital each day and fetched me in the evening. He had only expected to have us for three days but he allowed us to stay for a week after Peter came out of hospital, and was kindness itself. The garden round his house was a riot of colour, with azaleas and dogwood in bloom. There were Bluebirds courting in the trees and Ruby-throated Humming birds in the bushes. It was the perfect place to recuperate and relax.

While we were there we had the shocking news that Nicola was in hospital with two broken legs after a car accident so were pleased when we finally arrived home and could see her. The leg wounds were severe but she was remarkably cheerful.

After returning from the US we tried to lead a quiet life. Inevitably there were social occasions, some more fun than others. For me one of the most enjoyable was the annual gathering and lunch party for my brother Evelyn's Cambridge 'clique' which we hosted at our house in 1989. There were fifteen of us – only one was, sadly, deceased since the previous year's party. For fifty years we had kept in touch and now we gathered with our husbands or wives. They were as stimulating as ever and it was fun to look forward as well as reminisce. I was taking Peter back into a part of my life before he knew me and I was pleased that he liked my friends.

Other social occasions included dinner with the Captain Scott Society in Cardiff at the Royal Hotel where Peter's father had dinner on the last night before setting out in the *Terra Nova* for Antarctica. This is an annual formal occasion with speeches and it was our second time at the event. There are no women members of the society so I was one of very few female guests. The meal is identical to the one served in the same room on 13 June 1910.

We attended the handing-over ceremony of Peter's and John Winter's 14ft dinghy *Thunder and Lightning* to the Maritime Museum in Greenwich, and for Peter it was exciting to see his old friend John and the boat in which they had won so many races together.

During that summer Peter spent a lot of time designing the Wetlands Centre at Barn Elms and also planning a new visitor centre at Slimbridge. As long as he was doing creative work he was happy. The launch of the name-change to the Wildfowl and Wetlands Trust was arranged for 14 June. It was to be a major event, held in the Natural History Museum, with Prince Saddrudin as the guest of honour. Peter was not feeling well and I was anxious about him. As it was, he was taken ill while at the Museum. A kind friend drove us back to the Royal Thames Yacht Club, where we had a room in the basement. But how to find a doctor in London? The nearest one we contacted was stuck in a traffic jam somewhere on the outskirts. Max Williams turned up to give us support and finally we found someone who referred Peter to the Harley Street Clinic.

He was in hospital for a week after this severe attack of angina while I stayed first with the Shackletons and then with Peter's half-brother, Wayland. It was a desperate week, not made easier by a heatwave in London. Dafila read out Peter's speech at the Natural History Museum and Peter wrote in his diary: '... the organisation we started forty-five years ago as the Severn Wildfowl Trust is now the Wildfowl and Wetlands Trust, able by right of its title to take responsibility for the wetland habitat without which the wildfowl would be doomed. From being lukewarm about the idea at first, I am now fully convinced, and I believe it may release funds our way which would not have been possible with our more limited title.'

That interlude in London was the beginning of the end, although the end, when it came, was somehow unexpected. Peter died of a heart attack on 29 August after two days in intensive care in Southmead Hospital. I remained in a state of shock for some time after his death. I felt very strongly that he was still there. I felt his hand in mine, giving me strength. Whatever I felt inside there still had to be the public me and I knew that Peter would have wanted me to carry on his work for the Wildfowl and Wetlands Trust. It was my life as well as his.

Most important, I had at first to direct all my energies towards helping to raise money for the PSMAC (the Peter Scott Memorial Appeal for Conservation). Peter had set this up some little time before he died, its object being to benefit the WWF and the WWT in equal parts. I wrote many appeal letters, attended meetings and gave talks. That kept me busy, quite apart from replying to the one thousand condolence letters which I received.

Organising a memorial service in St Paul's Cathedral was rather like producing a theatrical performance. It was to be a celebration of Peter's life and had to have a cheerful note. Keith Shackleton was to give the address, and I was especially pleased when Prince Philip said he would come and read Psalm 104, which he chose himself. At first the Dean was surprised that I wanted the main body of the cathedral for the service, but when the day arrived the whole central part was full. People came from far and wide to honour my beloved Peter. Keith was brilliant, as I knew he would be. My brother Evelyn was a volunteer guide in the cathedral at that time, which made all the arrangements much easier for me, and June White looked after the tickets and logistics with her usual efficiency. The occasion was definitely uplifting and I thought Peter would have enjoyed it.

Later we had a repeat performance in the church at Slimbridge. For this I had arranged for a tape to be played at the end of the service of the sound of a flock of White-fronted Geese. Peter would have liked that. Just before the service I went up to make sure they had the right species but as the last words of the blessing ended and the tape started I was horrified to hear the raucous cry of a flock of Greylags. Possibly it was only I and a few others who noticed but I was shattered and very angry.

People were incredibly kind. An invitation to attend the opening of the Peter Scott Field Study Centre at Mai Po in Hong Kong gave me a wonderful opportunity to get away from Slimbridge for a while. Staying with Sue Earle, whom I knew from previous visits and bird watching in the marshes, was stimulating. There were dinner engagements every evening, all with people I knew. champagne flowed and I think I must finally have left after four days in a champagne haze. Certainly I was very tired by the time I arrived in Kuala Lumpur to stay with the McNeices in their little house at Fraser's Hill. Doing things which I had done with Peter, and which I now found myself doing without him, was difficult but there had to be a first time for everything.

After Fraser's Hill, and a few days' bird watching, we went back to Kuala Lumpur and on to Singapore. Staying with Peng and Percy in their house in the suburbs of Singapore was like coming home. I was able to visit the Sungei Buloh Wetland Reserve, with which the Wildfowl and Wetlands Trust had been very involved during its development. I was pleased to record twenty species of birds there.

From Singapore I flew on to Muscat in Oman at the invitation of Ralph Daly. There I found myself once again staying in the superb Bustan Palace Hotel. The object of this visit was to try to persuade HM the Sultan to give some money to IUCN, specifically for the Species Survival Commission. He had been so enthusiastic in his support for the Arabian Oryx and also for the Tahr (the rare goat) in the mountains and was genuinely interested in endangered species. He and Peter, who shared a love of Mozart, had got on well together on three occasions. That was all very well for Peter, but how was I going to cope with a male-dominated society?

The Sultan was on 'walkabout', visiting the different Bedu tribes in his country, but Ralph had secured an interview for me with the Minister for Finance and Economic Affairs at teatime on the afternoon of my arrival. Ralph came to brief me at lunchtime. Still rather jet lagged after my arrival in the middle of the night, and also awed by the responsibility which had suddenly been thrust upon me, I was escorted, again by Ralph, to the Palace of the Minister.

The Palace was like something from the Arabian Nights: huge and situated in a vast landscaped garden. At the front door, inside the archway, was a complete miniature village with palm trees, which were lit up after dark. We were taken past wonderful paintings in the passages, to a large drawing-room. There were beautiful rugs everywhere. Our elderly and agreeable looking host came in and we sat discussing the weather for a short time. He had great charm and a gentle manner which was reassuring. Before getting down to business he wanted to show me his garden which was certainly very impressive, with flowers, vegetables and an orchard with the largest grapefruit I had ever seen. Then it was back to the drawing-room to talk about money and endangered species. He made it all very easy for me and even indicated that he thought the Sultan might be sympathetic to my appeal for one and a half million Swiss francs for the SSC.

The Dalys were planning to take me to Yalooni to see the oryx again and the Minister said it was possible that we could all meet up there again as he would be joining the Sultan somewhere in that part of the desert. Driving into Yalooni this time gave me the chance to see more of the country. Some of the ancient irrigation systems are fascinating and the view from the top of the highest mountains in Oman across the plain to the sea was stupendous. Interestingly, there were fossils in the rocks.

The camp at Yalooni had been slightly enlarged since our previous visit. It was as friendly as ever, there were still gazelles to be seen from the windows and all the enticements of the local wildlife, including the oryx – but there was still the possibility of making contact with the Sultan. I needed to know if my efforts with the Minister had been successful. My mission was not completed until the Sultan had given his approval for the money.

Ralph was very keen to show me the wetland bird life on a lagoon at Khor Dirif on the coast, so we set off on the long drive the day after we arrived at Yalooni. We were about halfway there, having just passed a curious *wadi* (dried-up river bed) where the sand dunes were black and white, when suddenly there was a call on the radio to say that a helicopter had just landed at Yalooni. It turned out to be the Sultan's equerry and a party. They went to the house. Ralph was able to talk to one of the group on the radio but it was still not known whether the Sultan or the Minister would come the next day.

The lagoon, when we got there, was lovely. Surrounded by reeds and rushes, it was covered in birds: flamingoes, spoonbills, herons, stilts, avocets, godwit and masses of waders. I walked over the sand dunes to the sea shore and saw dolphins playing and Sooty Gulls and an immature Masked Booby.

The Sultan did not come, but on the following day there was a very high-powered visitation of four ministers, including the Deputy Prime Minister Qais Zawawi, with whom I had had tea in Muscat. It was a red-carpet kind of day, with everything being laid on at short notice for the VIPs. We viewed the oryx from Land Rovers, the Ministers lifted up their jelabas and paddled in a lake and we had a wonderful lunch in the warden's house. It was not disclosed whether the grant for SSC had been approved but I understood that the Sultan was sympathetic and only the formalities remained. I was satisfied and in due course the money did come through to IUCN. It was to be counted in with the Memorial Appeal money, which brought the grand total to well over a million pounds.

I was busy all through the summer of 1990. There were WWT Council meetings, Management meetings and, excitingly, my book *Lucky Me* was published. I remembered Peter telling me how special it was to hold the finished product in your hand for the first time and it was – almost like giving birth. There were several book launches and there were media interviews. I learned that you have to work to sell a book.

One of the greatest joys was having Elspeth Huxley in the house nearly every day of the week. She was writing Peter's biography and was witty, kind, funny and very good company. But my luck ran out at the end of the summer when a lump in my breast was diagnosed as cancer. It was frightening but I was sufficiently reassured by the surgeon to put off the operation for two weeks so that I could go to the private view of the Society of Wildlife Artists' exhibition in London. Two weeks later I was running through the house to the telephone and tripped and fell down the step onto the stone floor of the hall. I broke my wrist and cut my lip badly. Three days after that, with my arm in plaster, I went into hospital for the lumpechtomy operation. My hospital room was full of flowers, including a bunch from Elspeth with the note 'Have a nice day!'

In due course and with the help of friends I was fit enough in early September to join Keith and Jacq Shackleton on a visit to the Leigh Yawkey Museum in Warsaw, Wisconsin. This is a splendid Wildlife Art Museum which appoints a Master Wildlife Artist every year and has a big party of artists from all over the world. Peter had been Master Wildlife Artist in 1980 and Keith in 1986. It was kind of them to invite me and I was determined to go even though my arm was still in plaster.

With June's help I had managed to trace a large canvas of Peter's which he had painted a few years before and had hoped to sell in aid of WWF. Having been in Johannesburg, it somehow fetched up in the United States. The money for WWF was to be his renewal subscription to Prince Bernhard's 1001 Club. To my delight the Leigh Yawkey Museum had hung the painting in a very prominent position, where it looked lovely. What was even better was that they wanted to buy it and I was therefore able to send the money to the 1001 Club, for which they made me an Hononary Member. On my return home I was almost immediately back on the hospital round, having the plaster removed from my wrist and the beginning of four weeks' radiotherapy treatment.

During the summer I had received an invitation from Mike McDowell, ex-*Lindblad Explorer* and now running his own travel company, to join the *Lumba Lumba* on a two-week cruise from Ambon to Kupang in Indonesia. It was the most exciting thing that had happened to me since Peter died. The question was whether I could make it so soon after the radiotherapy and with a wrist that still ached. I told my oncologist and everything was geared to the departure date.

There was also the *Woman of the Year* Luncheon in London to be fitted in just two days before my departure. I was not at all sure what I was doing there but I found myself sitting at the top table between an architect and a banker. The Princess of Wales was the chief guest and Tracy Edwards, the yachtswoman, made an excellent speech. For an all-women event it was good value and I enjoyed myself.

Fearful that I might end up having to share a cabin, I managed to persuade Jacq to go diving with me in the Lumba Lumba. Many of our friends from previous diving trips were joining the ship at Ambon and we had a great welcome. Jacq and I enjoyed sitting in our cabin working out what fishes we had seen and drawing them in our notebooks. As with all diving holidays, there were a lot of early morning starts so that three dives could be fitted into the day, but the atmosphere was relaxed and everyone was interested in the fishes. I was especially pleased to be able to record eighteen different kinds of Butterfly Fish on one dive. Peter and I used to record them as 'Chetils' (their scientific name is *chaetodon*), which we reckoned was a measure of the richness of the reef.

While I was having radiotherapy I was not allowed to have a bath or to get my top half wet. About this time Penny Skelton rang me. We had been out of touch for some time. I explained my circumstances and told her how much I minded not being able to have a bath but that I was shortly going off on a scuba-diving cruise. She thought that was very funny, so I told her she should learn to dive because I could do with another buddy. She went off to Oban and embarked on a course. Negotiating the slipway at Gallanach near Oban, wearing a dry suit and carrying 35lbs, was hardly the ideal way to learn – she finished the course in the sunny waters of Jamaica wearing a T-shirt. From that time on Penny and I have gone on diving holidays together every year. Penny does all the work organising the people and the tickets. She calls herself 'Penny Package Tours'. Falcon was able to go with us until he was married and had a family, and the other members of our party were friends, relations or people we collected on our travels.

In 1997 Penny and I decided to go round the world visiting various enticing coral reefs. Starting from Singapore, where we each had friends to give us a bed, we flew on to Cairns in Queensland, Australia. After various land and sea excursions we arrived on my favourite island, Heron Island. There we spent Christmas and had a glorious week, diving every day, enjoying the birds, the sea, the sun and the food. For me, Christmas should always be in the sun.

We had various adventures, including being stranded for a short while on Castaway Island in Fiji owing to a cyclone in the neighborhood. It was on this trip that Penny had the idea that we, as scuba divers, should call ourselves the '150 club', the sum of our ages at that time. Since then we have been diving somewhere every year and as I write, this exclusive club is now called the '158 club' and will soon be the '160 club'. We are already planning our next underwater fish-watching holiday.

Epilogue

This book is very largely about the more domestic and sometimes frivolous parts of our lives. But for me there is one underlying thread – the Wildfowl and Wetlands Trust. It is like one of my children, and as with all children it can be difficult at times. For fifty-five years it has been the background to my life; physically it is the foreground, since I still live at Slimbridge in my own house overlooking Swan Lake.

When I joined in 1947 the Severn Wildfowl Trust (as it was then) was rather like a 'cottage industry'. There were very few staff and about 500 members, and we had a struggle to survive financially. In the early days there was a real family atmosphere. Since then it has become a nationwide organisation with nine centres open to the public in the British Isles, 100,000 members, a turnover of £2 million pounds and an international reputation. All over the world Slimbridge is still referred to as 'Peter Scott's place'.

Raising money was always a problem and it became more difficult after Peter's death. Prince Philip loves to tell the story of how, when he was President of the Trust and presided at Council meetings, he would ask, 'How will you raise the money for this project?' and Peter would reply, 'Oh, I'll paint a picture.' That was in the early days. But nevertheless we expanded and grew, and have continued to do so thanks to many dedicated conservationists.

At the time of Peter's death we were lucky to have as our Chairman Sir John Harvey-Jones, with his flair and business connections. Since he retired, chairmen and directors have come and gone, the world has changed, people and their expectations have changed.

During the past ten years two notable, and parallel, developments have taken place: the Millenium Visitor Centre at Slimbridge and the Wetland Centre at Barnes in London. It took all of eleven years to get Barn Elms off the ground and there were some frightening moments when we wondered if WWT could survive the struggle and risks involved; in fact we feared for the whole organisation. There was one terrible year when thirty people were made redundant. However, thanks to the dedication of our recently retired Chairman Hugh Mellor it is now flourishing. The Wetland Centre is working as a flagship and has won several prestigious awards.

No longer part of the management team, I am on the Council for life. I am happy that the child I helped to nurture for so many years has grown up and matured and I am proud of it.

Acknowledgements

First of all my most grateful thanks go to my 'literary guru', Barbara Cooper, who in the middle of moving house has acted as co-ordinator for the publication of this book and has been unfailingly and marvellously helpful. My step-daughter Nicky Starks uncomplainingly and laboriously typed every word and my enormous thanks go to her as well as to Jennifer Owen who coped with various problems, including unfriendly computers, and to Colleen Dunmall who kindly checked one of the many typescripts.

Lastly, and by no means least my thanks go to my brave editor, Judith Draper, who managed to reduce the number of chapters from 46 to 23, thus turning it into a much more readable book.

Slimbridge
August 2002

Index

Plates sections; *1* between pages 32–3: *2* between pages 128–9: *3* between pages 192–3